A significant shift in cross-cultural ministry has com of the world in such a relatively short time. Mobility h has provided a means by which more people are able to participate in short-term mission endeavors, producing many wonderful outcomes. However, one detrimental aspect is the unfortunate understanding of missions as being able to be accomplished in brief periods of time. Those who have yet to hear of the treasure of the gospel are the most difficult to reach, and this workbook addresses one of the central components necessary: grit lived out gracefully! Sue and Eva have blessed us with what I believe will be a central tool to prepare for, gracefully persevere, and navigate transitions in the work God guides each of us as members of Christ's body to engage.

STEVE COFFEY, DSL
Christar, US Director

I wish I'd had *Grit to Stay Grace to Go* in my resource library when I served in leadership and member care. It is an excellent book. The authors, scholars themselves with a great deal of life and mission experience, share vulnerably with courage and skill. The book is frank, no gloss here. It is a workbook that will connect with every reader. It begins with text, then moves into reflection questions, additional resources, biblical support, and proposed responses. The bibliography is robust and broad. The best audience for the book is new workers, leaders, member care staff, chaplains, and personnel overseers.

LAURA MAE GARDNER, DMin
Developer of Member Care, Wycliffe and SIL

How clearly I remember those difficult days when my husband and I decided we needed to leave Egypt. It was our seventh year in the country, and from the outside, the work we were connected to was going well. Our work with a semester abroad program that introduced Christian college students from the United States to all the religious and political complexity of the Middle East was in its third year and we were busy raising our family in a cross-cultural context when the whispers we both felt became conversations that always began with "Is it time to go?" I remember longing for a map of sorts, a guidebook that could help show us the way. Instead, we floundered through the process in lonely isolation. It is this story that brings me to endorse with gratitude *Grit to Stay Grace to Go,* the very guidebook that would have helped us through the decision-making process. Indeed, it is a book that is much needed in the libraries of cross-cultural Christian workers. While through the years a large body of work has emerged with memoirs, personal essays, adjusting, and reentry, this book offers something different, summed up in the sentence *"Do I stay, or do I go?"* Thick with practical advice, never glossing over the hard, offering insight from saints who have gone before, and lacing Scripture throughout, Eva and Sue will be your gentle guides as you read this excellent volume.

MARILYN GARDNER
Author, *Between Worlds: Essays on Culture and Belonging*
and *Worlds Apart: A Third Culture Kid's Journey*

Sue Eenigenburg and Eva Burkholder do my favorite thing—they "pull up a chair" and tell their stories, and I listened! With candor, authenticity and conviction, they share their own experiences and lessons learned while observing and working with individuals and teams during their years of service. They adeptly drive home the truth that serving cross-culturally will require both grit and grace, yet with grace they come alongside to nurture and nudge us with *practical* application. Their reflection, suggested response, and prayer challenge sets us on a new path, and then cements our foundation with an arsenal of good resources. Bravo for such an authentic read and a tool we can happily pass on to equip future generations.

DORCAS HARBIN
Executive Vice President, One Another Ministries International

I know you are not supposed to read the last chapter to see how the book ends, but if you choose to do so, I believe you will be drawn in by Sue and Eva's closing challenge. It is packed full of powerful insights to help you navigate the rough waters of a potential transition. It will entice you to read the chapters that pertain to your unique situation, linger long in the reflection questions (that make you pause and wrestle!), process potential responses, and delve deeply into the abundant resources provided. Thank you, Sue and Eva. May the Lord use the gift of this practical handbook to help both Goers and Stayers!

LORRIE LINDGREN
CEO/President, Thrive Ministry

I found the book helpful in so many ways. I enjoyed the personal illustrations from people who have both gotten it right and messed it up. The authors clearly have lived what they talk about and offer great advice, practical insights, and applications. This workbook will be useful for those going through transitions—either one of their own or someone near to them. I appreciate that this book looks at several sides to the issues: one who is trying to decide whether to stay or go, one who has already decided to leave and has to walk that out, and one who is staying while others leave. The use of Scripture is helpful and reassuring. I appreciate their ability and willingness to go deeper and acknowledge the pain and grief felt by everyone. Though not an easy topic to address, Sue and Eva present a realistic and balanced approach to the sorrows and joys of ministry.

STEVE MAYBEE
Member Care Director, TEAM

This is a wonderful resource for all of us who are called to do "the hardest work in the world." *Grit to Stay Grace to Go* overflows with the kind of biblical and practical insight I wish we'd had when my wife and I started our own missionary journey years ago. It tackles the tough questions that every cross-cultural worker encounters sooner or later, when the stakes are high and the answers feel elusive. Sue and Eva have given us a precious gift from their decades of experience.

STEVE RICHARDSON
President, Pioneers USA

In their book *Grit to Stay Grace to Go*, Sue Eenigenburg and Eva Burkholder provide nearly everything a cross-cultural worker needs in a single, stand-alone volume. Biblical wisdom and personal experience are woven together with practical steps and heart-focused reflection questions. This book will help you persevere through the challenges of cross-cultural ministry, sort through your emotions during times of transition and farewell, and discern whether it's time for you to stay or move on. *Grit to Stay Grace to Go* is a true "cross-cultural manual," and every worker needs a copy.

ELIZABETH TROTTER
Author, *Serving Well: Help for the Wannabe, Newbie, or Weary Cross-cultural Christian Worker*
Editor-in-Chief, missions website *A Life Overseas*

I'm glad Eva and Sue wrote this book because it is important to stay and thrive, but when it's time to go, to leave well.

JOAN WILCOX
Former cross-cultural worker on Eva's team

Grit to Stay Grace to Go is a must-read for all cross-cultural workers because it equips people at three key touchpoints in their overseas lives: when life is hard (very hard!), when you say goodbye as others leave (again!), and when you're discerning your next step. *Grit to Stay Grace to Go* is destined to become one of the books that makes the cut when you have to decide on your "keepers."

AMY YOUNG
Author, *Looming Transitions*
Founder, Global Trellis

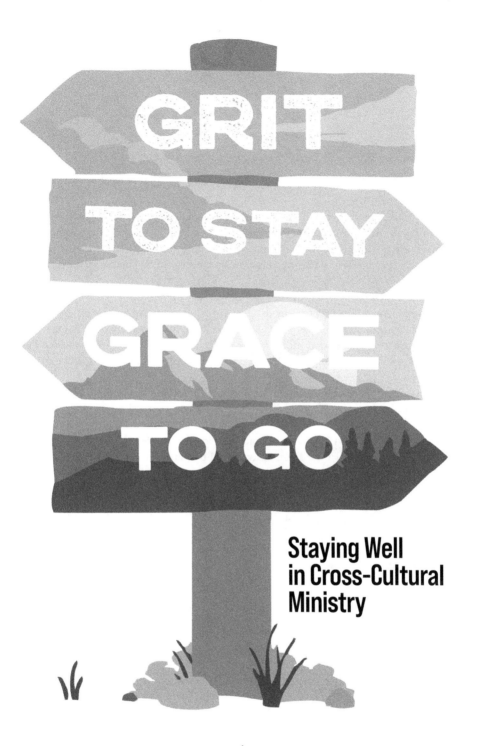

GRIT TO STAY GRACE TO GO

Staying Well
in Cross-Cultural
Ministry

Sue Eenigenburg | Eva Burkholder

WILLIAM
CAREY
PUBLISHING

visit us at missionbooks.org

Published by William Carey Publishing
10 W. Dry Creek Cir
Littleton, CO 80120 | www.missionbooks.org

William Carey Publishing is a ministry of Frontier Ventures
Pasadena, CA | www.frontierventures.org

Cover and Interior Designer: Mike Riester

ISBNs: 978-1-64508-483-9 (paperback)
        978-1-64508-485-3 (epub)

Printed Worldwide
27 26 25 24 23   1 2 3 4 5   IN

Library of Congress Control Number: 2023938179

Dedication

To my parents, Buck and Nell Downey, who modeled lifelong love and commitment in family relationships. To my teammates throughout the years who have displayed grit and grace in ministry. And to my husband Don, who inspires me with his faithfulness in loving our family and serving our God.—Sue

To my Lombok Team (you know who you are), who embraced me, loved me, believed in me, served with me, trained me, and let me go. I would not be serving other cross-cultural workers now without you and your influence.—Eva

Contents

Part Three: Deciding to Stay or Go—Grit *and* Grace Needed

Foreword

Cheryl and I loaded all that remained of our meager earthly belongings into a red and white Volkswagen microbus (think hippies of the 1970s era) and departed on the adventure of a lifetime. Just three years into marriage, I was the ripe age of twenty-four and Cheryl was twenty-one. The air was brisk that November morning in Kansas City, Missouri when we belted our two girls, aged three and five weeks, into the back seat. Every time we stopped or started our journey, we had to reassemble our floor to ceiling cargo to either release or reinsert our baby girls. We drove from Kansas City to Costa Rica, crossing four other countries to take the good news of Jesus to the underserved and forgotten (at the time) populations of Central America.

We had no vetting, no training, no theological studies, no orientation, no Spanish, no idea of what a missionary was or was not, and no solid organization to back us. We had entered the dense jungle of cross-cultural ministry where new and frightening creatures lay in wait behind every bush and tree. We began a collection (suitable for framing) of the issues that Sue Eenigenburg and Eva Burkholder deal with in this book.

The only thing that matched our boundless faith was our complete and total ignorance. We spent the next year learning Spanish in Costa Rica and pastoring as a side hustle. Next, we arrived in Nicaragua to witness the beginning of the Sandinista Revolution. With our impeccable timing, a year later we accepted the call to ministry in a young church in San Salvador just as that nation's bloody civil war erupted. In eight years, we traded in our microbus of possessions for a truckload of PTSD. (But let it be said that we also arrived in time for an amazing spiritual awakening, the effects of which continue to this day.)

How in God's name did we survive? Where was this book when we needed it? Besides the microbus and the 55-gallon barrel of stuff, we basically had two possessions—grit and grace. I can think of no other reasonable explanation. Purely by God's grace we made it, but many fell at our side. How we could have made better and wiser decisions armed with what Eva and Sue have compiled.

We learned. We grew. We matured. We returned to the United States, not due to danger, war, or even desire. No, we did not leave too early, did not stay too long, nor did we quit. We returned compelled by God to accept the call of our home church in Kansas City, even without fully understanding why. We DID NOT WANT to return to the United States— something understood only by some, like you, who have had the privilege of totally immersing yourselves in another culture.

Every ministry and every life has seasons and endings. The issue is where to draw the line that divides beginnings and endings, who draws that line, for what reason, and when to draw it. As Eva and Sue point out, their burden for this book arose from their concern to help cross-cultural workers be certain they were not leaving too soon or leaving for the wrong reasons. But as often happens in the evolution of book-writing, the layers of this question led to others. The result is an amazingly complete resource to assist cross-cultural workers in knowing when, where, how, and why to draw lines between the seasons of life and ministry and to find the grit and grace to endure the multiple pains, frustrations, hurts, confusion, challenges, betrayals, disappointments, and sacrifices along the way.

Here's what I love about this book:

- It addresses issues of attrition in the world of cross-cultural ministry.

- It is written by two women. First, two sets of eyes are better than one. Second, because of the complex and layered issues involved in cross-cultural ministry that affect entire families, immediate and extended, women often see things that men do not. In our (sincere) bravado to press on, suck it up, make it happen, and tough it out, we males tend to ignore or deny the little foxes that spoil the vines, to borrow a phrase from Solomon.

- The authors resist the temptation to offer formalistic answers to these complex problems. They do not pretend to be experts or have all the answers. They instead pose thoughtful and probing questions to guide readers to make their own decisions, coupled with stories, examples, and common-sense advice. The authors recognize that we are all unique and will never draw lines the same way or at the same time or for the same reasons.

- They suggest fabulous resources for further consideration on each topic.

- Their pragmatic approach is firmly grounded in biblical truth that they offer with thoughtful contextualization.

- They refer to this book as a manual or workbook. Though still deserving a thorough read-through, a workbook is something that one should return to repeatedly as the need arises.

Sue and Eva are my friends. I know and respect them and their weathered spirituality complete with scars and scratches. I have followed them through almost twenty years as a board member of Christar, the mission organization that unites us and is a worthy laboratory for learning and fine-tuning the lessons they share with you here. These two women have also known their share of pain and perils in other cultures. They are likewise survivors and thrivers by the grace of God and the grit provided by that same grace.

This is not a book of theory or spiritual niceties that you might expect from Jesus followers. No, this is a practical book of physical, emotional, mental, and biblical realities written by two warriors proven on these battlefields. As I have, they have witnessed the pain and confusion of Christian workers caught on the horns of a difficult dilemma. Do I stay? Do I leave? When is it just too dangerous? Am I putting myself or my family in unnecessary danger? Am I ruining my children's lives? I don't think I can take the stress any longer! What happened to my team? Does anyone know that I am here? Does anyone care? My parents need me now, is this the time I need to return home? Am I running to something or from something?

Cheryl and I faced real, clear, and present danger on an almost daily basis for the better part of a decade. But we also wrestled with loneliness, fear, betrayal, isolation, personal relationships, and the many other challenges that Eva and Sue consider in this book.

The day we returned to the United States in 1984 to accept the position as lead pastor of our home church, we prayed for safety to make it to the airport, passed a truckload of dead bodies taken off to be buried, and wept because we were leaving friends, adopted family, and what was "normal" to us. We had no one to talk to, no one who could possibly understand.

Little did we suspect that we had just moved not only geographically from Central America to Missouri, but spiritually from the frying pan to the fire. The greatest war and danger we have ever faced loomed behind the pleasant homes, comfortable church buildings, and apparent prosperity of our new abode. Thus, what cross-cultural workers face is not an issue of geography, personalities, or people groups, but rather a war of cosmic proportions, a spiritual war beyond our full comprehension and for which we mortal humans need grit and grace.

This is the reason I am so passionate about this book you have just opened. There is someone who understands. Whatever you feel, whatever you struggle with, I would be shocked if one or both of the authors has not felt the same or dealt intimately with people who have.

This book is a gift from God that can, prayerfully, enable you to learn some of the lessons we have learned and more, yet avoiding some of the many mistakes we have made along the way. I am pleased to recommend this work of my two friends, and I urge you to take full advantage and to consider prayerfully what they have to say. You are not alone.

JEFF ADAMS, PhD, Founder/President, Missional Impact

Introduction

By Sue Eenigenburg

My husband, Don, and I met in 1976 and got married two years later. They say—whoever they are—that opposites attract. I would say that rings true for Don and me. I am an extrovert. He is an introvert. I tend to think and talk at the same time. He thinks, and when he says something, it is meaningful. When we first met, I questioned whether he liked me. But he kept asking me out, so I remained hopeful. His facial expressions are reserved, and sometimes I don't know by looking at him whether he is happy, sad, angry, or excited. I think almost everyone can tell what I'm feeling—even from a distance. These differences were attractive. Of course, we also had things in common like our faith, our calling, our enjoyment of sports, love of family, and desire to minister. But the differences helped draw us together.

I don't know how long it was after our wedding day that those same differences we admired in each other became annoying. We began trying to make the other person like ourselves. Both of us failed. After some time, we came to appreciate those differences once again. How happy we are that we didn't quit too soon. We weathered the storms. Our love for each other grew because, by the grace of God, we remained committed to our relationship.

I can understand why marriages fall apart. I also understand how not quitting too soon brings great blessing. When marriages fail after a short time, it makes me sad. I feel this same sense of sadness in missions when teams fall apart. People give up during the annoying stage and fail to hang on until they can appreciate one another again. In relationships we often quit too soon, but if we persevere there can be great blessing, fruitfulness, and an evident growing love for one another.

In cross-cultural ministry, and possibly every area of our lives, the temptation to quit too soon looms large. Wanting to quit could stem from team dynamics, unfulfilled expectations, feeling ineffective, or not finding our niche quickly enough. Often, cross-cultural ministry doesn't look like we thought it would. People disappoint. A major theme of this book is not leaving too soon.

We need grit.

We began writing this book at the end of 2020. What an interesting time to write about grit. The year that brought about mask fatigue. People couldn't leave their homes, and transportation came to a standstill. The COVID-19 pandemic crisis stole opportunities to be with family for joyous reunions or grievous funerals. Trips and conferences were canceled. Zoom. Always Zoom. If there was ever a year that required grit by all people in the world, this was it!

When I talked with Eva about working together on this project, she asked why I wanted to use the word grit. I know more biblical terms exist like endurance and perseverance. So why grit instead of those terms or more member care-type words like resilience or hardiness?

I've seen grit defined as courage and resolve; strength of character. The Cambridge Dictionary describes grit as "courage and determination despite difficulty." Grit shows "firmness of character; indomitable spirit; pluck."[1] Just reading the definitions makes me desire to be a person of grit.

---

1 *Cambridge Dictionary*, "Grit."

Grit brings an image of hard work, determination, and stick-to-itiveness that is earthy and tough. In missions, as spiritual as ministry is, a lot of down-to-earth toil also takes place.

Ministry doesn't just happen in the miraculous; it shines through the mundane. And because God works through it all, he receives the glory. Sometimes we feel his presence and ministry flows. Other times, though we know God is present, it takes sheer determination on our part just to get through one more day.

As a child, I watched the movie *True Grit*. The story involves a young woman who set out to capture the man who killed her father. Nothing could deter her. She faced dirt, danger, thieves, killers, discouragement, tiredness, ridicule—and she just kept going. She endured. She persevered. She showed true grit.

As I look back on my life and ministry, many times I have wanted to quit. I felt like leaving my family because I felt overwhelmed and unappreciated. I wanted to give up cross-cultural ministry because planting a church seemed impossible considering the obstacles. Government spies and secret police opposed missionaries sharing the gospel. Acquiring visas and keeping them required cutting through red tape. Struggling team relationships and lack of resources slowed progress. An earthquake struck. Terrorists attacked different places around the city. Closed hearts and blinded eyes characterized the people we wanted to reach for Christ. I tried to figure out what role my own inadequacy played and what role spiritual warfare played in the lack of tangible results. I didn't even mention missing my extended family, grieving alone when friends and family died back home, and all the pulls of the familiar that called to me in the foreignness that was my life.

If you read my life story without knowing me, I look adventurous. I've traveled to over forty countries. I've walked where people say land mines remain. (I didn't know this at the time.) I rode on a plane which performed a spiral landing to avoid potshots by extremists. (I also didn't know about that.) Whatever adventure you see in my life is likely due more to ignorance than boldness.

In one place where we served, a bomb detonated down the street from our apartment. A deranged man shot into a hotel that we planned to visit the next day. (We didn't visit, by the way.) The police tapped our phones and routinely opened our mail. They deported or imprisoned other global workers. We stayed until we were no longer permitted to stay even though I wanted to leave when my husband went in for questioning the first time. Actually, when we landed at the start of our first term and I saw the soldiers with machine guns at the airport, I wanted to turn around and get back on the plane. Scared and longing for safety, I wanted to flee.

Big things made me want to leave, but so did smaller things. Things like feeling overwhelmed at not being able to choose a box of milk in a grocery aisle. Having the electricity go out in the middle of a call. The stove running out of gas. Being stared at, misunderstood, unsure of what to do or when to do it. Battling fear over the unfamiliar. Figuring out how my washing machine worked. Getting used to not having a dishwasher and then feeling guilty when I had one. Germs, sicknesses, and spiritual dryness when my soul needed refreshment.

But I didn't bolt. Partly because my husband, a rock under pressure, steadied me. I also wanted to follow God's leading, and he gave me strength to trust him as I clung to his word and prayed like never before. I sought to live out in my life what I said I believed in my soul. I desired to model a life of faith for my children.

My urge to flee when facing challenges comes naturally to me. Grit does not. But grit can be developed. Angela Duckworth points this out in her book entitled *Grit*:

> Like calculus and piano, you can learn the psychology of grit on your own, but a little guidance can be a tremendous help. The four psychological assets of interest, practice, purpose, and hope are not you have it or you don't commodities. You can learn to discover, develop, and deepen your interests. You can acquire the habit of discipline. You can cultivate a sense of purpose and meaning. And you can teach yourself to hope. You can grow your grit from the inside out.[2]

Maybe by staying I've learned a few things that helped grow my grit. The Apostle Paul writes, "Be patient in affliction" (Rom 12:12). As we are patient through affliction, we develop more patience which produces endurance. Endurance begets the ability to persevere even more. That grit can be learned encourages me.

My fear of disappointing people, not quite so exemplary, played a part in staying as well. Churches and supporters prayed for us, partnering with us in ministry so that we could serve least-reached peoples. I felt a sense of responsibility. Maybe pride played a part—I could do this even when others left. Perhaps I felt a bit superior because, even though I was a wimp, I stayed. I could stick it out. I wouldn't be a quitter.

Searching my heart almost always uncovers a bit of good and a bit of not-so-good. The truth is the not-so-good runs deeper than I know. Let's call it what it is, sin, and I'm not always aware of it. I'm uncertain of my own motives, but God knows I seek to do his will and follow his leading. He has led us to stay sometimes and led us to leave at other times.

Both decisions take grit. It takes grit to stay. It also takes grit to leave, to know when to go and follow God's leading no matter what people think or say.

However, I don't want to just stay on the field to say I stayed. My desire shouldn't be to just survive, to show grit in my own strength and barely hang on, becoming bitter, angry, and tired. Staying just to stay is useless. It may even be disobedient. Relying on my own strength is futile. I don't have enough. No one does.

We also need grit when God leads us to leave. The Lord guides people to different ministries in different ways. He opens and shuts doors. He exerts the final word on visa approvals and refusals. Challenging events aren't the only reasons people leave. They may be very happy and fruitful in their ministry, but their giftings may be needed more in other avenues of ministry. Family concerns can make choosing to leave the best thing to do, even if ministry is a good fit. Saying yes to moving on when you feel content where you are causes heartache.

After sadly leaving our first field of service, we moved to a different country. Two years later, our family needed more help than we could find in that location. At the same time, our US office offered us positions there. After twelve years of ministering overseas, we relocated to America. Hearing people say, "You used to be missionaries" made me feel misunderstood. Our focus hadn't changed, just our location. God used our gifts and abilities for his kingdom even in the US. Twelve years later, we headed back overseas. Five years in South Asia and then seven years and counting in Europe. Who would have thought our journey would be such a winding road?

When we first joined our agency over thirty-five years ago, the president challenged all those who joined to "leave their bones" in their host country. Perhaps this was his definition of grit. That was our plan. However, the country we felt called to didn't want our bones!

---

2 Duckworth, *Grit*, 92.

We needed a plan B. Plan B became plan C. Plan C became D. I think we are currently on plan E awaiting plan F.

Leaving isn't always bad.

Staying isn't always good.

But how do we know what God is leading us to do?

When we lived in South Asia and prayed about moving to Europe, I did some soul searching. Life held many challenges for me where hot peppers burned my mouth even in milder dishes. Overt idol worship emphasized spiritual darkness. I couldn't understand English because of the unfamiliar accent. Though I felt uncomfortable, I didn't want to run from the challenges. I wanted to run to what God was calling me to do. Where did he want me to go? I didn't want to be looking for an easier place to live where I would be more comfortable. I wanted to be where God wanted me to be. Discerning my own motives can be complicated. But I wanted our decision to be based in leaving for, not running from. Deciding required waiting and looking to the Lord, which proved a beneficial, though not always comfortable, place to be.

By Eva Burkholder

Language school and survey trips completed. The decision finally made. With our two small boys, my husband and I left the expat-saturated city to set up home and ministry in a new field on an eastern island in Indonesia. After furloughs and travel, the whole team was finally together on the ground—five families and one single man. We excitedly began to settle in, strategize, and get to know each other.

Just a few months later, the phone rang in the early hours of the morning. The frantic voice of my teammate called out, "We've been robbed. My husband's been cut. Send help." He had, in fact, been seriously wounded and her call started a chain of events that altered our team and our lives. What began as a dream team of eleven ended with two families looking at each other, wondering what had happened and what we were going to do about it.

We planned for our team to work together long term. When I signed up to serve cross culturally, I expected a long-haul endeavor. After all, my parents were still serving in Papua New Guinea at the time, completing a second Bible translation project. Mastering a language, planting a church, or translating the Bible requires many years. Missions takes commitment, resilience, perseverance—grit.

Instead, we barely had time to say hello, to determine each other's gifts, styles, and ways of working together before most were whisked back to their passport country.

The first teammate and his family left for what I considered an "acceptable reason." Their family needed to heal from a tragic near-death experience. The second family's situation seemed a little more tenuous in my mind: mental breakdown due to the stress of the previous event revealing deep-seated anxiety. The third family finished their research and moved on. Fourth, the single man took a position at the mobilization center.

With our team leader and friends gone, the newest families remained to figure it out. The other couple was thrust into leadership, changing our peer relationships into hierarchal ones overnight. Forget ministry, we just tried to survive.

Over the next six years, we watched teammates come and go in sync with each crisis that disrupted life. Engage, goodbye, adjust. Engage, goodbye, adjust. Repeat.

I wish that I had had a guidebook, a way to think through the aftermath of my teammates' exits. Experiencing hurt and feeling judgmental forced me into new uncomfortable territory. Why did I need to forgive someone for leaving? Why did I feel superior for not copping out or quitting too soon? Why would God bring someone all that way, provide financial and prayer support, training, and language skills, only to send them back again? How does this work, anyway?

Then my turn arrived.

I remember sitting cross-legged on the floor in the circle of women. Looking around at my teammates and dearly loved friends, I began to weep.

"What's the matter?" the one next to me asked, putting her arms around me.

"I don't know why," I said through my tears, "but I have this overwhelming sense that I'll never again be in this circle with you all." I had no real proof for this other than my husband had begun to have another bout of restlessness and increased anxiety. While not new, this time felt final.

My husband's wrangling disturbed me. We couldn't quit. We didn't have a good reason. Acceptable reasons included a midnight stabbing like our teammate had experienced, or the children of expats being diagnosed with something that our host country could not provide adequate support for. Tropical sprue (a rare digestive disease) also justifiably took out a family or two. Even repeatedly contracting dengue fever would qualify.

But restlessness about his exact place on the church planting team? That couldn't be defined within acceptable categories. It sounded weak. And anxiety? He had sought help and experienced some relief. Yet my husband, feeling farther and farther out of his comfort zone, wanted a change.

We did enjoy living cross-culturally. We loved our teammates who had become dear friends. We lived on a beautiful tropical island. It wasn't all bad. Except for the crises that hit our team every year. We became known as the team who "wrote the book" on crises. Dengue fever—evacuation. Stabbing—evacuation. Riots—evacuation. Broken arm—evacuation. Exploding stove—evacuation. And then death. Twice.

These crises alone should have taken us out. But they didn't. We stayed through them all. But as often happens with living cross-culturally, these stressors revealed deeper issues and unresolved emotional trauma. My husband's increased anxiety and unhealthy coping mechanisms, along with the growing awareness that we served on a different side of church planting than our giftings, proved too great to ignore. We needed the courage to simply admit that we desperately needed more help and that our giftings did not lie in pioneer church planting.

While we were on home assignment, my husband and I spent time wrestling, praying, receiving counseling, improving our emotional health, and finally making the excruciating decision to leave the mission field after twelve years. We had no guidebook. I found many verses in Scripture (which is one way God directs me), and pastors and mentors advised us. But we made mistakes. We could have done better. We hurt and offended dear friends and teammates in the process.

Where many resources now exist for those leaving and repatriating to their passport countries, we don't see many for the ones left behind. And as a member care provider, I hear their stories. They feel betrayed, left out of decision-making, forced to accept that the choices of others drastically affect their lives. They have to pick up the pieces, fill in the gaps, take on extra work, and revisit ministry plans because someone else left—again.

These ones try to endure tough situations, even if reluctantly. Why should they stick it out when it feels like teammates have thrown in the towel? How do they let their teammate go without judging them? How might their perception of the events be inaccurate? How do they heal, pick up, and carry on while wholeheartedly blessing the one leaving?

When Sue approached me about collaborating with her, I knew we had to write the handbook we lacked when we wanted to quit, when teammates left unexpectedly, and when we made our decision to leave.

About This Workbook

In the first part of this workbook, I (Sue) want to encourage people to not leave too soon. To endure by God's grace and under his leading, we need to understand the challenges requiring grit: continual adjusting, balancing two worlds, juggling roles, finding our niche, rootlessness, different expectations, navigating priorities, loneliness, messy relationships, and the desire to escape.

Questions arise as we wrestle with all of these challenges. What is our calling? How will we know exactly what to do? Where can we find available and needed resources? How do we recognize the lies we believe and the truths we must cling to instead? We would never say out loud that we believe these lies, but in practice we may not see that we live the lies without realizing truth has gotten lost along the way.

As we seek God's will, examine our challenges, and look for guidance, we eventually decide what to do:

If he leads us to stay, let's do so—with grace, humility, and continuing dependence on the Holy Spirit.

If he leads us to leave, let's do so—with grace, humility, and continuing dependence on the Holy Spirit.

Those who stay will end up saying a lot of goodbyes to those who leave. Maybe the leavers go too soon and their departure seems ill advised. Perhaps the timing appears perfect. Either way, they still leave and those who stay must bid them farewell.

The second part of this handbook, which Eva focuses on, is a snapshot, zeroing in on one aspect of staying that is particularly difficult—saying goodbye to colleagues who leave. It's for those who help their teammates pack, who may feel betrayed, alone, angry, disappointed, overworked, or even a tad jealous. How do we respond when those with whom we had intended to change the world leave us and our seemingly shared vision? Or perhaps there has been team friction or a traumatic break in relationship and we feel relieved that teammates are leaving. Either way, we still experience change. And we need to be open to healing and forgiveness. How can we grieve and adjust in a healthy manner? What does it look like to truly bless those who leave and let them go? How does the stayer refocus attention on their responsibilities and invest in their present reality? Whether we see God's hand in it or not, we still must deal with the aftermath of change and transition.

Through Scriptures and reflection questions, we will guide you to process the "stayer's" common reactions and look at how messengers of the gospel can respond to rebuild and move forward.

Finally, in the third section of the guidebook, we tackle the in-between process when deciding what to do. How do we know which way God is leading? What are factors we consider and emotions we experience? Determining God's will has always been a heartfelt desire for believers. What have people done and how have they decided? We will discover some practical ways as well as some spiritual practices to help in discerning whether to go or to stay.

While Sue focused on part one and Eva part two, we both edited each other's words and added comments and personal insights so that our touch is on each other's work (especially in part three).

We will not have all the answers, but we will ask clarifying questions and present factors to bear in mind. One certainty remains: deciding is rarely easy. Going, staying, and being left to carry on are all hard and each one requires grit and grace!

How To Use This Workbook

This book is meant to be a guide, to help both the goer and the stayer process their feelings and make decisions related to leaving or staying on the mission field. While you may find yourself on one side of this coin, we think it would be most beneficial to read through all sections. Understanding each other's process, feelings, and struggles will create empathy and grace for one another. We suggest you take the chapters in order, but we want you to proceed in the way that works best for you.

Each chapter will contain some of our stories and those of others who have also walked this road. We have garnered testimonies and examples from surveys, comments during webinars, emails, and interviews, which we share with their permission. Sometimes we use real names, other times aliases, and sometimes we leave a story anonymous.

We'll look at what Scripture has to say and posit questions you can use to reflect on your situation. As with all guidebooks, you will get more from this if you truly interact with the material, allowing the Holy Spirit to direct you to consider what he is showing you. We have concluded each chapter with other helpful resources that focus on that particular topic if you need to dig deeper.

If you decide to stay, may God help you to stay well. If you decide to go, may God help you to leave well.

PART ONE

Challenges to Staying Well—Grit Needed

Introduction

During my pre-field training, I heard about challenges in cross-cultural ministry. But I didn't realize the extent to which those challenges would affect me. Theory is much easier than reality.

As I think about my life, the lives of others with the same heart for the nations, and all I've learned through the years—missions is indeed hard! Stress levels soar. Our teams are normally under-resourced and under-staffed. Needs seem unending. Fruitfulness looks unachievable.

In a recent webinar called Field Onboarding and Retention, Elliot Stephens points out that 47 percent of workers, who felt called to long-term service, leave by year five and that 70–80 percent leave by year eight—the year when workers start becoming most fruitful.[1]

Believing that a lot of attrition can be prevented, Stephens addresses what organizations can do to help people stay and thrive in their ministries. However, our book focuses on the practices missionaries themselves can do. This is what I picture King David doing when his distress felt overwhelming:

> Moreover David was greatly distressed because the people spoke of stoning him, for all the people were embittered, each one because of his sons and his daughters. But David *strengthened himself in the LORD his God.* (1 Sam 30:6 NASB 1977, emphasis added)

When troubled, we must strengthen ourselves in the Lord. Oswald Chambers wrote in *My Utmost for His Highest*, as he reflected on Jesus overcoming the world: "Spiritual grit is what we need."[2] We prepare ourselves to stand firm, face challenges, and develop spiritual grit for the great commission.

Peter and Ginnette wrote in their recent prayer letter about some challenges (and blessings) they've faced as they serve cross-culturally:

> *We've walked through trials ...*
> We've said painful goodbyes to teammates who left.
> Another year of infertility has been written in our story.
> We've lost hours wading in government restrictions and bureaucracy.
> There has been much conflict and relational confusion.
> We've navigated the effects of major restructuring in our organization.
> The societal fallout of the pandemic has been disorienting and lonely.
> We've wept over the state of the local church around us.
> We've been away from family during some of their hardest moments.
> We've been away from friends during some of their best moments.
> Peter has sought wisdom in the midst of many challenging roles.
> Ginnette has battled depression and despair, a first for her.
> Our daughter has become comfortable in our new country, but not completely—
> both are trials.
> *We've also seen blessings!*
> We've welcomed new teammates with joy and gratitude.
> Our family of three has bonded deeply and made wonderful memories.

1　Stephens, "Webinar: Field Onboarding and Retention."

2　Chambers, *My Utmost for His Highest.*

We've stepped out of language study and into many opportunities to use our new language in real and important situations!

There has been much reconciliation and relational wisdom.

We've been able to network with and learn from new co-laborers.

We have experienced some significant events in our host country's history.

We've seen the fruit of obedience and perseverance in the church.

We've been with family during some of their best moments.

We've been "with" friends during some of their hardest moments.

Peter is learning to honor, to be humble, to be patient, and to forgive.

Ginnette is learning to trust, to persevere, to hope, and to have courage.

Our daughter has become comfortable in our new country, but not completely— both are blessings.

As their letter so beautifully describes, cross-cultural messengers face many challenges in life and ministry. I appreciate their list of blessings that could only come through enduring the challenges. For this workbook, I chose ten challenges for us to consider. When facing these hardships, we may begin to believe lies that can affect our decision to stay or to leave.

We may choose to leave for numerous reasons: God shuts one door and opens another. Our gifts are needed in other areas of ministry. Challenges seem insurmountable. We see no tangible fruit. Our agency needs us elsewhere.

We also find many reasons to stay: Language is progressing. Our lives emit light in dark corners of the world. We don't want to leave too soon just because it is more difficult than we thought. We don't want to give up when our once-held-dearly dream looks more like a nightmare.

How can we recognize these challenges and prepare better for them? If we choose to leave, we must do so with truth ringing in our ears. If we choose to stay, let's place truth as our solid foundation, with no place for lies.

Chapter 1

It's Harder Than I Thought
Missions Is Difficult

I am not a theologian or a scholar,
but I am very aware of the fact that pain is necessary to all of us.
In my own life, I think I can honestly say
that out of the deepest pain has come the strongest conviction
of the presence of God and the love of God.

—Elisabeth Elliot

Life, in general, is challenging. A life of faith is tough. Believers experience spiritual warfare and struggle (Eph 6; Phil 1:30; Rom 15:30). We battle against sin, labor for godliness, and strive to do good (Heb 12:4; 1 Tim 4:10; 1 Thess 5:15).

Beyond this, cross-cultural service adds another layer to an already complex life. The Apostle Paul writes about ministry being difficult, using words like "labor" and "toil" (2 Thess 2:8). He mentions physical challenges like hunger and lack of sleep (2 Cor 11:27). He talks about his labor and suffering in ministry (Phil 1:22; 2:16; Col 1:24). In his desire to see spiritual maturity in fellow believers, he describes "strenuously contending" (Col 1:29; 2:1). He mentions working hard so that he wouldn't burden the church (1 Thess 2:1, 9; 2 Thess 3:8).

Paul also commends his coworkers for their work. Epaphras not only worked hard but wrestled in prayer for the Colossians (Col 4:13). Mary, Tryphena, Tryphosa, Persis all worked hard for the gospel (Rom 16). Timothy endured hardship (2 Tim 4:5). He considered the soldier, athlete, and farmer as he determined his work ethic in life and ministry (2 Tim 2:3–7).

While Paul normalizes the challenges in ministry, I am still often shocked when they interrupt my life. I find myself inadequately prepared for how overwhelming they are and how frequently they tempt me to quit for an easier life, especially when I feel stuck and unsure of how to make progress.

Whether I stay or leave, I want to do God's will. I want to be resilient. Sometimes resilience feels like grit. Maybe these two terms are synonymous. But the picture in the words feels different to me. Resilience is a beautiful word, seen from God's perspective. He knows we aren't strong enough on our own to endure, to persevere. He gives strength and we recognize that we can be resilient. But sometimes, when my soul feels crushed, resilience feels like grit. I barely hold on and strive with all my might to keep walking by faith. Only when I look back can I see how God held me up. At the time, I couldn't see his hand.

At one point in ministry, we faced a difficult time as a family. Tensions ran high. I pictured my husband Don and me in an ocean. Both of us attempted to stay afloat with bellowing winds and heaving waves all around us. But we had only enough strength to keep ourselves above water. Neither of us had the extra energy to help the other. Now that I look back at that, I see God had us securely tied to a lifeline and to each other. We weren't at the mercy of the storm, even though it felt like it. Grit can sometimes look like the human picture of divine resiliency.

Not every problem feels overwhelming. Some seem manageable. However, even when you successfully juggle several at the same time, stresses can build. In missions, lots of things happen at once. Therefore, overseas workers operate at a higher stress level than is considered average according to results from the Holmes-Rahe Stress Inventory, an assessment tool for measuring total stress levels. In fact, they often live above the serious illness level. (Elliot Stephens, in his webinar, highlights high stress levels especially for those in their first term.[1])

Herbert F. Lamp, in his book *Journey With Me*, gives testimony that stress can lead to a crisis of calling and cause us to leave too soon. Or we can allow God to use these stressors and problems to grow us. Lamp writes:

> Early in my missionary career I was faced with a crisis of calling. After about two years on the field I sensed God calling me into a deeper and harder work than I thought I could handle. During this struggle, I started to evaluate what I had accomplished and found little fruit. I asked God, "If you really want me to sacrifice even more, will you let me know it is worth it?" I wanted a clear affirming sign that God was at work. But guess what? Things only got worse, and my sense of failure grew even more. I wondered what was happening and if we should consider returning home. But then I started to pay attention to what was really going on in my life. I could see that every difficulty I encountered, every failure I experienced, became something God was addressing and solving. Rather than my problems being a barrier too difficult to surmount, I saw amazing ways in which God was present with me. I started seeing God in all my circumstances, and I regained perspective on God's calling and my commitment to stay.[2]

We cannot possibly be totally prepared for the reality that hits when we serve overseas, but we can be better prepared and ready to pay attention to what God is doing in and through us.

When thinking about how hard this life can be, we are tempted to believe lies. We know truth, but in the face of hardship, truth dims and lies shine brighter. In our heads, we would not acknowledge we believe these lies. But they show up in our hearts when life looms harder than we thought possible.

Lies we are tempted to believe when we are in over our heads:

Obeying God and following him should make life easier, not harder.

I didn't fight God or disobey him. I left home, saying goodbye to family and all that was familiar. That was the hard part. The rest shouldn't be. So where is the blessing? Where is the fruit? Or as one global worker put it, "Where is the honeymoon period? I didn't get that. It was hard from the first moment I landed."

My definition of success defines who I am and determines my significance.

When I left for my first term, I had envisioned such great ministry successes. Looking back, many of those expectations were unrealistic, outside of my gifting and strengths, and based on what I thought I "should be" or "should do."

---

1 "Webinar: Stephens, Field Onboarding and Retention."

2 Lamp, Jr., *Journey With Me*, 109–10.

After some time, if I'm not accomplishing what I came to do, why should I stay? I have my goals, my vision, my list of what I do so that my life can be significant or gain significance. Additionally, supporting churches can ask success-based questions that cause me to question if I deserve support. "You've been there one term, how many souls have you led to Christ? How many disciples?" I feel like it would be easier to achieve what constitutes "success" from the comfort of my home country. I mistakenly catch myself thinking that I must be at a certain level of success for God to value me.

Everything in my life would be easier if I left the mission and returned home.

I know that I'm experiencing selective memory when I start seeing life in Europe as much harder than life in South Asia. When I have trouble with bureaucracy here, I forget bureaucracy exists everywhere. I can remember so many positive things about life and ministry in the Middle East or how much easier life was when my kids were younger. Everything looks better somewhere else or at some other time when we face hardships. In every foreign place I've lived when I felt overwhelmed, I wanted to go home where life seemed much simpler. I fail to remember the issues I encountered in my home country.

Truths we must embrace to face challenges with power and courage:

Obeying God and following him brings us joy along with suffering.

Joy and suffering often go together in the New Testament. Luke records that after being flogged, "The apostles left the Sanhedrin, rejoicing because they had been counted worthy of suffering disgrace for the Name" (Acts 5:41). God's worthiness counted more than their suffering. They felt honored to suffer for his name. It gave them joy. Paul connects joy and suffering as he looks at the results of trials in our lives:

> Not only so, but we also glory in our sufferings, because we know that suffering produces perseverance; perseverance, character; and character, hope. And hope does not put us to shame, because God's love has been poured out into our hearts through the Holy Spirit, who has been given to us. (Rom 5:3–5)

We rejoice in hope because our sufferings bring about good in our lives. Peter writes in his first letter,

> Dear friends, do not be surprised at the fiery ordeal that has come on you to test you as though something strange were happening to you. But rejoice inasmuch as you participate in the sufferings of Christ, so that you may be overjoyed when his glory is revealed. If you are insulted because of the name of Christ, you are blessed, for the Spirit of glory and of God rests on you. (1 Pet 4:12–14)

Three major authors in the New Testament combine joy and suffering as part of our lives, which is an important aspect of our ministry and calling as believers and ministers of the gospel.

My definition of success matters little compared to fulfilling God's purpose for me.

As believers, we find our significance in Christ because he loves us, not because of what we can do for him. We are weak and helpless to save ourselves. However, our value is not dependent on our actions but in his declaration that we matter to him.

The Psalms are filled with verses about fulfilling God's purpose in our lives. David wrote, "I cry out to God Most High, to God, who fulfills his purpose for me" (Ps 57:2 ESV) and "The LORD will fulfill his purpose for me; your steadfast love, O LORD, endures forever. Do not forsake the work of your hands" (Ps 138:8). Luke refers to the purpose of God for David as well: "Now when David had served God's purpose in his own generation, he fell asleep" (Acts 13:36a).

A gap existed between my perceived purpose and God's purpose for me. As I realized my faulty thinking, I let go of my version of success and looked to God. I experimented with various ways of serving, failing, and succeeding. Basing my significance on my view of success undercuts the gospel. However, true success is found in fulfilling God's purpose for me.

I do not have to achieve my version of success. I need to know how God made me and serve him where he has placed me. I must be obedient to him and use the gifts he's given me knowing they are for the common good (1 Cor 12:7), not my own significance. My life is not about me. It is about my Lord. Life is for his purposes, done in his ways, for his glory, not my own.

Challenges exist in every place I live and in everything I do.

I sometimes look at other places and think life would be simpler there. Or, to the other extreme, I can feel guilty that life is easier here and ministry would be more important or my life more significant in a more challenging area of the world. No place is perfect. Every stage of life and phase of ministry has its drawbacks and benefits. No ideal situation or totally wonderful stage of life exists anywhere in this world.

Life and ministry are hard, for everyone. Satan is against us. We grow weary. We serve. Challenges come. Almost everyone has felt like leaving at some point. We try to decide whether to stay or go. But praise God that he is at work in us. He helps his children endure.

The Holy Spirit empowers me to do God's will and fulfill his purpose for me. Giving up on that purpose isn't an option. I need to walk in the power of God to do the will of God and follow where he leads—even when it's hard.

REFLECTION

What have been some of your biggest challenges in ministry?

How have you defined "success" for your ministry?

What lie(s) have you been tempted to believe?

RESPONSE

Write a list of the challenges you might face if you lived in your passport country.

Compare it with the challenges you face in your current location.

Ask God to help you believe truth and not lies.

PRAYER

Lord, Paul reminds us in Romans 15:5 that you are the God who gives endurance and encouragement. May I look to you as I seek to work hard and persevere. May I remember to put on the armor that you have provided for me. Thank you for your grace and the power to do your will. Amen.

RESOURCES

https://www.youtube.com/watch?v=ulswQICDAk0 _____
(The Armor of God by Tony Evans)

https://www.youtube.com/watch?v=CazArZlwePM _____
(Your Spiritual Battle and the Armor of God by Priscilla Shirer)

https://kennethacamp.com/13-challenges-foreign-missionaries-face/ _____

https://lausanneworldpulse.com/perspectives-php/924/04-2008 _____

https://www.valeo.global/services _____

https://www.imb.org/2018/08/16/5-considerable-challenges-todays-missionary/ _____

https://globaltrellis.com/prayer-of-examen-for-the-ways-we-define-success-in-cross-cultural-work/ _____

For training options: https://www.grow2serve.com/ _____

Amy Young, *Getting Started: Making the Most of Your First Year in Cross-Cultural Service* (Independently published, 2019).

Corella Roberts, *Colliding with the Call: When Following God Takes You to the Wilderness* (Independently published, 2020).

Chapter 2

I Feel Like I'm Always Adapting
Continual Adjusting

The best things in life are on the other side of your comfort zone.

—Neale Donald Walsch

Thinking about all the adjustments we make as we seek to serve across cultures feels formidable. We adapt almost daily and the changes we must make seem unending. Research shows that people are the most vulnerable during the first term.[1] One missionary wrote, "I would say the time I wanted to leave the most was early on. I felt unstable. I was learning language and felt useless."

We all know that acquiring a new language represents only a small portion of the learning needed to adapt to a new culture that feels extremely foreign. On her first term in a new country Erin wrote in her prayer letter:

> Culture shock has also made an appearance. When nothing is familiar and your brain is constantly stimulated, sometimes the smallest things can be the straw that breaks the camel's back. I am thankful that those who have been here for many years were able to give me perspective as I begin wrestling through the normal frustrated emotions that come along with entering a new culture long-term.

I remember our early days trying to adapt in new cultures. In my home culture it is considered rude not to respond to people, regardless of their gender, when they ask a question or invite conversation. However, in the first country where we served, responding to a stranger of the opposite gender could be perceived as acceptance (or an invitation) to an immoral relationship. When I didn't converse with men I didn't know, I felt rude. In that culture though, I was seen as respectable.

Trying to figure out all the ins and outs of living in a different culture produces challenges. We will always mess up, choose wrong, or miss cues. Then, because we don't understand the customs of our new culture, we judge it as inferior to our own. We grapple with when to adapt and when not to adapt with cultural customs that may go against Scripture. We struggle to learn to be hospitable in a new context, what to say at weddings, funerals, and births. We constantly learn appropriate ways to greet people and how to say goodbye. Quitting may look easier than persevering, but we usually learn and change—a lot in the beginning.

As we learn and adapt to our new culture, we function outside of our comfort zones. Many of us had counseling, formal or informal, to help us deal with life issues and prepare us to minister across cultures. However, during stressful times outside of the familiar and

---

1 "Webinar: Stephens, Field Onboarding and Retention."

away from our normal support systems, the struggles we thought were resolved reappear. And they are stronger than ever! Marital issues we thought we fixed come back with a vengeance. The marriage relationship becomes strained as our newly developed ways of communicating give way to the old patterns.

For married couples waiting, unable, or not wanting to have children, the new culture has opinions on that. Questions are asked that may seem rude in our home culture. "Have you had your period yet?" "When will you have a child? You've been married one year!" These awkward questions can strain couples' relationships as well as relationships with the people who ask such questions.

Healing from previous sexual trauma seems to come undone when facing harassment on the streets of one's host culture. Staying home seems safer than going out. Asking for help, then finding the professional assistance needed to cope with these issues overseas can be challenging.

We may start our first term physically healthy, but with the stress of living overseas and the new set of germs we encounter, we get sick. Diarrhea becomes a dreaded and frequent enemy. We lose weight due to stomach issues, heat, stress, and increased walking. When my husband's mother came to visit us in the Middle East, Don met her at the airport. She burst into tears. He thought she was happy to see him. We found out later she cried because he had lost so much weight that she thought he looked sick.

Arriving to the field with children increases the challenges for families adjusting to new cultures. Of course, parenting isn't simple in our home cultures. We referee fights, determine when and how to lovingly discipline each child, encourage them to grow, and pray for their salvation. But parenting overseas adds even more challenges. A long-lasting battle with lice almost put me (and Eva, too) over the edge. Children can feel isolated and lonely. They also go through culture stress. As children deal with all their feelings, they may have more emotional outbursts which can leave everyone reeling. Discerning how to let them vent without becoming disrespectful is tricky. Figuring out what parts of the culture to protect them from and when they need to learn how to handle what comes their way seems murky. It's challenging navigating decisions we've never had to make before—and this for people we love more than life itself.

Children get sick, and effective treatments for some illnesses aren't readily available in some countries. When a child is diagnosed with emotional issues, physical challenges, or learning disabilities, parents feel uncertainties about being able to stay in their country of service.

Education can bring even more issues for families. Schooling options may change. What we thought would work for kids, doesn't. Boarding school, which we assumed we wouldn't consider, becomes the best option.

How much is too much for our children? Many times I wondered if I was permanently damaging my children because of the extra pressures they faced living in a different culture. Our endurance meant they had to endure as well. They had no choice. Parents feel a lot of pressure as they try to decide what is best for their families: to stay or to leave. The answer is rarely clear cut and always emotionally draining.

Single teammates have struggles married ones don't. Some cultures perceive them as lacking or immature (no matter their age) since they aren't married. Neighbors and new friends ask prying questions that seem impolite. Pressures arise to marry a national friend's cousin—anything would be better than staying single. Single people also have some of the same issues married people do but without a life companion with whom they can process their experiences.

In missions, we must keep in mind that it often gets worse before it gets better, especially in the early years.

Lies that can surface in the "worse before it gets better" stage—when adjusting feels overwhelming, unending, and pretty much impossible:

I will never adjust. There is too much to learn.

Just when I thought I was making progress, something happened to make me realize how far I still had to go to feel well-adapted.

After serving in the Middle East for more than a decade, I'd been teaching in my new language for about a year. As I was counseling a student, she began sharing a burden. One word kept recurring which I didn't know. I excused myself for a moment, went to find the definition of the word, and came back to continue our conversation. I needed that information and felt discouraged that after all those years I still didn't know that word.

We should never feel that we have arrived. Of course, at the beginning of ministry all of this feels more like a tsunami. Thankfully, as we gain exposure and experience, adapting becomes less overwhelming. But flexibility remains a vital need.

I am on my own.

If I tell my home church how hard cross-cultural ministry is, they may stop supporting me. If I tell my family, they will ask me to come home (which is where they want me to be anyway). If I tell my team, they may judge me. My team leader might see me as the weak link. I already feel inferior next to my more experienced teammates. This will be just one more way I appear needy.

When my family went through a challenging time, we wanted people to pray for us but didn't know how much to communicate about our situation. We worked on a prayer letter and sent it out. I feared the responses and how it might affect our support. Instead, an outpouring of love, empathy, and prayer support came and it amazed me. All of our partners face challenges. All other global workers face challenges. Everyone in the world faces challenges. We don't tell everyone everything, but we need people to hear our burdens and enter into life with us. I needed to stop worrying about people's opinions about me and realize we are in the body of Christ to love and serve one another.

I can't ask for help.

If I ask for help, I will be judged as unproductive. I worked so hard to raise support to get here. All the things I said I was going to do now seem beyond my reach, and I feel like a liar. If I share my true feelings, I may be asked to leave the ministry before getting started. I should be able to do this on my own.

I remember sitting in church and looking around at people there. No one seemed bothered. But even as I saw them looking serene, I knew some of their struggles. Maybe I looked serene on the outside to others who may have been looking around as well. But many times I wasn't. It's almost like we consider weakness or a need for help as sin and are afraid to let people in on our pain.

Truths we must cling to so that we don't shrivel, give up, and run away:

It takes time to adjust. Don't rush the process.

Be ready to make mistakes. Embrace them. Mistakes help us learn. On my first language test, I missed every single question. I started studying more and planning more visits to practice language and make new friends—as much as I could with four kids while trying to stay sane.

We can maintain our sense of humor as we adjust. I chuckled (and still do) when I asked a little girl, in my new language, what her doll's name was. She said, "Lisa." I thought that was a name like in my own country. When I replied that Lisa was a pretty name she looked at me like I was confused. I later learned *lisa* meant, "not yet." She hadn't named her doll yet. No wonder she thought my reply was strange. Everyone makes mistakes. Nothing is simple. Life cross-culturally takes more time. Everything moves more slowly. Relax.

Remember we are not only learning about our host culture, but we are also learning about ourselves and God. While adjusting to a new culture, I felt so over my head, I knew I needed to rely more on the Lord. He met me and was my rock in the sea of my bewilderment. James reminds us of how God uses trials in our lives to produce perseverance and maturity:

> Consider it pure joy, my brothers and sisters, whenever you face trials of many kinds, because you know that the testing of your faith produces perseverance. Let perseverance finish its work so that you may be mature and complete, not lacking anything. (Jas 1:2–4)

I am not on my own. I can ask for help.

For new arrivals on the field, Duckworth in her book *Grit*, mentions mentoring can be a tremendous help.

> Encouragement during the early years is crucial because beginners are still figuring out whether they want to commit or cut bait. Accordingly, Bloom and his research team found that the best mentors at this stage were especially warm and supportive.[2]

How can we receive the help we need if we aren't open to letting people in? And even for those with experience, they can't go it alone. Duckworth points out the different motivational needs of beginners from those with experience:

> For now, what I hope to convey is that experts and beginners have different motivational needs. At the start of an endeavor, we need encouragement and freedom to figure out what we enjoy. We need small wins. We need applause. Yes, we can handle a tincture of criticism and corrective feedback. Yes, we need to practice. But not too much and not too soon. Rush a beginner and you'll bludgeon their budding interest. It's very, very hard to get that back once you do.[3]

Everybody needs a little help and a lot of encouragement. Asking for help is good.

I have a terrible sense of direction. I used to try and hide it, but it really is impossible to hide when you must always ask which way to turn. It can be embarrassing. I remember a time when we were visiting family. Their house is a sprawling ranch, and I was unfamiliar with its layout. We spent the night in the guest room. I slept later than Don, so when I woke up in the morning, he had already left the room.

---

2 Duckworth, *Grit*, 107.

3 Duckworth, *Grit*, 108.

After I got ready for the day and when it was time for breakfast, I opened our bedroom door. There was a long hallway, we were in the middle room and there were two doors on either end. Both were closed and I didn't know which way to go. One door led to breakfast. The other door was our hosts' bedroom. I didn't want to open the wrong door.

I thought, when Don notices I am not there when breakfast starts, he will come let me know it is ready and lead the way. So, I waited. And waited. He didn't come. It was now past time for breakfast. I felt so embarrassed and silly. They must have thought I was running late. Nope, I was stuck because I didn't want to open the wrong door. Then brilliance struck. I will text him to find out. So, I did. He didn't respond. Eventually I had to call him, letting my in-laws know I got lost, even indoors.

Asking for help reveals my weaknesses to others. Asking for help requires humility. My heart can be proud. But everyone has weaknesses and everyone has strengths. We need each other. That is why God put us in the body of Christ. Under his direction, we each serve as he has gifted us and we help each other.[4]

With all the adjustments and help we need, ignore the desire to portray a strong image. Abolish pride. Understand the limits of independence. As we re-focus on truths, we can ask for help when we need it.

REFLECTION

What have been some of your hardest adjustments to living cross-culturally?

How does your season of life affect how you adjust?

What lies have you found easy to believe during this season?

---

4 Adapted from Eenigenburg, "Hiding Weakness Doesn't Make Me Strong."

What truth can you cling to?

RESPONSE

Imagine that a less-experienced missionary comes to you for advice about what they need to know as they adjust to your location or field. Write out what you think would be most important for them to know.

PRAYER

God, you are the one who never changes. Your faithfulness continues through all generations. You are with me as my circumstances change. I am never alone. Thank you for being my unmovable rock, my unshakeable fortress. You hold me tight. I can face whatever changes come my way because you are my strength. Amen.

RESOURCES

https://missionarycare.com/coping-with-change.html _____

https://missionarycare.com/uncompleted-transitions.html _____

https://screamsinthedesert.wordpress.com/2022/03/31/what-i-would-tell-my-younger-me-starting-out-in-cross-cultural-ministry/ _____

Christine Caine, *Resilient Hope: 100 Devotions for Building Endurance in an Unpredictable World* (Nashville: Thomas Nelson, 2022).

Tanya Crossman, *Misunderstood: The Impact of Growing Up Overseas in the 21st Century* (UK: Summertime Publishing, 2016).

Sarah J. Simons, *The Art of Transition: A Creative Process for Navigating Change* (Great Britain: Springtime Books, 2020).

Chapter 3

I Must Keep My Footing
Balancing Two Worlds

If you're spending an excessive amount of time on social media and feelings of sadness, dissatisfaction, frustration, or loneliness are impacting your life, it may be time to re-examine your online habits and find a healthier balance.

—LAWRENCE ROBINSON AND MELINDA SMITH

Cross-cultural workers today face a pressure that we didn't face in our early years—social media and the internet. Despite its drawbacks, social media has some wonderful benefits, too.

Benefits involve staying in closer contact with loved ones and supporters and keeping up with news and current events in home cultures. Communication overall is easier. Partners in our home country keep current with our ministry and recent successes and challenges. Many resources for our spiritual development and for our ministries are also readily available.

Drawbacks include the emotional upheaval we experience when others post photos and about family events. Every time we log on, we realize anew how much we miss. Years ago, we knew we missed out on things, but we didn't have a constant flow of information to keep reminding us. With more frequent communication and ease of travel, we also hear more pleas to come back home for special family events. Saying yes can be nice, but responding no or explaining why we can't come can affect relationships.

I am thankful I can keep up with family. But I am also now consistently aware of everything I miss by not being there. I feel sad and happy at the same time. Nate and Danielle, returning to their host country after a summer home assignment, described these types of feelings well:

> There were difficulties back in America with family and friends—health issues, struggling relationships, and for the first time since we've been away, the death of a dear friend. It is hard to be so far away when people we love are struggling and hurting.
>
> It is a strange thing to have two lives—one in America, and one here in our host country, both with people and things we love and enjoy—but no matter where we are, we are always missing someone, or thinking of what could happen in our time away, realizing it will be longer than we want before we see them again, and then accepting that there are no guarantees of any of our plans anyways.

For some, social media breeds comparison. Ministry snapshots of people serving in an amazing way makes it look like that is the norm for everyone but me. Other ministries and lives appear to be going seamlessly and productively. I don't see stories about the sweaty, no makeup, can-barely-make-it-out-the-door (or bed) days. It doesn't show the times when people don't show up to the Bible study. Nor when my kids throw a tantrum and we can't go visiting. Or when I throw the temper tantrum and don't want to go. Social media can add fuel to the fire of comparison that I already have a hard time keeping under control, anyway.

We must remember that social media doesn't tell the whole story. When others post things and photos that make everything seem good, we forget that behind the smiles of color coordinated family photos can lie broken hearts and fractured relationships. Sarah Deal, a co-laborer in the gospel and gifted writer, posted some comments on Facebook about what was going on underneath her beautiful smiling face:

> This lady [referring to herself] has a lot of practice putting on a happy face. It's what she does, and it comes as natural as breathing. But can I let you in on a little secret? She's struggling.

> Within literally twelve hours of hubby getting staples and stitches out from his collision with a deer on a motorcycle ride last weekend, she ended up back in the ER with her fourteen-year-old waiting for an x-ray and stitches for a busted elbow after a nasty fall.

> Friends, this is the metaphorical tip of the iceberg of the emotional tension in my heart these days, and I covet your prayers.

> I am reminded often in this season of how weak I am.

> Despite the smile you see, I am often trembling inside. I am not strong in myself. I feel unable to handle even the seemingly small interruptions and ordeals that come waltzing into my tidy little world I try frantically to keep in order. At times I even lie awake at night, scheming about how to maneuver things in such a way so that I can feel normal again—with stresses and pressures lightened and only dishes and laundry and some semblance of normal life to maintain.[1]

Karl Dahlfred writes about social media on his blog, *Gleanings from the Field*. In the post, "Should Missionaries Use Facebook and Twitter?" he mentions four dangers of social media: time consumption, distraction, escapism, and overestimating its importance.[2] I can so easily get sucked into looking at post after post, scrolling mindlessly. The more time I spend on social media, the less time I can spend in my host culture. The less time I spend in my host culture, the less time I have to adjust, learn, and orient myself to it.

Cross-cultural workers face the unique challenge of what to post. Some frequently post a lot of personal information, and others don't post anything because they dislike the scrutiny. If they post a vacation picture, will supporters think they get paid too much or are wasting time? If they post a picture of serving in a poor village, does this exploit the people they serve? How can they communicate what they do while respecting those they serve and those who send them?

While recognizing the challenges, Nate and Danielle describe the benefits of communicating with family and friends for their sons. "While I have a love-hate relationship with electronics, I am thankful that the boys are able to stay connected with family and friends on the other side of the world, and that does help bridge the gap between our two lives."

I don't think we could or should give up social media. We need to proactively consider how we use it, how often we use it, and if it is useful or damaging. I've set limits for myself for how much time I spend on social media. I've messed up, but I get back on track. Others I know have stricter limits or have even deleted certain accounts and some have increased their social media presence for ministry purposes.

---

1 Sarah Deal (@sarah.l.deal.7), Facebook, October 6, 2021.

2 Dahlfred, "Should Missionaries Use Facebook and Twitter?"

As we balance the worlds we live in, we must be intentional to limit time focusing on our home culture and set social media boundaries according to our own circumstances. If we don't, living well in our host homes may be more difficult. Straddling both worlds too much can keep us a little in both, but not a lot in either.

Lies we may believe while balancing our worlds and trying not to fall include:

Pictures tell the complete story.

We can make ourselves look better online—lighting, clothing, how to sit or tilt our chin. We can choose what stories to tell, what milestones we achieve, focusing on telling stories that make us look successful or even more successful than we are. But images can lie. Believers get into trouble when their public images become more important to them than their inner spiritual lives. With social media, we can deceive ourselves into thinking we control our public image until we too believe the lie that we are what we portray to others.

On the other side of the coin, we naively can believe the things others post to be who they really are. Then we're shocked when we discover the crumbling pieces of their inner person—they can't maintain the public image of a super-spiritual-kingdom-influencer—and we catch a glimpse of reality.

I can easily control time on social media.

We deceptively think we have more self-control than we do, proving the need to regularly examine ourselves and how we use our time. My iPhone gives me a weekly update on how much time I've spent scrolling. I remember being shocked the first time I saw the report from a particularly uncontrolled week. Yesterday morning I rode the metro in my city and noticed every person looking at their smart phone. No longer was anyone talking to others in the car.

One of the biggest challenges for parents today may be helping their kids control time spent online. Children need time in the real world and outside, not only within a digital world of games or seeking approval from their virtual friends. Parents who have difficulty monitoring their own time on electronic devices can end up modeling addiction to social media to their children.

Truths we must embrace for wisdom as we straddle two worlds:

God values me even if I have no followers or don't tweet.

Often when I post something on social media, within minutes I check to see if I have any likes or comments. It's as though I'm in junior high school again, looking to others to validate my worth. Even if I have no comments, likes, or followers, or if someone writes negative comments, this does not affect my value as a person. Why am I so concerned about it?

God loves me all the time, in every way, no matter what. Though the world is against me, I care only that God is for me. Time and again, I must reject the pervasive ideology that responses to me or about me on social media reflect my value as a person.

Believers live for an audience of "One." This thought keeps me focused on who I am really living for and whose approval matters. And when I know that the audience of One loves me no matter what, the likes or dislikes on social media cease to matter.

The Holy Spirit empowers me to do God's will.

I need not bow to the mercy of my own strength. When I fail at keeping a commitment—whether limiting my time on social media or following through with a task—I don't just give in and say I couldn't help it or decide that since I messed up I should just give up trying. No, we ask for help to keep progressing. God gives strength to the weary and wisdom to those who ask for it. He never leaves us powerless.

Paul reminds us in 2 Corinthians 12 that God's power becomes evident in our weakness. He also writes that we resemble clay pots (2 Cor 4). All glory goes to him when his strength shines through our weakness. We are in trouble only when we think we must be strong enough on our own to handle what comes our way.

I can find creative ways to deal with the sadness of being far away.

When our granddaughter, Penelope Sue, was born, we lived in South Asia. The news of her birth gave me such joy. Seeing pictures of her made me realize anew that I lived a world away from the newest member of our family and I couldn't stop crying. I wanted so much to meet her in person.

I tried praying for me and for her but ended up sobbing even more as she stayed in the forefront of my mind. To help my thoughts and emotions get to a more normal state, I tried what I now call "Monk therapy." I watched an episode of Monk, the obsessive-compulsive TV detective, and "escaped" for about forty-five minutes. That brief escape gave me time to breathe, think of other things, and relax. Not exactly a spiritual remedy, but we are physical, emotional, and social—interconnected—beings. Sometimes a little bit of an escape is good.

As we straddle two worlds, we will benefit from taking the time to discover the things we can and need to do to keep our footing.

REFLECTION

How has social media affected you emotionally?

What advantages of social media excite you?

What adjustments do you need to make regarding your time on social media?

What lies have you struggled with around social media?

What truths would be helpful to you as you straddle two worlds?

RESPONSE

Consider which of the four dangers of social media (time consumption, distraction, escapism, or overestimating its importance) you are facing.

Write out a plan that addresses how to deal with it.

Evaluate again after one month.

PRAYER

God, it is tricky balancing my two worlds. Help me use social media wisely. Forgive me when my mindless scrolling becomes obsessive. Empower me to look to you for strength as I work to get my footing. I want to know what is going on in my passport country, but I also want to stay focused on what you have for me here. By your grace, I choose to live for you, my audience of One. Amen.

RESOURCES

https://ourgoodwinjourney.com/overseas-worker-speaks/ _____

https://blog.eastwest.org/gods-power-is-revealed-in-our-weakness _____

https://www.desiringgod.org/articles/the-blissful-and-trivial-life _____

Netflix: *The Social Dilemma*

Tony Reinke, *12 Ways Your Phone is Changing You* (Wheaton: Crossway, 2017).

Paul David Tripp, *Reactivity: How the Gospel Transforms Our Actions and Reactions* (Wheaton: Crossway, 2022).

Chapter 4

I Can't Anticipate Everything
Unexpected Challenges

> *Unexpected turbulence creates an opportunity*
> *to experience more of God.*
>
> —LEAH DIPASCAL

We are usually prepared for the arrival of teammates. Rarely, though, are we prepared for the changes that occur after their arrival. Unexpected things happen. Circumstances change.

When choosing where to serve, future teammates may look at members of the teams they want to join. They desire to work with quality leaders and proven teammates who have experience in local ministries. They want to work with people they resonate with in personality or have gifts that fit well together. But by the time they raise support and finally arrive, the leader may have left and other team members relocated.

Not only do teammates change but also what the organization implies in training may differ from reality on the field. For example, a person who wants to be involved in youth ministry may be given a green light by the organization's mobilizers. However, they may hear a different message from the field side. A team leader might say that youth ministry isn't possible in their culture. Field leadership may determine they need more people to fill out current teams before starting work in a new city. (These unexpected changes highlight the great need for mobilizers and field leadership to maintain good communication about locations and specific ministry needs.)

Illnesses invade. Personal illnesses happen unexpectedly that change our plans and those of our teammates. Brain cancer. Thyroid issues. Dementia. Heart attacks. Divorce of family members or the death of loved ones back home affects where in the world we need to serve as well as how we are able to serve.

Sin corrupts. Loneliness brings strong temptation to fill the void with relationships we wouldn't have considered in our home setting. Using social media to reconnect with old flames can lead a lonely person down a path where moral failure looms. Relationships fracture. Bitterness blossoms. Forgiveness isn't sought or isn't given, and the unity that should portray the church gives way to division.

Gossip infects. Gossiping could be described as the work of a grown-up tattletale. Someone tells a person something in confidence, maybe as a prayer request. Before you know it, other people know. Possibly a leader felt the need to pass the information on to their leader (without informing the person who shared it).

New believers backslide. Someone comes to know Jesus and they begin growing in their faith. They join a newly planted church. Then they stop spending time in the Word. They miss fellowship times and don't return calls. We grow discouraged when they disengage from us.

A teammate's love for Jesus wanes, as well as their desire to serve or love others. The Word becomes stale. Prayer morphs into a duty to get through a list rather than a desire to know God or recognize dependence on him. Possibly, our own spiritual life becomes lackluster. Quiet times slip. Other things take the place of time with God. More sleep, more TV, more social media. When anything becomes a habitual escape from reality and from our pursuit of God, we enter a danger zone. We all go through periods where time with God is more a duty than a delight, but staying there can lead to a diminished walk with God.

Schools close. Language schools lose teachers or finances. Our kids' schools lose students when families transition or teachers move on. Even minor losses become major if the schools can barely cover expenses. So, they close, or their quality drops, or their tuition increases beyond the reach of missionary budgets.

Visas are revoked. Perhaps with no warning. Some workers are taken straight to the airport and deported. Others are given twenty-four to forty-eight hours. Still others are allowed to stay until their current visa expires. Even if they know the possibility of deportation still exists, it still feels unexpected when it actually occurs.

Leaders mess up. Miscommunication or lack of communication frustrates everybody. Some missionaries, especially single women, feel they have no voice (one reason they leave their team or organization). Learning to deal with a directive leader when you prefer a facilitative one can be challenging. Leading a person who needs more direction when you value independence can frustrate you. Sometimes mistakes prove costly. Other times, there are just hiccups along the way that can be resolved or tolerated.

One missionary woman wrote, "There were times when we felt very alone, and did not feel like leadership really understood what was going on or had our backs. We wondered what they actually believed about us. We did not feel like anyone really knew us or cared to know us."

It can sometimes be difficult for leaders to both supervise and provide member care. In some cases, only when someone's issues become critical are extra steps taken to provide or ask for more professional care. Some team leaders won't visit a field or work with a person unless a crisis necessitates it. Putting out fires already burning keeps them so busy that they can't help to prevent other smoldering embers that can eventually burst into new flames.

Followers don't follow as leaders think they should. Maybe they want to share ideas they think will enhance the ministry. Possibly they see mistakes the leader makes and want to address them. Maybe they have a differing vision or philosophy. Some leaders, when challenged, feel attacked and become defensive. Or maybe the leader leads well, but the follower just doesn't want to follow. They want to go their own way. They want to be the leader. Feelings get hurt on both sides.

When teammates don't receive the help they need from their leaders, following is more challenging. When leaders don't listen to or care about their followers, leadership weakens. When teammates ignore the advice and experience of their leaders, leaders feel demeaned. When teammates constantly disparage their leaders, leaders feel discouraged and want to quit leading.

Leaders need to learn to hear ideas and vision from newcomers without automatically rejecting them because of their lack of experience. Some people arrive on the field with great ideas and fresh vision for how to get things moving. They desire to be heard. However, leaders expect the new arrival to understand that because of the leader's experience, they already know what works and what doesn't. We all need to discover ways to share ideas and vision with humility and openness.

New arrivals also expect to be supported by people who understand their struggles and empathize with them. But sometimes they hear, "This is nothing! You should have seen it when we first arrived. It was way worse than what you are experiencing," or, "Just suck it up. Of course, it is hard. Did you think it would be easy? This is the way it is. Get over it." These aren't the responses they need or want to hear.

We could go on and on about the unexpected. Political coups take place. Borders close. Wars start. Kidnappings are threatened or take place. One messenger shared, "There was internal conflict in my country of service (suicide bombers, coup attempt, etc.), team conflict ... I couldn't get my residency permit in the city I was living in (had to move back to the capital), and six teammates were forced to leave in the stretch of a year and a half." What a lot of stress.

There is no way any of us can prepare for all the unexpected. If we could, it wouldn't be unexpected. But there are things we can do. We can do our best to think through our expectations, ask about others' expectations, and communicate clearly about it all. We can do risk assessments and work on contingency plans specific to our places of service. When the unexpected happens, we can take time to debrief and work through the implications.

We can become more emotionally aware. We can learn how we react to stress and sudden change so that we can be alert to our symptoms. We can get to know our teammates so well that we know their stress signs and learn to be a support to each other. Even though we sometimes respond to the unexpected as if we are alone, ultimately, we face the unexpected together.

Lies we may be tempted to believe when encountering the unexpected:

My team should be and will always be my main source of support.

Almost every training event I've been involved in conducts sessions on conflict management. Yet team friction still seems to come as a surprise.

Having enjoyed being on a team where we all moved in the same direction, had weekly meetings, and supportive relationships, I automatically assumed all teams were similar. Then we joined a team going in various directions. Meetings weren't weekly and, as a result, not as supportive. It took a while for me to determine that this team was different. Once I figured out that I could not change our team dynamics, I started looking for more supportive relationships elsewhere, outside of my team. This way, team relationships worked, but I did not depend on them for my well-being.

One messenger of the gospel wrote, "Both times I left the country were because I didn't have a team left at all. … And I was struggling with burnout from feeling like I constantly had to try to find a way to glue the broken pieces of our team back together."

Leaders never make mistakes.

I'm not sure anyone would ever say they believe leaders never make mistakes, but when upset with leaders, we can unknowingly assume it. And as anyone who has ever been in leadership knows, this obviously isn't true. Leaders make mistakes. Followers make mistakes. Messing up is a part of being sinful humans. Working through these mistakes and the results that follow takes a lot of grace. (Thankfully, God has that in abundance, and he gives it freely to us—to share, not hoard.)

One responsibility of supervisors is supporting those who report to them while also holding them accountable. Team leaders want to know their supervisors have their back. Sometimes this can cause team members to feel unheard because supervisors seem to only support team leaders.

Sometimes team members want leaders to know what they need without asking. Some leaders micromanage, resulting in frustration for those who want more freedom. Some teammates want more direction, but their leader is a hands-off type of leader. Expectations play a role in how we view leaders as good or bad.

Communication takes place whenever I say or hear something.

On the surface, communication appears easy. You talk. I listen. I talk. You listen. Because it seems simple, we think we've communicated. Then, when we misunderstand or are misunderstood, we are surprised. Hidden assumptions and mistaken expectations take place between conversations.

Recently, someone gently confronted me about a wrong I had done. I felt awful, and I apologized. I came to understand what went wrong. But I feared I had damaged our long-standing relationship. I couldn't sleep. I kept picturing several devastating outcomes. I cried for several days. I finally called the person to talk to them again to get a better perspective and ensure our relationship was in good standing. The other person had already moved on. But because I had not, I assumed they couldn't either. I was wrong. We were good. We put a new plan into place and nothing more was said about the wrong I had done.

While miscommunication can take place when we share the same culture, the potential increases between different cultures. An Asian sister held a workshop for North Americans about communication mishaps. She asked us how we would interpret an invitation out for lunch. I would have thought, "Oh, we are building a relationship." However, for her, lunch provided an opportunity to communicate about a need. Also, she explained that if she didn't speak up during a team meeting, North Americans would assume that she agreed with all the decisions. But in reality, she didn't want to publicly disrespect the leader, so she remained quiet about the issue until she could communicate her opinion through a third party.

As we learn about the different cultures of our teammates, we may try to adapt to theirs even as they try to adapt to ours. Friends from the Middle East may decline coffee the first two times to be socially polite and then accept on the third time. But when westerners try to be culturally appropriate and say no the first time, the Middle Easterner may take that as a true no since they've learned that westerners are more direct. Miscommunication continues.

Truths we must remember and understand when working through the unexpected:

I must be proactive in staying well while overseas.

When something isn't working (relationships, my own well-being, ministry progress, etc.), it won't help me to waste time blaming others. I need to focus on what I need to do to stay well. If I feel physically sick, I go to the doctor. Yes, I pray. I also take medicine and follow the doctor's orders. Likewise, when I feel emotionally unwell, I need to seek help—talk with my team leader, pray with a friend, confer with a counselor. Sitting back doing nothing, waiting, and hoping things improve are not effective strategies for thriving.

We must keep pursuing our relationship with God. Practicing new spiritual disciplines, staying in the Word, and working on our prayer life are all important ways to stay healthy spiritually. Take steps to find a spiritual mentor. Have a sabbath rest. Be proactive in developing sacred rhythms or holy habits.

Music can also enhance our soul's wellbeing. Whether we sing songs or listen to them, meaningful words and melodies can soothe and encourage us. Though not musically inclined, I find listening to a worship song as part of my time with God meaningful. We suggest creating your own playlist of songs about spiritual grit (like Stephen Curtis Chapman's "Don't Lose Heart," or "Battle Belongs" by Phil Wickham). We must spend time on life-giving activities. Eva says that life-giving activities are more than recreation and leisure or simply relaxation. While those are important too, life-giving activities truly re-create. They give refreshment and restoration. They leave the partaker energized to get back to the hard stuff, the daily grind—that task they have been avoiding. For many people these activities double as their hobby but not necessarily—things like gardening, playing a sport, creative writing, art, journaling, photography, hiking, reading, or puzzles.

Eva also encourages global workers to start by evaluating their current soul care routines. To discover this, make a chart, a list, or use your planner or calendar to look at your rhythms. Make a column for daily, weekly, monthly, and annual activities. Write down how you pursue your walk with God (Bible reading, prayer time, meditation, etc.), your time with others (church, small group, accountability partner, coffee date, etc.), and your self-care (fitness, life-giving activity, sleep, vacation, fun, etc.). Determine if any changes need to be made in order to stay well. You can find a sample worksheet in Appendix One.

A good rule of thumb is to take (in addition to your daily time) at least one hour a week, one day a month, and one week a year for attending to your soul in personal retreat.[1] Remember, we cannot view soul care as a charging station that we visit only when our battery registers low. Soul care is a lifestyle, rooted in constantly abiding in Christ.[2]

Grace must be given and received in team relationships, especially with leaders.

Bitterness and lack of forgiveness are consistent themes in missions. Feeling unappreciated seems common. We can be stingy in offering words of affirmation and lacking in encouragement. Quickly pointing out others' mistakes comes easily. We tend to give ourselves grace and expect more from others.

I often wonder how Nehemiah led such a diverse group of workers in rebuilding the walls of Jerusalem—people from all walks of life—perfumers, families, goldsmiths, rulers, daughters, sons of rulers, priests. But even there we read about the dissension of the nobles who would not stoop to lend a hand and serve their Lord (Neh 3). Grace was needed then and is needed now in all of our relationships.

---

1 Others suggest one hour a day, one day a week, one weekend a month, and one week a year.

2 This illustration comes from Steve Sweatman of Mission Training International at the Mental Health and Missions Conference, 2015.

Forgiveness is essential. Read (and maybe reread) the chapter on forgiveness in part two. Untreated bitterness is fatal. Team covenants can help keep relationships strong. You can find a sample team covenant in Appendix Two.

Communication always involves work and needs evaluation.

While most resources on good communication among believers addresses marriage, all relationships require healthy communication. Communication demands work. One conversation is seldom enough for making bigger decisions as a team. When I think I've communicated clearly and well, I should always double check.

One team of five, all from North America, faces some upcoming big changes. An older couple will transition back to the States. A younger couple on the team is also expecting to move, leaving one, single teammate. In a team meeting, the five discussed hosting short termers the summer before all of these transitions. The two couples thought they should proceed with hosting since the single desired teammates. The single man, due to time constraints, seemed reluctant. The two married couples didn't want to push an agenda and sought to listen to him. They urged him to cast the deciding vote, since the outcome would affect him the most. However, their attempt at deferring to him only stressed him out more.

Fortunately, through further conversations, the four apologized and worked toward resolution. Through the challenging conversations, they understood each other's boundaries and worked together for a common cause with unified effort.

Diligently pursuing good communication must be a high priority for teams and goes a long way in resolving unexpected challenges.

REFLECTION

What are some of the unexpected things you have encountered?

What are some healthy ways you might deal with the unexpected?

What stress symptoms do you need to watch for?

What lies seem true to you when facing unexpected events?

What truth is most meaningful to you in your current situation?

RESPONSE

After writing out your current soul care rhythms, ask yourself:
What works well for me (or doesn't) in my soul care?

What is missing or out of balance?

Do I have enough rest for the work I am doing? Am I retreating too much?

What will bring life to my relationship with God? What new disciplines can I add?

In what ways am I experiencing a lack of care from others? Where can I find support?

In what ways might my body be suffering from lack of adequate care? How can I improve my physical well-being?

What activity most replenishes and feeds my soul? How can I incorporate this into my life or routine?

What might be keeping me from practicing healthy soul care?

What changes will lead to more attention to my soul care?

Start this week to put into practice what you have discovered.

PRAYER

Lord, you never lead us where you haven't been. You are never surprised by the unexpected challenges that catch us off guard. You always know what is next for us. You also know our heart and the hearts of our teammates. May we pursue spiritual health, give grace to one another, and seek to communicate well. Give us strength to work hard to build trust and understanding. May our love for you and each other be evident for your glory. Amen.

RESOURCES

https://themissionsexperience.weebly.com/blog/expectations-factors _____

https://www.desiringgod.org/articles/six-lessons-in-good-listenings-in-good-listening _____

https://krystalrsimpson.com/four-principles-of-effective-christian-communication-2/ _____

https://www.youtube.com/watch?v=saXfavo1OQo _____
(William Ury, "The Power of Listening")

https://www.saritahartz.com/ _____

Ruth Haley Barton, *Pursing God's Will Together: A Discernment Practice for Leadership Groups* (Downers Grove: InterVarsity Press, 2012).

Ruth Haley Barton, *Sacred Rhythms: Arranging Our Lives for Spiritual Transformation* (Downers Grove: InterVarsity Press, 2006).

Adele Calhoun, *Spiritual Disciplines Handbook: Practices that Transform Us* (Downers Grove: InterVarsity Press, 2015).

Stephen W. Smith, *Solo: Creating Space with God* (Independently published, 2021).

Letitia Suk, *Getaway with God: The Everywoman's Guide to Personal Retreat* (Grand Rapids: Kregel Publications, 2016).

Gary Thomas, *Sacred Pathways: Nine Ways to Connect with God* (Grand Rapids: Zondervan, 2020).

Chapter 5

I Must Navigate Priorities
Juggling Multiple Roles

Even the most regular, seemingly unimportant tasks of my life must be shaped and directed by a heartfelt desire for the glory of God.

—PAUL DAVID TRIPP

When we first arrived overseas with young children, I had extra roles and responsibilities added to my life. No longer just a wife, mother, homemaker, and ministry partner, I also became a full-time language student. Whereas my husband, once away from his responsibilities as a seminary student, painting business owner, and church volunteer, had fewer roles. His main ministry focus narrowed down to learning a new language. His stress level decreased. Mine increased.

Of course, we both added the roles of teammates, church planters, and support raisers. Team membership and relationships involved both blessings and challenges.

For those who come into missions from the corporate world with a defined workday and clear-cut guidelines, adjusting to setting their own routines and outcomes can be stressful. They not only have to learn different roles but also need to set their own schedules and timelines. Team leaders and mentors can help, but a lot of activities in missions require self-motivation.

Describing a typical day when missionaries have various roles and responsibilities can be difficult. I resonate with this post by Linda and Ron Sheppard:

Hmm ... people keeping asking me to outline what a "typical" day in my life looks like. Oh my gosh. It kinda makes me want to laugh because I don't know that there is a "typical" day in my life or a "typical" day in the life of really anyone that lives in Haiti, or a typical day in the life of a missionary.[1]

Global women have multiple roles. Marguerite Kraft, in her book *Frontline Women*, summarizes the struggle of balancing roles well:

Balancing the juggling act of wife, mother, and homemaker can be a challenge of the highest order on the mission field. Missionaries typically comment that simply the act of living requires much more time for them, and perhaps no one feels it more than the missionary wife and mother trying to manage a busy household in a foreign land.[2]

Homeschooling, hospitality, team meetings, communicating with supporters, and trying to get away for a date now and again adds up to a huge time commitment.

---

1 Sheppard, "Juggling Multiple Roles as a Missionary."
2 Kraft, *Frontline Women*, 140.

When we first started out in missions, I remember being asked how much time I spent in ministry and, separately, how much time I spent with family. Through the years I've come to know that time invested in my family is ministry. Whether playing games with my kids or mopping floors, cooking, cleaning, washing dishes—all these things can be done with a heart of joyful service to the Lord. Paul wrote, "Whatever you do, work at it with all your heart, as working for the Lord, not for human masters, since you know that you will receive an inheritance from the Lord as a reward. It is the Lord Christ you are serving" (Col 3:23–24). Knowing how much time to invest in the different spheres of ministry needs to be revisited regularly as life changes. My schedule as an empty nester differs from my schedule as a mother with children at home.

My friend, Suzy, a single worker with over 30 years of experience in cross-cultural ministry says that single missionaries tend towards workaholism. People expect them to do more because they supposedly have all this "free time." Married people tend to forget that single people must do everything on their own while married people can split their responsibilities. It could be that married people think single peoples' lives are freer and judge them more harshly when they say no to ministry opportunities. They do have more flexibility in their time—a blessing—but they might not have someone to support their refusals when others pressure them to say yes.

Men juggle priorities as well. I watched my husband balance many roles: his job in the community, role in the team, time with the family, commitment to church planting. These different roles were often intertwined. When our kids were smaller and he worked out in the community, I and our kids helped him determine when we needed him at home—sometimes verbally and sometimes with tears. The kids didn't always use words, but it became evident when they needed to see more of their dad.

When team issues came up, he knew he needed to invest more time in those relationships. Sometimes his job took more hours, sometimes family did. Schedules fluctuated, and he became adept at knowing what to do when and where to do it.

One man wrote about managing his roles:

> I do know that I will probably drop something accidentally due to the juggling; I try not to. As missionaries, I feel destined to wear different hats frequently. I am in a different role now than when I was in Asia. In my new country the four roles I'm juggling are: family man, missions training center teacher, mobilization center founder, church elder. The number of hours is fairly consistent in both places, but the importance or emphasis of tasks varies wildly from week to week. Yes. Juggling roles has caused me to consider quitting ... or at least consistently wish for just one role instead of multiple ones.

A member care provider pointed out that for some, there are brain wiring issues that makes juggling more than one thing very difficult. That adds underlying stress that others might not understand. As much as we can, we must learn to prioritize as we juggle. We can and should say no to some roles. However, some roles last a lifetime. Some seasons of life are busier than others. For me, compared to the roles I juggled in my younger years, this season of life is less stressful and hectic. But I still juggle and decide on priorities daily.

Lies we may be tempted to believe when juggling roles:

I should always get it right.

The truth is I don't. Everyone messes up. For perfectionists, this is unsettling. We want to get the juggling act right all the time. When we've read accounts of all the positive things missionaries have done through the centuries, serving well can look like a simple thing. It's important to keep learning and to be sensitive to when we might be off course. As sinners, we mess up. As learners, we can grow in discerning how to juggle better. As we talk with others and watch their examples, we can discover changes we need to make. But we will fail at times.

Family is getting in the way of "real" ministry.

My home church sent us to the field to see fellowships planted, to evangelize and disciple the nations in this little corner of the world. People give and pray so that we might serve the Lord in this dark, spiritually needy place. When we spend time with family, we might miss the importance of that responsibility. Cleaning house, buying groceries, or cooking meals doesn't feel as important or look like serving God.

What do we write in our prayer letters when family schedules have kept us so busy that our ministry outside of home looks unimpressive? We don't want to go overseas and end up only raising our families. Nor do we want to be so busy in community ministry that we lose our families. How do we communicate about and find balance in both spheres of ministry?

No one else struggles as much as me.

It often looks like others have an easier time. We know our struggles. We know the argument we had this morning. Others seem more consistent in their time with God, their ministries more fruitful, the doors more open for them. We may feel our language isn't as fluent or priorities as well defined. We readily see higher energy levels in go-getters. For those who have been overseas longer, their relationships appear more meaningful. Why does everyone seem to be handling things so much better than we are? We need to remember everybody struggles, though often the struggles remain hidden.

Truths we must cling to while juggling and maybe dropping some balls:

I can revisit and evaluate my roles regularly and adjust.

Because I choose to invest more time in my home and family ministry this year doesn't mean next year will look the same. Annual reviews present excellent opportunities to examine the past and make needed changes for the future.

Evaluation doesn't only have to take place once per year. In fact, we benefit from regular reflection about our roles and ministry. Lamp writes, "Without periodic reflection, our work can become burdensome because we lose the perspective that God is with us and upholding us in our ministry."[3]

At some point in time, most people come to a place where they realize they can't do it all. To use time wisely, some hire household help so that while someone cleans the house, they can spend time on other ministry opportunities. Others purchase timesaving devices

---

3 Lamp, *Journey With Me*, 57.

that aren't always as common in certain places of the world, like dishwashers, fully automatic washing machines, and dryers. Depending on where people live, they get outside help with water, firewood, cooking, and driving.

Different people decide how to strategize in different ways with a lot of variety. Those who choose not to hire a cook should not judge those who do. God guides us in various ways so that we can serve him in all that we do. The goal is to serve the Lord, using time and energy wisely.

Reflect. Adapt. Juggle. But let's do so wisely and intentionally as we think through what is needed during this life season in our own contexts and circumstances.

I serve Jesus in all I do.

One of my strongest convictions is that ministry is 24/7. How I love and serve my family, my team, my community, and my world should all stem from love for God (which stems from his love for me). Vacation. Sleeping. Sabbath rests. Eating. Serving. In whatever I do my desire should be for God's glory.

Sometimes, missionaries base their work solely on the needs around them, and they end up exhausted, serving others while snapping at them. While needs are unending, our energy isn't. Recognize limits, develop healthy life rhythms, serve well, and do all for the glory of Jesus.

In the early days, my household chores were much harder to do overseas than in my home country. I lacked some appliances. I needed to learn to cook from scratch. I worked longer and harder to keep up with four kids and my husband. While studying the gospels, I read, "Many women were there, watching from a distance. They had followed Jesus from Galilee to care for his needs" (Matt 27:55). I remember thinking, *Well, if I was caring for Jesus's needs it would matter more.* And then, of course, the words of Jesus from the parable about the king came to mind, "The King will answer and say to them, 'Truly I say to you, to the extent that you did it to one of these brothers of Mine, *even* the least *of them*, you did it to Me.'" (Matt 25:40 NASB 1995, emphasis added). Serving my family, serving strangers, serving anyone at any time equals serving Jesus.

I need time with God for spiritual refreshment and to maintain vision.

In the busyness of life and ministry, time with God can get pushed aside. Lots of studies show that ministers often get so busy serving that their own walks with God suffer. This, in turn, affects their serving. In 2007, I researched global women for the book *Expectations and Burnout*. For those women who spent regular time with God, only 10% experienced burnout. For those who didn't, the rate of burnout increased to 30%.[4]

We need time with the Lord to receive strength, truth, conviction, comfort, challenge, hope, and joy. Paul wrote, "For everything that was written in the past was written to teach us, so that through the endurance taught in the Scriptures and the encouragement they provide we might have hope" (Rom 15:4). The Word teaches us endurance and provides encouragement. The Scriptures lead us to hope.

Through the years, I've learned the important lesson that we need to keep trying new things to develop our walks with God. Whenever we traveled, I tried to keep up with the same devotional pattern that worked so well for me at home. But all the unknowns, schedule

---

4 Eenigenburg and Bliss, *Expectations and Burnout*, 60.

changes, and disruptions regularly interrupted me. I kept repeating the same thing and the only constant result was guilt. When the kids lived at home, my quiet time pattern that worked on weekdays didn't come as easily on weekends. So, I experimented with different approaches on weekends and while traveling. Like reading a different portion of God's Word or not always journaling the same way. I also sometimes packed smaller journals because of limited luggage space.

Because of the uncertainties during travel, Eva suggests cross-cultural workers come up with two plans for time with God. One is their regular quiet time routine. The second is a modified plan for traveling. A short devotional reading, for instance, or a prayer app. Having a pre-determined, time-with-God travel plan has helped me to have some connection with the Lord rather than give up on my quiet time all together.

Through the years different Bible study methods, prayer times, spiritual disciplines have ministered to me in different ways. This year I am reading through the entire Bible. I celebrated the day I finished Leviticus! It is vital that we keep learning and growing using different means so that we don't get stuck in ruts or become stale in our thinking and practices.

REFLECTION

What factors contribute to deciding where to invest your time?

What do you need to juggle your roles well?

What roles or responsibilities should you refuse?

How do family values influence your priorities?

What are your lifetime roles and how are you honing your gifts in these roles?

Which of these lies (or other ones) have you believed as you juggle your roles?

Which of these truths (or other truths God brings to mind) are important to remember as you determine your priorities?

RESPONSE

Schedule time for an annual review now. Don't wait for the new year.

Use one of the guides suggested in the resources below or find your own.

Follow through and make the necessary changes.

PRAYER

Lord, sometimes I feel like I cannot handle all the roles I have to juggle. I desperately need you to enable me to fulfill the responsibilities you have given me. But I also need your discernment to sort out the things I should let go of. As I reflect, open my eyes and heart to hear you and then give me courage to act. Amen.

RESOURCES

https://catalystintl.org/conferences/breathe/ _____
(refreshment for missionary families, singles)

https://catalystintl.org/conferences/traction/ _____
(refreshment, training for missionary men)

https://thriveministry.org/ _____
(refreshment, training for missionary women)

https://ginabutz.com/transition _____

https://globaltrellis.com/ _____

https://www.seebeyond.cc/ _____

https://nfppeople.com.au/2018/02/how-to-get-more-done-when-youre-juggling-multiple-roles-in-your-nfp/ _____

https://communicatingacrossboundariesblog.com/2013/10/29/the-security-blanket-of-busy/ (communicatingacrossboundariesblog.com) _____

Chapter 6

I Feel Alone Even When I'm Not
Loneliness

You are never left alone when you are alone with God.

—WOODROW KROLL

"To some extent, loneliness and anxiety are inherent to missionary life," Amy Newsome with Mission to the World (MTW) points out in an interview.[1] I agree. Both married and single people face loneliness adjusting to a foreign place, new people, and an unfamiliar culture. Building friendships takes time, more time than we would like. Even when we join a team, those relationships are normally recent ones. Every time we've moved internationally—six times—I've always experienced loneliness in the beginning. I understand my surprise the first time, but I continued to be dismayed each time I felt friendless and thought I would remain stuck there forever.

Feelings of loneliness intensify when we come from a place where we have close ties with family, deep friendships, and supportive networks to a place where we must start afresh.

In an article from Within Reach Global, the author writes:

Loneliness is magnified on the mission field, especially when involved in cross-cultural missions. We are in a foreign country, away from family, away from little luxuries and comforts that we are used to. Most likely, we are surrounded by people speaking a language that is not our own. We don't have the same strong support structure that we would have back home.[2]

In the same article, the author also shares that loneliness is not a sin. Loneliness calls us to intimacy. When we are alone, we reach out more intentionally to our Lord. Additionally, loneliness can be turned into incense, meaning it invites us to trust in Jesus and lay this need at his feet. And last, we can never be as lonely as Jesus was on the cross. That puts things in perspective as we remember that alone he took the penalty for our sin.[3]

Ronald Koteskey points out that loneliness has nothing to do with being alone; it has to do with relationships. He also lists reasons loneliness appears so commonly in missions. As you read through his (adapted) descriptions, note the ones that resonate with your experience:

- Part of being a missionary is moving from one place to another. Singles do not even have a spouse to talk with when they first move.

- If you do not move, other people from your agency are likely to.

- Part of working cross-culturally is living in a place far from acquaintances in your past.

---

1 Shaughnessy, "Pandemic, Missions, and Loneliness: Q&A with MTW's Member Care Network."
2 "4 Truths to Help Overcome Loneliness on the Mission Field."
3 "4 Truths to Help Overcome Loneliness on the Mission Field."

- Perhaps you had heard how friendly people were in your host culture, but you find them quite distant.

- You may not be accepted by the people you came to serve and feel rejected, even by people serving in your agency.

- You came to serve, but you find that political or social forces in your host country discriminate against you because of your passport country, your race, your religion, your gender, or even your singleness.

- You long to share deeply with others, but you are not able to find anyone in your agency or in your host culture who wants to do so.

- You do not want to become too close to anyone because you know that either they or you will be moving soon.

- You do not understand how to interact well in your host culture—or maybe your passport one.

- Having low self-esteem or lack of self-confidence [makes] it difficult to get close to anyone, single or married, in any culture.

- Personal problems in adjustment prevent you from interacting adequately with other expats or nationals.

- You grew up in a farming community or small town, and the large city in which you serve has no similar sense of community.[4]

Though Koteskey categorized his article for single people, we must keep in mind that married people also experience loneliness.

When we moved to South Asia, I only had three phone numbers in my phone. My husband—that really doesn't count because he must be on there. My two teammates, which was good. They were wonderful. But again, did they really have a choice? We needed to stay in touch. After several months, I attended a conference for women ministering overseas. One night they asked everyone who lived in my area to gather in a corner of the room and I returned home with nine new numbers in my phone. I cannot express how deeply thankful and happy that made me. After the conference, I met regularly with many of those women and still treasure those friendships from more than a decade ago. That night I found my community.

We also don't want to overly depend on people to satisfy our longings. One single worker mentioned that loneliness can be a potential trigger for moral failure, or at least a strong temptation to look for our needs to be met in people. She said that men she wouldn't normally consider pursuing due to their religion or marital status, began to look attractive. Everyone who feels lonely is perhaps more susceptible to temptation to rely on people, even the wrong people, to fulfill their needs.

Pursuing our walk with God is a more fruitful way to deal with loneliness. I recently read a book on spiritual disciplines. Since my goal was to learn spiritual disciplines, I committed to pausing after each chapter in order to put the specific discipline into practice. I felt more disciplined by deciding that before I even started reading! While this meant going through the book slower, it also made my life richer.

---

4 Kotesky, "Missionary Single Issues: Loneliness."

Then I came upon a chapter about solitude. I was not excited. I dreaded it. As I already often felt alone, more time alone didn't seem to be something I should consider. I talked with teammates and they pointed out the huge difference between being alone and choosing to spend time in solitude with God.

So, I scheduled a five-hour date with God—just me and him. I was skeptical. Then I was surprised. With no schedule to follow or commitments to keep, I spent a longer time praying. I read, relaxed, and reflected on Scripture. During the time, I became aware of heartfelt burdens I had been ignoring. I hadn't been intentionally burying these concerns, but because I had neglected to dig deeper and spend extended time praying about them, I didn't realize how heavy and normal they had become. The joy of walking without that weight was something I had forgotten.

I left my date refreshed and feeling more connected with God. I also came away with a project that I knew God was leading me to do. I did it. God used it. My burdens felt lighter and my soul freer as I drew nearer to God.

This time of solitude was so meaningful that I now set aside one full morning each month to spend with God. I guess it is still called solitude, but I don't feel alone. I know his presence with me. I've gone to cafés, sat outside, hung out in my living room, and taken walks. I've read, prayed, journaled, sang, drew, and cried. I sense God's delight and my own as the Holy Spirit ministers to my soul.

In the busyness of life and chaotic pace of ministry, we may keep serving without abiding in the One we serve. I want to keep developing practices that will help me spend time alone with God and hear his voice so that I notice his presence when I feel lonely.

Developing our personal relationship with God and building friendships with others help us deal with bouts of loneliness and enrich our lives. Loneliness can help us learn to draw near to the Savior and friendships encourage us as we seek and serve the Lord together.

Lies we may be more susceptible to when we feel lonely:

I should go home where I have friends.

I remember getting together with friends in my home country over coffee and enjoying rich conversations without even trying. But in the midst of loneliness here, I can forget I also had times of loneliness there as well.

We picture the past in our mind and when we feel lonely, we may tend to idealize that memory. Feeling lonely can make us want to go home or move back to a previous location. Finding new friends can be challenging, so while we wait, we may think going back home would fill that void. Loneliness drives me to want the friendships I once had where I had them. I long for comfortable settings with comfortable people—home.

I will never make friends, so I give up and wallow in despondency.

Feeling lonely makes us miserable. We may grow discouraged and believe we won't ever make friends. It can be tempting to stay home, watch TV, read books—anything to avoid and escape this sense of not belonging and not being known.

When we do make friends, they leave, and we face yet another goodbye. We can give in to the temptation to stop searching out friends because it doesn't seem worthwhile. Goodbyes hurt, especially after developing good solid friendships. Why work at building friendships when they will most likely end with someone leaving? When workers stop seeking to make friends, loneliness can become so normal that hopelessness sneaks in and stays.

I am alone.

Sensing that I stand alone against all that comes at me, that no one will help, and no one cares feels devastating. When I feel lonely, I sense a disconnection from others which can lead to depression and anxiety, especially if I keep these struggles hidden.

In the Within Reach Global article mentioned at the beginning of this chapter, the author writes, "Loneliness is not a phenomenon exclusive to people on the mission field, but I believe that it's one of the reasons why we can find such disheartening statistics regarding missionary attrition."[5]

When we feel alone, our souls chafe because we were created for community. Paul writes, "Just as a body, though one, has many parts, but all its many parts form one body, so it is with Christ. For we were all baptized by one Spirit to form one body—whether Jews or Gentiles, slave or free—and we were all given the one Spirit to drink. Even so the body is not made up of one part but of many" (1 Cor 12:12–14). We grieve with one another. We rejoice with one another. We stay connected under the headship of Christ.

Truths we can claim when we find ourselves in the depths of feeling unendingly lonely:

I am never alone.

We must always remember that Jesus said he would never leave us or forsake us. Because of this, we are never really alone. The Holy Spirit indwells us. In many of the Old Testament passages God tells his people not to be afraid and assures them of his presence. Jesus says, "And behold, I am with you always, to the end of the age" (Matt 28:20).

In our loneliness we must never forget Jesus, our true friend. Dane Ortlund, in his book *Gentle and Lowly*, writes about having the companionship of Christ:

> But Christ's heart for us means that he will be our never-failing friend no matter what friends we do or do not enjoy on earth. He offers us a friendship that gets underneath the pain of our loneliness. While that pain does not go away, its sting is made fully bearable by the far deeper friendship of Jesus.[6]

I can make new meaningful friendships.

I treasure my friendships from my passport country. We share a common history. My childhood friends influenced how I grew in Jesus. What rich and loving memories fill these relationships. However, after living in multiple new places, I discovered that in time new friendships can become lifelong. My global worker friends and I share common experiences in cross-cultural life that friends and family back home can't fully understand. We've celebrated language and ministry milestones together, knowing the high cost of both. It may feel like one group of friends is better than the other, but they are both valuable, just different.

Even knowing I have friends isn't the same as feeling a kinship with others. After church one afternoon as people drank coffee and ate cookies, everyone had someone to talk to, except me. It felt lonely. Even though I knew almost everyone there and considered them friends, I felt like an outsider. I entered several conversations. But eventually, I just left. I wasn't angry or

---

5 "4 Truths to Help Overcome Loneliness on the Mission Field."

6 Ortlund, *Gentle and Lowly*, 120.

sad, just off. Thankfully, this doesn't happen often. If it did, I would need to take some action in order to develop deeper friendships and a better support system.

God will use loneliness in my life to build into me something he can't do when I keep busy with other people.

When feeling lonely, we are more open to hearing from God because we are more aware of our dependence on him. Loneliness drives me to talk with him frequently. I read his Word looking for help. Then as a result, I can hear him speak to me because I am less distracted and busy. When God brings us through time of loneliness, even before making physical friendships, we learn to make Jesus our friend.

In the article, "The Gift of Loneliness," Shana Schutte writes:

> When we sink into loneliness and allow it to do its redemptive work by embracing it, it can be a powerful teacher. And as Henri Nouwen writes in his book, *The Inner Voice of Love*, we may find our "loneliness not only tolerable," but even fruitful.[7]

REFLECTION

When have you been most lonely?

What have you learned through loneliness?

Why might you hesitate to reach out to new arrivals in the missions' community?

What is meaningful about being a part of the body of Christ?

---

7 Schutte, "The Gift of Loneliness."

How might new friendships help combat loneliness?

What lies draw you in when you feel lonely?

What truths encourage you when you feel lonely?

RESPONSE

Decide on a day this month to schedule a morning of solitude.

Spend some time alone with God, reading his Word, praying, journaling, walking, singing—whatever helps you intentionally focus on time with the Lord.

PRAYER

Jesus, you are always with me. I am never alone. You know the pain of rejection and loneliness. You understand sorrow. So not only are you with me, you are in me, and you know exactly how I feel. Thank you for your kindness. May I never forget your presence and that you invite me to know you as I walk with you. Amen.

RESOURCES

https://omf.org/us/lonely-missionaries-why-and-what-can-we-do-about-it/ ____

https://velvetashes.com/you-belong-here-too/ _____

https://www.openbible.info/topics/i_will_never_leave_you_nor_forsake_you __

https://omf.org/us/lonely-missionaries-why-and-what-can-we-do-about-it/ ____

Elisabeth Elliot, *The Path of Loneliness: Finding Your Way Through the Wilderness to God* (Grand Rapids: Revell, 2007).

Chapter 7

Why Can't We All Get Along?
Messy Relationships

> *In most conflicts, each party quite easily sees the misbehavior and sin of the other. We tend to create inner narratives that magnify the other person's weaknesses and minimize our own contribution to the dispute.*
>
> —ALFRED ELLS

The saying "Ain't nothing easy" is especially true in relationships. Relationships are messy. Moving to a new culture adds stress even on the most stable family relationships. Don and I had been married eight years and had three children when we moved overseas for the first time. We knew a lot about each other and how to relate well with one another. We were even more in love than at the beginning of our marriage and our commitment was strong. But once overseas, we forgot almost everything we had learned. We needed to work hard to keep communicating and loving one another well.

Joining teams made up of people we don't know well (and struggle to get along with) may be one way the great commission suffers. Lamp states, "In fact, my personal belief is that world evangelism is harmed more from inner fighting than outside persecution. We are our own worst enemy!"[1] Various personalities, visions, and philosophies of ministry also contribute to the challenges. Teams formed before arriving overseas discover that, despite their good training and solid friendships, fissures can develop during cross-cultural stress and ministry. And heightened stress levels only add to the difficulty of learning to relate well. Lamp also points out, "Unfortunately, interpersonal conflict stemming from poor team dynamics seems to be the norm rather than the exception in the mission community."[2]

In the introduction, I wrote about how opposites attract in marriage. Those same things that drew Don and me together now threatened to tear us apart. Only after showing grit, staying together, and working through things could we again appreciate the differences that once sparked our interest in each other.

While team life isn't a "till death do us part" relationship like marriage is intended to be, team relationships can go through the same testing period as marriages. At the beginning, differences are appreciated. In time they grate on us. So, we leave because the idea of working together seems impossible. We can quit too soon. However, we can stay and work through— as much as possible—our differences because we have Jesus in common. He gives us the power and love that holds us together.

---

1 Lamp, *Journey With Me*, 129.

2 Lamp, 129.

Team friction remains a major reason people leave teams, countries, and organizations. I remember some stressful team meetings when I wanted to leave. Through the years, we've talked with many global messengers struggling with stressed relationships. People try hard but somehow are unable to work together. Personality, vision, and philosophy differences all come into play.

One couple wrote of the constant transitions of teammates and the difficulty of continuing to work on team development, only to have members leave. Bruce Tuckman wrote a theory of team development in 1965 that included five stages: forming, storming, norming, performing, and adjourning.[3] This couple bemoaned that forming and storming ensued but, because of constant change, the chance to work and be productive as a team never materialized. The norming and performing as a team proved elusive. I think that too often some teams jump from storming directly to adjourning.

This jump presents additional challenges for relationships between team members and their leaders. By the time people admit to serious relationship issues, it is often too late for leaders to work toward resolution, which might have enabled their teammates to stay. On the other hand, teammates might face the problem that when they bring up a relationship issue or other challenge, leaders wait too long to step in and help. Or they ignore issues. Or the leaders are the issue.

Lack of leadership or a very different leadership style can also cause people to leave, or at least want to leave. One gospel messenger wrote, "I believe the expectations from leadership caused much stress and anxiety for me. Throughout my time on the team, I didn't feel like I had a voice. I wasn't heard. Seeking help, I felt ignored and didn't get the assistance I needed until it was considered 'critical.'"

Another cross-cultural worker didn't feel cared for by mission leadership. After moving to a new place, no one in leadership debriefed her or asked about the transition. The leader later did apologize for this, but trust had been shaken. Looking beyond her team leadership, she identified changes in the organization as a whole. These changes hurt her because she had no voice in what was happening. When she asked about a policy, she was told, "This is the way it is now."

Single people, married people, mixed generations, varying levels of experience, strengths, weaknesses, and expectations—all create a beautiful opportunity to model the love of Christ in God's family. However, without care and intentionality, these differences can erupt in division and bitterness. We've seen both.

Consider dating relationships for singles on teams. If you come to a team married, no one has any say about your choice of spouse. But if you are single, teammates may offer unsolicited advice about who you date. While perhaps necessary, this counsel may or may not be appreciated and adds stress to an already complicated scenario.

Good relationships also require ongoing, clear communication. When listening, hearers can be so busy thinking of a response that they don't truly listen. Derek Johnson, a counselor and member care provider for our organization, lists four practices to enhance listening.

- Don't *judge*: "That wasn't very smart." Do practice reflective or active listening. Repeat the person's word verbatim, "So I hear you saying that you are angry because of the way you were treated."

---

3 "Tuckman's Stages of Group Development."

- Don't *defend yourself*: "The reason why I did that was ..." or "It wasn't my fault that you ..." Do define certain words: "I'm not sure what you mean by upset? Angry, sad, confused?"

- Don't *give your opinion* but do clarify: Ask questions like, "Describe to me how you are feeling. What was going on? Where were you?" You are the detective trying to get more information. You are not there to fix it or them.

- Don't *solve their problem*: It is their problem. Do compare or evaluate what they are going through to another thing they have gone through: "When you got angry, was that like when ...?" or "Tell me when you felt, thought, or experienced that before in your life."[4]

Working hard on communication is always a win. Caring enough to stay silent and thinking about what the other person says may be one of the strongest ways to build trust in relationships. Lamp gives the example of Howard, a global servant in Brazil, who wrote, "One of the most powerful tools in missions is listening."[5] When we don't listen, we aren't truly communicating. For more good listening tips, see "Six Lessons for Good Listening" from David Mathis in Appendix Three.

One missionary wrote, "Someone once told me, 'God is always working on everyone in the room.' This has helped us realize and count on God being at work in others, even if we can't see it, and to focus on what he wants to change and do in and through us, as we do our best to love others well."

Difficult people can sometimes make us better. They can also make us bitter. A lot depends on our attitude and how much we think about ourselves. Recently I asked myself, "What is it like having me for a teammate?" I started thinking of how much I like to talk, the stories I tell repeatedly, the times I forget what I already told people, my selfishness, lack of mercy, and desire for things to be done my way. I am so grateful for kind and forgiving teammates.

Each of us needs to be open to taking responsibility for some of the messiness in our relationships. May we give and receive grace freely.

Lies we might believe when relationships are far messier than we had ever imagined:

It's always their fault.

We typically give grace to ourselves and judge others more harshly. We suspect other's motives more than our own. We can see ourselves in the best possible light and see others at their worst. We can be quick to judge. We think we know someone's thoughts. We hear what we want to hear. We lay the blame squarely on their shoulders, especially if there is a history of repeated offenses and no change. As relationships spiral downward, taking offense at one another grows easier and occurs more frequently.

If I was on a different team or in a different organization, relationships would be better.

Without working through issues and challenges, our capacity to thrive diminishes. Remember the illustration of the caterpillar who needs to wiggle out of his cocoon in order to fly. Without the struggle he wouldn't have the strength in his wings to fly. The same applies to relationships. As we encounter difficulties and work through them together, we build relationship skills that

---

4 Derek Johnson, e-mail message to Sue Eenigenburg, January 14, 2022.

5 Lamp, *Journey With Me*, 98.

can help us improve as teammates. Without that, when we go to a different team or different organization, our baggage comes along with us.

Confrontation is always bad.

Even knowing that confrontation is necessary, many of us hate it. Confrontation can go poorly in so many ways (as we've all unfortunately experienced) which makes us want to avoid it even more and think of it negatively. We can be afraid that the other person will get angry and dislike us. We don't like rocking the boat or upsetting people. If I confront someone, what if they confront me back? How can I know when I'm judging unfairly? How do I know when to confront? How does forgiveness fit in? What if confrontation makes the situation and relationship worse? With all that is necessary to know and do for confrontation to go well, we can feel overwhelmed. Confrontation appears too risky.

I came to serve the lost, not my teammates.

Most missionaries come ready to love the unlovely among the lost. We know we need to show patience and love for our national friends to come to know Christ. However, we are less prepared to love our teammates when they seem unlovable to us. We assume that since our teammates are mature believers, they should be able to handle life and ministry without help from us, especially if serving them takes us out of serving in the community.

Truths to keep us grounded when we're rocked by conflict:

Sometimes it is my fault.

I hate to be wrong. But sometimes I am. I love it when I'm right. And sometimes I am. Pride can be an issue in both scenarios.

I need to be open to the reality that I make mistakes. What do I bring into the relationship that has rubbed my teammate the wrong way? What have I done poorly that I am unaware of? How are my assumptions of others' thoughts and feelings affecting my relationships? When have I not spoken up and should have? When did I speak when I might have listened?

Sometimes, no one is at fault at all. Our personalities are simply different and don't mesh. Our organization uses the Myers-Briggs Type Indicator® and GRIP-Birkman® personality testing for teams to better understand each other. We also discuss values and preferred leadership style. We take the FIRO-B® and talk about calling so that teammates can understand each other. These assessments are not meant to label one another or put people in a box. They are tools that help us recognize potential conflict areas with another person due to our personality, not necessarily our behavior.

We are called to love one another as a demonstration of our discipleship (John 13:35). Paul challenges us to do this more and more (1 Thess 4:10). This may entail accepting that I could be at fault or that I need to accept my teammates as they are without trying to change them. Or perhaps we simply need to bear with them and overlook their faults (Col 3:13).

Grace and forgiveness are always possible by God's power.

As a teenager, I co-taught a Vacation Bible School class of fifth and sixth graders. One student asked me about Catholicism. I loved to teach and so I proceeded to instruct even though I had never been a Catholic. My co-teacher was raised in a Catholic church. As I waxed eloquent, it hit me that I should have let my co-teacher take the lead, since she knew more than me and could teach effectively. After class, I apologized to my friend, and she forgave me. Though many years ago, that memory of conviction and grace stands out fresh in my mind.

I also remember the first time someone confessed to me a sin they had committed. About to judge harshly, I remembered my own sin and the grace that God lavished on me. How could I hoard that for myself? Why would I judge someone severely when I was shown mercy?

In one of my graduate school classes, we studied the parable Jesus told of the workers in the vineyard (Matt 20:1–16). A landowner hires some workers. Some start working early in the morning, others at 9 a.m., others at noon, and still more at 3 p.m. He then hires a final group at 5 p.m. At the end of the workday, he pays them all the same wage. The first group grumbles. "These who were hired last worked only one hour," they said, "and you have made them equal to us who have borne the burden of the work and the heat of the day" (v. 20). Jesus replied, "Are you envious because I am generous? So the last will be first, and the first will be last" (v. 15–16).

I didn't like this story and didn't understand why the workers received the same pay. The professor, seeming to read my mind, explained that we may not appreciate this parable nor understand it. He said, "If you think this isn't fair, it is because you associate yourself with the wrong group." And he was right. I put myself in the position of those who worked all day rather than in the place of the one who was hired at the end. This has now become one of my favorite parables because I am so aware of the grace of which I am in desperate need.

The Apostle Paul commands us, "Be kind and compassionate to one another, forgiving each other, just as in Christ God forgave you" (Eph 4:32). Strength and power can come from meditating on God's amazing grace towards us. As we stay aware of it, we become a conduit of that grace to others.

Invest in relationships so they can withstand withdrawals.

Don and I lived overseas when our kids were younger. When the time came for a parent-teacher meeting at their school, I felt rather busy and thought Don should be the parent to attend. Rather busy himself, he thought I should be the one to go. We had several "discussions" about this. In the end, I went but not with a very good attitude. I was mad—so mad that I didn't want to talk with Don or be near him.

Soon after this squabble, we had a team meeting at our apartment. I'm not sure what I expected to happen, but I was still so angry I didn't care. I sat across the room from him at the meeting. Did I think no one would notice? My teammate could see that there was an issue since Don and I normally sat next to each other (and talked to each other). After our meeting, she came up to me and asked, "Did you and Don have an argument?"

"Yes, we did," I replied. Before I could go into the unfairness of me having to go to the meeting, she simply said, "Get it fixed!"

Now, my friend is one of the sweetest, kindest, most compassionate women I know. When she said this, I knew she was right. After the team meeting, I got it fixed.

One reason she could confront me, and I could accept it, is that I knew she loved me. In the "bank account" of our friendship, she had been making many deposits. She called regularly to check on me. We babysat each other's kids, did ministry together, took care of each other when we were sick, prayed for each other, and worshiped together. I could turn to her when I had an awful day.

I remember one morning specifically. Picture a frazzled mom, four little kids, a pair of scissors, and a cut-up curtain—all before breakfast. After the school bus picked up two of my kids and the other two settled into preschool, I ran to my friend's building and knocked on her door. Unannounced and unexpected, I stood there weeping. Still in her robe and quite busy herself, she took me in, and let me cry and talk as she listened, comforted, and prayed with me. I left her apartment—not with solutions, but with a strong sense of being cared for and supported.

Sometimes what happens on teams, or any friendship, is that the relationship "bank account" has too many withdrawals—confrontations, criticisms, misunderstanding, poor communication—and the relationship can't handle the strain of yet another withdrawal when there have been no positive deposits.

Teammates who care enough to proactively love us and to humbly confront us are precious soul mates. Friendships can handle the hardships, stressors, disagreements, and differing opinions when the relationships are strong due to the loving deposits we make by caring, listening, serving, and praying.

REFLECTION

What is it like having you for a teammate?

How can you make deposits in your team relationships?

What are the components of good confrontation?

What lies have you been believing about relationships?

What truth will you meditate on in the coming month?

RESPONSE

Read Acts 15 and notice strategies for dealing with conflict and different outcomes of conflict. Choose one strategy that you can implement in your messy relationships and begin to apply it.

PRAYER

Father, you consistently show me grace. I recognize I am not always a conduit of that grace to others. Forgive me for withholding from my teammates what I so obviously need and receive from you. May grace and compassion mark my life. I want you to be honored in the ways I interact with others. Convict me when I'm wrong. Strengthen me to do your will for your glory. Amen.

RESOURCES

https://www.boundless.org/faith/its-my-fault/ _____

https://irvinechristiancounseling.com/how-to-fix-a-toxic-relationship/ _____

https://peacepursuit.org/quickstart-guide/ _____

https://www.instagram.com/p/CgykrpQOHRc/?igshid=NDBlY2NjN2I%3D __
(A Liturgy for Expat Relationships from Liturgies for a Life Abroad)

https://www.seebeyond.cc/blog/2022/8/25/our-top-strategies-to-get-ready-for-that-difficult-conversation _____

https://www.seebeyond.cc/blog/2022/7/19/what-went-well-the-pain-and-the-joy-we-found-in-conflict _____

Laura Mae Gardner, *Healthy, Resilient, and Effective in Cross-Cultural Ministry* (Condeo Press, 2015), chapter 13.

Alfred Ells, *The Resilient Leader: How Adversity Can Change You and Your Ministry for the Better* (Colorado Springs: David C. Cook, 2020), chapter 3.

Chapter 8

I Must Sort Through Shoulds, Coulds, and Wants
Finding My Niche

> *Who you are as a person—and specifically how well you love—*
> *will always have a larger and longer impact on those around you*
> *than what you do.*
>
> —PETER SCAZZERO

Wading through the shoulds, coulds, and wants makes cross-cultural ministry difficult. Before our first term, we have an idea of what missionaries do since we've read their biographies and heard them speak. When we join an agency, we learn their goals and vision and how we can contribute. As we catch that vision, we get excited and think we know how to accomplish those goals. We arrive at our place of service. We study, learn, grow, and stretch until we know enough language and culture to minister effectively.

And then some of us get stuck trying to find our niche. For married couples, sometimes one spouse finds their niche before the other one, which can cause tension. For single people, there might not be a colleague to encourage them to keep searching for their unique place in the ministry.

In organizational training, often the talk is about the ideals of team life. However, upon arrival, we find out that what we should do and what we can do don't match. We discover the perfect team doesn't exist and the role we thought we'd play isn't realistic.

Our team needed gifted evangelists. I can share my faith as a seed sower, but my gifts lie in teaching and training. But in those early days, I felt useless and stymied because we had no believers to teach.

Sometimes our wants, what we desire to do, coincide with our strengths. We love to do what we love to do. Other times our shoulds aren't necessarily what we love, but they need doing and we can offer to serve.

When we were well into our second term of ministry, the international church we attended needed someone to direct their vacation Bible school for children. I had done that many years before but serving in the church wasn't the reason we lived in that country. On the other hand, this opportunity would reach many children with the gospel who might not ordinarily go to church. Talking with Pastor Dave Petrescue, I told him I could serve, but I didn't really have a burden for that ministry. I will never forget his reply, "Without involvement, there can be no burden." So I volunteered and developed a burden for the children and their families to hear the gospel and feel welcome at the church.

I only served in that ministry for the short term, but I met a need for a time and participated in a small part of that outreach. Choosing to engage a "should" is beneficial, though we don't want to invest most of our time in those areas. In our early years, though, those shoulds can help us discover our gifts and strengths.

Being older, I hear a lot about *convergence*—spending all our time only serving in our gifting—but I see dangers in complete convergence. In Scripture, we read about kings who became so powerful and successful in their rule that they became self-reliant and pride led to their downfall (2 Chr 12:1; 26:16). When we frequently feel confident, we are tempted to think we can serve on our own and may stop relying on God. We can benefit from attempting things we aren't naturally good at. Doing so keeps us growing as learners and not fearing failure. I want to spend most of my time serving in my areas of strength. But I also want to teach children or serve at a community center. These keep me grounded and remind me that I need the Lord and other people to support me. These practices also help me gain a deeper appreciation for the gifts and strengths of others—especially in those areas where I am weaker.

As we work through and try different shoulds, coulds, and wants we consider various factors in order to find our niche.

Knowing when to say yes or no to opportunities can be problematic. Expectations of others and expectations of ourselves can battle with reality. We all want to be effective and fruitful in ministry. But how do we measure effectiveness? Especially when we work among least-reached people groups? Take John, for example. John felt challenged to know how to work from home with his spouse daily, year after year. He puzzled over whether they did too much or too little because measuring "seed planting" in evangelism seemed impossible. At the end of the day, he rarely felt satisfied that he had done good work.

When someone wants to join our team, my husband inquires about their strengths. He doesn't try to make them fit into a preconceived position or mold. He wants them to use their gifts and abilities to add to our mission, not end up frustrated because they labor in areas without having what they need to contribute.

How can we help people find their niche? How can we find our own? And how can we love and encourage each other along the way?

We've seen that trial and error can be helpful to us in finding our fit. Coaches, also, can help us discover our niche in ministry. Having someone ask us questions, giving us time to think and answer, and then listening to our responses gives life. This time of interaction can help clarify direction.

Using a spiritual gifts inventory and asking others what they see in us gives us valuable input. Taking any of the assessments mentioned earlier helps as well. We usually know where we excel, but sometimes we'd prefer something we view as more sensational. Instead, we need to embrace our gifts and thank God for those of others.

I would suggest that looking back over ministry history and identifying what has been constant will help point to our niche. For instance, I served in women's ministries, led small group Bible studies, and loved to teach and write. In my early church planting days, I also planned retreats for other women missionaries. When I had small children, I participated in a women's Bible study. Later, my involvement included sharing my faith, discipling, training, mothering, and housekeeping—lots of different things—but I noticed some constants, like leading Bible studies and working with women, throughout.

When we see the constants, these point to our niche. Once we have an idea of our niche, it can be helpful to write a purpose statement so we can plan and work with our niche in mind.

Last year, I wrote out my life purpose in less than twenty words for the first time ever. If I had done this helpful exercise before, I think it would have shown how my purpose has shifted according to the seasons of life and my roles in work and ministry. It would also have been harder for me to be this concise in my younger years, except for when I was in language school and my four kids were six years old and under. During those seasons, my life purpose might have been only two words: to survive!

Because I am now in my mid-sixties, I have a much freer schedule and the ability to choose where to invest my time. I can also look back over thirty years and see the consistent parts of my ministry. I am aware of my strengths. I know my gifts. I also see many of my weaknesses.

As I considered the past and present, as well as the future, I wrote this for my life purpose:

Communicate through teaching Scripture and sharing personal experience to encourage others in life and ministry for God's worldwide glory.

Once I had that worked out and written down, planning became easier. My goals, desires, and overall ministry plan for the coming year flowed from my purpose with my strengths in mind. My niche is also clearer to me now, so I know where and how to focus my time and energy.

From that life purpose statement, I wrote down some personal goals for the coming year. For the rest of my career, the skeleton will stay the same, but the activities and applications will change.

To honor God by seeking him through prayer, his Word, spiritual disciplines, and time spent with him. This will keep ministry flowing from my relationship with God. My own walk with him must continue to flourish if I have any hope of finishing well and serving faithfully.

To serve God by investing in those in my circle (praying, writing, teaching, listening, planning, coaching, mentoring). This keeps me aware of those in my circle—co-workers in my organization, on my team, and in my church—and how I can serve God by investing in them.

To serve God by investing in those outside of my circle. Who can I influence through broader means? A lot of the activities remain the same, but with people outside of my normal spheres. People I wouldn't normally meet. I love the picture of the ripple effect—me in my apartment in Spain, encouraging and teaching others around the globe. Hearing now and again from people who have read my books and how they were a help is a great encouragement to me. Ripples! What a lovely thing to ponder as we serve where we are and touch lives in ways we might not realize.

To bless God by blessing those he gave me in my immediate family. This has changed through the years from when my children were little, to young adults and now all over thirty and moving quickly toward forty and beyond. I continue to pray for them and be their biggest fan. And now there are grandchildren. How can I bless and encourage them from afar? What can I do to bless my dad, sister, nieces, and nephews? Being intentional about my goals in each of these relationships helps me do more than if I hadn't thought through each of these relationships.

To worship God by serving alongside and loving Don. Don and I have been married since 1978. We were called to serve together and love one another for a lifetime. What are we doing together and how can I be a blessing to him as we serve on the same team and in the same church plant?

As we grow older, our niche becomes clearer, and we can work well in it. However, just yesterday I talked to a friend about the importance of also continuing to work not only outside of our giftings, but without recognition. I make coffee and serve snacks. I wash the coffee pot and take out the trash. I try to communicate in languages I don't know. I share my faith and plant seeds with strangers. No one may notice or care when I do these things except God. And that is enough.

Lies we may be tempted to believe when we are working to find our niche:

I am not needed.

We feel this way especially during language study and early cultural learning. We go from being confident in ministry to not knowing how to find the bathroom. And when we find it, figuring out how to use a squatty potty or locating the flusher increases the difficulty. If others on the team have lived there longer, we feel we don't fit as well as they do and might not for a long time.

Friends who would love to see us return to our passport country quickly point out the many needs around them. Their comments convince us we could be of more use where we came from than where we currently reside.

Furthermore, the role I thought I came to fill no longer exists. So, what will I do now? Finding my niche doesn't seem possible.

Others' gifts are more important than mine.

When I look at others and their fruitfulness in areas I lack, I question the necessity of my own gifts. I battle jealousy. I relate to what Tim Challies wrote about envying those with the gift of evangelism:

> When I look at those friends who are greatly gifted in this way, I am tempted toward guilt and from guilt it is only a short step to envy. I hear them describe all the opportunities they had, they created, they took, and I feel my heart sink a little. I can begin to envy this gift, to wish I had it. Why shouldn't I be gifted in this way? I want to reach the lost, I want to be a skilled evangelist, I want to share the gospel with friends, family and neighbors.[1]

When we believe this lie, we can become resentful and wary of others. Resentment disrupts unity and love in the body of Christ.

If I had different gifts, I could help the ministry more.

When we look at the needs of the ministry and the gifts that our team lacks, we think we might have a better idea of what we need than God does. If only I could be who our team needed! Why would God gift us like he has if I'd be more effective with another gift?

Truths to dwell on while battling lies so that we don't give up and leave too soon:

God gave me my gifts for the common good of the Body of Christ.

At times, I have thought that God gave me my gifts for me. I've looked at them as the source of my significance or proof of my spirituality. However, my gifts are not given to me for my good, but rather for the good of others.

---

1 Challies, "Gift Envy and Gift Projection."

I met Don during my second year of college, and we began dating. Sometimes I bought a candy bar for me and one for Don. I would eat mine and plan to give the other one to Don so that he would know I thought of him. However, if I didn't see him right away, the candy bar would look better and better to me as the day wore on. So, I would eat it, too. Later, when I would see Don and tell him I bought him a candy bar, his eyes would light up, until I told him I ate it. After this happened several times, he finally told me he would rather not know I bought him a candy bar if I was going to eat it.

At times in my life, I have viewed spiritual gifts like those candy bars. God gave me spiritual gifts to benefit others, but I begin to think the gifts were given to me for me. This is wrong. My spiritual gifts have no influence on my significance to God. They are for the common good of the body of Christ and the glory of God. You serve in your gifted areas, and I serve in mine.

Give the chocolate away! Use your spiritual gifts for others.

Who I am is more important than what I do.

As cross-cultural workers raising support, our prayer letters focus on our activities. Our presentations in churches describe our ministries so that they know how to pray and continue their support. While we need strategies and plans for ministry, we also need to know who we are in Christ and keep that relationship our primary focus.

Peter Scazzero, in his book, *The Emotionally Healthy Leader* writes, "Spiritual deficits typically reveal themselves in too much activity. Unhealthy leaders engage in more activities than their combined spiritual, physical, and emotional reserves can sustain. They give out for God more than they receive from him."[2] We aren't receiving from God in order to have something to give to others.

I've appreciated our agency's emphasis on spiritual health and maintaining our walks with God. I need reminders I am a child of God, his treasured possession, a reflection of him, and that he loves me, not what I do. When schedules get full, we can focus so much on what we do that we forget the importance of our identity in Christ.

God is interested in my journey, not only in the end results.

When I look at goals, I tend to make them all important. Don't get me wrong, we should keep them in mind. But I also need to be concerned about the process and who I am on the way toward those goals.

Cross-cultural servants quickly learn that God has to do a lot to work in them before he can work through them. I thought I was spiritually mature and ready for ministry when I arrived on the field, but quickly discovered I wasn't. I was angry, proud, and self-serving. I didn't realize I struggled with any of these issues in the comforts of my home country, but they quickly came to the surface once I got off the plane in a foreign land.

God delights to work in and through the lives of his children—now. Just think about the years Joseph spent falsely imprisoned and then forgotten by the man he had helped. Remember Moses in the wilderness, David as a shepherd, Esther in the harem, Ruth and Naomi as widows, Peter as a fisherman, Lydia selling her purple cloth—God worked in them long before they knew his plans for them.

Let's not rush the process and think only of what we'd love to see happen. Let's remember that we walk with Jesus along the way, in his presence now, not just after we meet our goals.

---

2 Scazzero, *The Emotionally Healthy Leader*, 25.

REFLECTION

What are your strengths?

How do we measure fruitfulness?

How can you find your niche?

What lies do you find yourself believing as you work to find your niche?

What truth do you need to remember today as you seek your niche?

RESPONSE

Write out your life's purpose statement. Aim to keep it as concise as you can. See if you can keep it to twenty words or less. Share it with a good friend and ask for their input.

PRAYER

Lord, thank you for your work in my life. I open my heart to you and ask that you would keep molding me to be more like Jesus. You have given me gifts to use to benefit others and honor you not as the means to my significance. May I serve you wholeheartedly. Lead my steps, when to say yes to opportunities and when to say no. I long to do your will. Amen.

RESOURCES

https://melanieschitwood.com/find-your-ministry-niche/ _____

https://studypracticeteach.net/2018/05/12/spiritual-gifts/ _____

https://velvetashes.com/ill-find-my-niche-someday-the-grove/ _____

https://high5test.com/ _____

https://www.gripbirkman.com/ _____

https://www.desiringgod.org/articles/where-is-your-identity _____

https://qideas.org/qmoments/discovering-your-purpose/ _____

Marcus Buckingham and Donald O. Clifton, *Now Discover Your Strengths* (New York: The Free Press, 2020).

Robert S. McGee, *The Search for Significance: Seeing Your True Worth Through God* (Nashville: Thomas Nelson, 2008).

Amy Young, *Becoming More Fruitful in Cross-Cultural Work: How to Be Free in Christ and Rooted in Reality as you Fulfill Your Call* (Independently published, 2022).

Chapter 9

I Sometimes Feel Rootless
Transitions

> *This side of eternity, we'll always be somewhat ill at ease in our surroundings because this is not our "forever" home.*
>
> —VINITA HAMPTON WRIGHT

With all the comings and goings of missionaries themselves, teammates, and other friends, a sense of rootlessness ensues. I think that all missionaries—married and single, young and old, new and experienced—battle feeling rootless. My friend shared a way rootlessness shows up in her life as a single worker:

> [I] feel like there is no one I can count on long term. With changes in teammates and the community surrounding me, there is no one I can count on to be physically in my life five years from now. There are a small handful that I would place a higher likelihood of still being here, also assuming I'm also still here. But the fact remains that the only people whom I feel I can count on to be a consistent part of my life are on the other side of the world. There is no one to really count on sharing my life with is a major way that feeling rootless shows up for me.

As a married person, I know what contributes to my feeling rootless. A couple of summers ago, Don and I drove around the States from home-to-home visiting family and supporters. We said lots of hellos and goodbyes. We saw family and dear friends for a short time and then left. Once we visited friends who live in a small town. When they walked into their local diner, everyone knew their names. They belonged. Another time we watched our son's softball game, played with the grandkids in the park, and went to an ice cream stand together. It felt so happily normal. Then when we got into the car to leave, I cried. On one of the long road trips, I turned to Don in the car and said, "I feel rootless." I mentioned this to him several times, trying to express this sense of not belonging, not having roots anywhere that could be called home.

Global workers often feel like we have no roots. We don't fit in with our host cultures and when we come back to our passport country, we don't exactly fit there anymore either. When we left to go overseas for the first time many years ago, I didn't think much about roots. I think I focused more on what was above ground—what I could see. I concentrated on what I would do in ministry. However, upon our arrival, I couldn't communicate, which made ministry impossible. I couldn't find my way around to serve people, and I couldn't have Bible studies with women because I couldn't read the Bible in their language. I felt rootless and useless.

I was shaken. During this time I discovered that my relationship with God was actually quite shallow. I thought I knew God deeply, but God knew me deeply and knew that I really needed to know him better. In my weakness and frailty, God showed me how strongly I had been depending on myself and only feebly on him. He did not merely invite me, he propelled me to grow deeper. As hard and painful as it was, I rejoice he brought me through the trials and challenges so that I could know him better.

I was born in Ohio, went to school in Chicago, met and married Don, and moved to Texas. We started our cross-cultural career in the Middle East thinking we would live there our whole lives. After twelve years, we went to work at the Christar US mobilization center (at that time) in Pennsylvania. We then lived in South Asia for about five years, and currently live in Europe. People ask me where I'm from, and I try to think of short answers like I was born in Ohio, or, my address is in Texas. (I am pretty sure that my kids hate this "Where are you from?" question more than I do.)

Whenever I sense that rootless feeling, God reminds me of my roots. Remember my car ride with Don where I talked about feeling rootless? As soon as I said it a third or fourth time, the Holy Spirit brought to my mind a prayer from Ephesians 3:14–19. Paul prayed that because the Ephesians were rooted and established in love, they would have the power to know the love of Christ and be filled to the measure of all the fullness of God. They were rooted not in their home communities, their church family, or even their blood families, but their roots were in the love of Jesus. I was not and am not rootless. I am firmly rooted in Jesus.

Paul says more about roots, "So then, just as you received Christ Jesus as Lord, continue to live your lives in him, rooted and built up in him, strengthened in the faith as you were taught, and overflowing with thankfulness" (Col 2:6–7).

These significant verses—especially for those of us in cross-cultural ministry—remind us that receiving Christ by faith only begins our journey. Our natural desire is to walk by sight; we want to know why things happen, how our support will come in, what we should definitely do. But God desires us to continue walking by faith. One day we will walk by true sight. We will see Jesus. Until then, we continue in this adventurous walk of faith.

Paul reminds us that in this walk of faith, we stay rooted, deep and secure in the Lord. In a hurricane, the palm trees bend but they are not torn from the ground. Winds and storms (trials and challenges) will come our way and may seek to uproot us, but they cannot. God holds us securely, whether we get an unexpected diagnosis from the doctor, a change in direction of ministry, or betrayal by a friend. We may feel shaken, but we cannot be shaken loose.

Our citizenship is in heaven, our true home is with Jesus. Wherever you go, whatever you face, whatever your earthly address and however long you remain there, remember it is only temporary. Your roots are eternal.

Lies we can believe when we feel rootless, especially when everything keeps changing:

I am rootless and have no home.

I feel this most keenly in my passport country, visiting people with obvious roots. I also experience this when I face challenging situations in my host country due to a lack of language ability and cultural understanding. This lie also pops up when something special happens in my family while I'm far away. I can feel lost and alone when others get together at home.

Listening to people tell stories of recent gatherings with their friends from grade school or high school leaves me feeling left out, alone—rootless.

Others who stay in their home country have fewer problems.

Those who stay in their home country seem to always know where to go to get their necessities and how to do it. They know how things work and can complete transactions in their own language. This ease appeals to us when we get lost in the cross-cultural mazes we live in as we try to get things done. We become convinced that no one has the problems we face and think that if we went back home, our life would be stress free.

I am hurting my children's future by raising them overseas.

When our children struggle, we can believe that it's because we are raising them in another culture. Though they might have similar difficulties in their passport countries as other children, third culture kids can sense rootlessness possibly more than their parents. They are far from their grandparents and might not have the same relationship with them as their cousins do. When my daughter was five years old, she clearly expressed this lack of connection and sense of home. As we came through immigration to the US, the official asked Kristi, "Where are you from?" (She knew she was born in Texas, had lived in Jordan, moved to Egypt, and was coming to Ohio.) She looked at the official and said, "Now that is a good question." A little bit funny, but also tough that she couldn't articulate where her roots were.

Enrolling children in a school where they were among a handful of foreigners brought about stressors we didn't know about until they changed schools. Two of our children got lost (and found their way home) in a city of 15 million people and one was slapped by a neighbor and ridiculed for his faith. Navigating how to help them through these cultural stressors and sense of not belonging anywhere is rough.

Truths we can affirm to refute lies
when they sneak in and we start to believe them:

I am a citizen of heaven.

No matter what passport I have, as a believer in Jesus, I am a part of God's family, a member of the body of Christ. I find my citizenship in heaven (Phil 3:20). That is my true home. As such, we will not feel totally comfortable in any location on this earth. Feeling rootless hurts sometimes, but also reminds me that my forever home is yet to come.

When God calls me, he calls my children.

When God called me and Don to go, he also called our family, but he did not promise all would go well for our kids. We faced challenges we would not have faced in our home country, like going to the zoo and becoming (us, not the animals) the exhibit that everyone gawked at. Eva's first trip to the zoo with her baby in a baby carrier remains among the most stressful experiences of her cross-cultural life. She felt more on display than the animals in their stark, empty cages.

Our kids also remember the zoo. They fed giraffes and hippopotamuses, saw lions, and watched monkeys play. Not all the experiences were negative. The kids also saw a lot of historical sites over the years. They learned about other languages and developed an appreciation for different cultures. They attended school by the Great Pyramid of Giza, enjoyed trips to the camel market, and walked on streets where Jesus and Paul also walked. They grew to be sensitive to others, friendly, considerate of other societies, and our friends loved them. They had amazing role models in their "aunts and uncles" on our team.

Raising our kids overseas and in America came with benefits, but also drawbacks. Especially adjusting from what they knew in their "home" to living in their passport country. I remember when we moved back to the US, Don and I happily went back to what we considered the "normal way" of celebrating Christmas and went to visit our parents. But our kids asked, "When can we go back to doing Christmas the way we've always done it?" Their normal and ours were different. But eventually they added this new normal to the mix and created wonderful memories with their grandparents.

I asked our oldest son, Stephen, who faced his share of difficulties overseas and in his passport country, if he regretted being raised overseas. He said definitely not. He was grateful for the opportunities he had and all he learned along the way. Michael, our second son, while acknowledging some sense of rootlessness in international living wrote, "Now that I am older and have kids, I want them to go to other places around the world, experience other cultures, and be able to love people much different than themselves."[1]

I guess God's work in my children resembles his work in me as I followed his call. I faced challenges, some days I struggled. But God was weaving all those experiences (positive and negative) to mold me more into the image of Jesus. If he is faithful to do that for me, he will be faithful to our children.

Living for the temporary isn't as meaningful as living for eternity—forever.

Linda Ellis, a poet and author, wrote a poem called "The Dash." In it she refers to the dash on tombstones that reflect the time spent between birth and death. She mentions the importance of knowing life is short and how we invest our time matters. She wrote:

> For it matters not, how much we own —
> the cars … the house … the cash.
> What matters is how we live and love
> and how we spend our dash.[2]

As we live out "our dash" we must consider eternity. How we invest our time and what we pursue have consequences. Knowing Jesus, following him by faith and in obedience all reflect eternal values. When we go after our own ways and think only of what we gain in the here and now, we fail to consider what really matters in the long run.

Jesus tells us about this:

> Do not store up for yourselves treasures on earth, where moths and vermin destroy, and where thieves break in and steal. But store up for yourselves treasures in heaven, where moths and vermin do not destroy, and where thieves do not break in and steal. For where your treasure is, there your heart will be also. (Matt 6:19–21)

Being cross-cultural messengers doesn't ensure that we will always live wisely and finish strong in our walks of faith. It is all too easy to get caught up in our earthly pursuits no matter what our career is. Keeping our eyes on eternity while we work diligently here helps us remember that we find our secure roots in Jesus and in our forever home in heaven.

---

1 Eenigenburg, *More Screams, Different Deserts*, xi.

2 Ellis, "The Dash Poem."

REFLECTION

Describe a time when you felt rootless.

How is being rooted in Christ significant to you?

What temptations keep you from living with eternity in view?

What lies have you been believing when you feel rootless?

What truth would be good to think about in your current situation?

RESPONSE

Write out and pray through Ephesians 3:16–21 for yourself. Share your thoughts with your team and pray for one another.

PRAYER

Lord God, you have given me roots and a citizenship in heaven. Help me to remember my deep roots in you. You hold me tightly so I can never be shaken loose. Even when I feel rootless, help me remember my rootedness in you. Amen.

RESOURCES

https://communicatingacrossboundariesblog.com/2021/10/12/now-is-the-time-of-goodbye/?mc_cid=1dadf42639&mc_eid=a4bb63d8ba   _____

https://www.youtube.com/watch?v=86dsfBbZfWs&t=1s   _____
(Rope Illustration by Francis Chan)

https://www.compass-ministries.net/   _____

https://www.instagram.com/p/CezlRCBtfWC/?igshid=NDBlY2NjN2I=   _____
(A Liturgy for Getting Too Much Attention)

https://thriveconnection.com/2003/04/15/raising-radiant-daughters-part-i-dispelling-the-silence/   _____

https://thriveconnection.com/2003/06/01/raising-radiant-daughters-part-ii-telling-the-truth/   _____

https://evaburkholder.com/2019/04/05/the-certainty-of-change/   _____

Gina Brenna Butz, *Making Peace with Change: Navigating Life's Messy Transitions with Honesty and Grace* (Grand Rapids: Our Daily Bread Publishing, 2020).

Marilyn Gardner, *Between Worlds: Essays on Culture and Belonging* (Doorlight Publications, 2014).

Marilyn Gardner, *Worlds Apart: A Third Culture Kid's Journey* (Doorlight Publications, 2018).

Lauren Wells, *Raising Up a Generation of Healthy Third Culture Kids: A Practical Guide to Preventative Care* (Canby: Independently published, 2020).

Chapter 10

I'd Like to Escape
Wanting Easier

The truth about missions is that it's a long, hard slog.
More often than not, I think missionaries feel ineffective.
Crossing cultures in Jesus' name is downright painful.

—JEN OSHMAN

Some days I just want life to be easier. The Psalmist, Asaph, writes in Psalm 74 about the destruction of Jerusalem, the temple trashed and burned down. The enemy has the upper hand in everything. There are no prophets, no one proclaiming hope. Waiting on God takes a long time. Asaph records, "We are given no signs from God; no prophets are left, and none of us knows how long this will be" (v. 9).

Some days seem longer than others, and we all experience periods of prolonged stress we think will never end. Sometimes we suffer in crisis mode. Other times, we face extended pressure, high risk, or murky uncertainty. We try to anticipate when the struggle will end. But the resolution remains hidden. So, we keep going, but we'd prefer to quit or at least know the trial will be over soon.

Jim Collins writes about the Stockdale Paradox. Admiral Jim Stockdale was tortured over twenty times in his eight years as a prisoner of war in Vietnam. He didn't know when or if he would be released. Collins had the opportunity to meet Admiral Stockdale and wanted to discover how he survived such atrocities when he didn't know what the outcome would be. In an excerpt from his book, *Good to Great*, Collins shares:

> If it feels depressing for me, how on earth did he deal with it when he was actually there and did not know the end of the story?
>
> "I never lost faith in the end of the story," he said, when I asked him. "I never doubted not only that I would get out, but also that I would prevail in the end and turn the experience into the defining event of my life, which, in retrospect, I would not trade."
>
> I didn't say anything for many minutes, and we continued the slow walk toward the faculty club, Stockdale limping and arc-swinging his stiff leg that had never fully recovered from repeated torture. Finally, after about a hundred meters of silence, I asked, "Who didn't make it out?"
>
> "Oh, that's easy," he said. "The optimists."
>
> "The optimists? I don't understand," I said, now completely confused, given what he'd said a hundred meters earlier.
>
> "The optimists. Oh, they were the ones who said, 'We're going to be out by Christmas.' And Christmas would come, and Christmas would go. Then they'd say, 'We're going to be out by Easter.' And Easter would come, and Easter would go. And then Thanksgiving, and then it would be Christmas again. And they died of a broken heart."

Another long pause, and more walking. Then he turned to me and said, "This is a very important lesson. You must never confuse faith that you will prevail in the end—which you can never afford to lose—with the discipline to confront the most brutal facts of your current reality, whatever they might be."

To this day, I carry a mental image of Stockdale admonishing the optimists: "We're not getting out by Christmas; deal with it!"[1]

We would be wiser to not try to guess when things will get easier or when the crisis will end. Rather, we need to know that the end of the story benefits us despite our current reality. We can do that by forging ahead in our faith in God and trusting in his good purposes for us.

If my situation involves crises or unending stress, I must choose to trust God through it. I won't set a timeline of when the trial should be over and when life should get easier. I will hold the timing in an open hand, trusting him in the midst and hanging on to the end. No matter when that comes.

Remember God is always with us:

God is our refuge and strength, an ever-present help in trouble. Therefore we will not fear, though the earth give way and the mountains fall into the heart of the sea, though its waters roar and foam and the mountains quake with their surging. (Ps 46:1–3)

Notice especially the second verse, "Therefore we will not fear." Because I am a fearful person, I love that I don't have to fear because God is an ever-present help "in trouble" (v. 1). Not always does he protect us from trouble, but he always goes with us through it. No matter what happens all around us, despite dangers, God remains our constant help through everything.

Looking back, my times of spiritual growth and maturity in my faith came during those desperate times when I realized my utmost dependence on the Lord. Easiness doesn't forge the deeper relationship with the Lord. Hardship does. Nor does ease of life strengthen relationships as much as going through flood waters. Elliot Stephens mentions "clinging fiercely to God" as imperative for missionaries.[2] We experience this clinging when we know we can't endure on our own. We find God faithful again and again. Our trust grows. We stick it out.

I want to be like Nehemiah. He faced threats from those who wanted him to give way to fear.

They were all trying to frighten us, thinking, "Their hands will get too weak for the work, and it will not be completed."

But I prayed, "Now strengthen my hands."

One day I went to the house of Shemaiah son of Delaiah, the son of Mehetabel, who was shut in at his home. He said, "Let us meet in the house of God, inside the temple, and let us close the temple doors, because men are coming to kill you—by night they are coming to kill you."

But I said, *Should a man like me run away? Or should someone like me go into the temple to save his life? I will not go!*" (Neh 6:9–11, emphasis added)

Because of his faith in God and his constant prayer, he didn't run away.

In the trials and tribulations that I face, in my homesickness, and desire for ease, may I stand strong like Nehemiah. As a person of faith, I want to say, "Should a woman like me run away?"

---

1 Collins, "The Stockdale Paradox."

2 Stephens, "Webinar: Field Onboarding and Retention."

Lies we are tempted to believe when we see escape as the better option:

Easier is always better.

Easier is my default mode. If I have two recipes, one that looks hard and one that looks easy, I will choose the easy one nine times out of ten. If I choose the other one, I will probably look for short cuts. This may be my personality. It may stem from having four kids and learning to cook from scratch in my early years overseas. It might be my preference anyway—even without living overseas. But easier isn't always better.

It is easier not to exercise, but worse for our health. It is easier to sleep in than have a quiet time, but my relationship with God suffers. It is easier to stay home than to follow God's call into missions. But we love God and seek to obey him by faith. When God calls, how can we not follow?

Easier isn't always better. I propose that it rarely is.

God doesn't want me to struggle.

Rather, God wants me to obey and sometimes that causes struggle. Angst rises in my soul as I count the costs.

When we dedicated our first two children to the Lord, I felt serene and confident as we acknowledged these gifts from God belonged to him. But when we dedicated our third child, we planned to move overseas in about six months. I was a wreck. I cried and felt far from serene. I didn't know what the future held for her or us. I struggled to dedicate her because of all the unknowns.

Since we chose to move to the Middle East, some people questioned our plan due to concern for our safety. These questions unsettled me as I sought to follow God's leading but struggled with fear of what obedience might mean. Others might not understand or approve of me if obedience goes against their opinions.

I hear a lot of teaching, not about struggling, but about what has been termed the *prosperity gospel*—the guarantee of financial gain and good health if you have enough faith. I like money and feeling vigorous. I don't like to struggle. Many say, "If God really loves me, it can't be his will that I have a hard time."

Even the often-used phrase, "God has a wonderful plan for your life," focuses on the positive. And ultimately, it is. But Jesus calls us to take up our cross and follow him. He says to lose our lives for his sake to find them (Matt 16:24–26).

North American Christians may need to grow in our understanding of the theology of suffering instead of praying to avoid it. I define spiritual maturity by wanting Jesus to come back because I love him, not because of something awful I am about to encounter. Too often, I only want him to come back because of my desire to escape suffering.

Blessing always equals deliverance.

I love being kept out of trouble—being protected from something so that I don't go through hardship. But often God calls us to endure *through* the suffering. In our weakness, we lean on his strength and find out we really can do all things through his power.

I think most people enjoy reading Hebrews chapter 11 and how God delivered heroes of the faith. We like the miracles. But in the second half of that chapter, we encounter more heroes who are delivered only in eternity, not on earth.

My earthy mentality wants deliverance now and to be blessed in such a way that trials end here. I mistakenly think strong faith means I get the ending I want when I want it.

Truths to remember when facing hardships which leave us feeling that escape is better because it seems easier:

God gives strength to the weak who desire ease.

When I think about wanting easy, I need to remember those who chose obedience and faith over ease. It would have been easier for the Israelites to stay in Egypt (as least they thought so in the middle of the desert. It didn't seem like it was easy when they had to work as slaves). It would have been easier for Esther to keep quiet about her nationality. It would have been easier for Shadrach, Meshach, and Abednego to bow down in front of the idol. It would have been easier for Peter to keep fishing. It would have been easier for Jesus to avoid the cross. But how different outcomes would have been. How much richness and fullness to their lives and stories would be missed. Our one way of salvation would be unavailable to us. Desiring ease is a temptation when we feel weak.

I used to be ashamed of my weakness and timidity. But now I recognize how much I need to depend upon the power of God. We normally celebritize strong people. Self-starters. Pioneers. Go-getters. People who don't need anyone and seem to do everything well. People can do amazing things. We just need to be careful that we never seek to depend on ourselves.

Esther realized her need for prayer and sought others to join with her before she approached the king to intercede for her people. Terrified, not knowing if she would live or die, she went anyway. And God received the glory.

Paul, bold and audacious, admitted his weakness. He didn't view himself as eloquent (1 Cor 2:1, 2 Cor 11:6). He went to the Corinthians in weakness, fear, and much trembling (1 Cor 2:3). He wrote of God's grace to him:

> But he said to me, "My grace is sufficient for you, for my power is made perfect in weakness." Therefore I will boast all the more gladly about my weaknesses, so that Christ's power may rest on me. That is why, for Christ's sake, I delight in weaknesses, in insults, in hardships, in persecutions, in difficulties. For when I am weak, then I am strong. (2 Cor 12:9–10)

God gives strength to the weak. Being weak enables us to serve in his power and for his glory. The Lord doesn't look for superheroes. He looks for servants, jars of clay (2 Cor 4:7), where his glory, not ours, can shine through.

God commands me to be joyful when facing trials.

We long for deliverance, yet James teaches us that perseverance leads to maturity:

> Consider it pure joy, my brothers and sisters, whenever you face trials of many kinds, because you know that the testing of your faith produces perseverance. Let perseverance finish its work so that you may be mature and complete, not lacking anything. If any of you lacks wisdom, you should ask God, who gives generously to all without finding fault, and it will be given to you. (Jas 1:2–5)

God uses trials in our lives to grow us. We learn to persevere. We grow in maturity. Our faith deepens. We develop grit. As we increase our dependence on him, our history of experiencing his faithfulness gives us hope for current trials.

We keep our eyes on eternity. James reminds us, "Blessed is the one who perseveres under trial because, having stood the test, that person will receive the crown of life that the Lord has promised to those who love him" (Jas 1:12).

We are people of hope with our eyes on eternity. Paul David Tripp wrote in his book *New Morning Mercies*:

> But eternity also fills this moment with hope. Because I know that this is not all there is, I also know that the sin, trials, and sufferings of the present will not last forever. For God's children, eternity promises that sin will die, suffering will end, our trials will be no more, and we will live with God in perfect peace forever and ever and ever. You just can't make proper sense of life without viewing it from the perspective of eternity.[3]

Yes, we face affliction. But trouble doesn't defeat us. Instead, God uses trials to strengthen us as we look to him. We anticipate the day when we meet Jesus face to face and our earthly pain fades away. Paul writes, "I consider that our present sufferings are not worth comparing with the glory that will be revealed in us" (Rom 8:18). And also, "Therefore we do not lose heart. Though outwardly we are wasting away, yet inwardly we are being renewed day by day. For our light and momentary troubles are achieving for us an eternal glory that far outweighs them all. So we fix our eyes not on what is seen, but on what is unseen, since what is seen is temporary, but what is unseen is eternal" (2 Cor 4:16–18).

Consider your trials. Keep your eyes on eternity. Forever makes the temporary struggle worthwhile.

Blessing involves trusting in and waiting on God.

As we serve and face hurdles, we trust our Lord. The Psalms call us to wait on the Lord. As we wait, we pray.

In *Journey With Me*, Lamp discusses a quote from Richard Foster's book, *Celebration of Discipline*:

> Richard Foster correctly identifies what our posture ought to be before God. ... Not surprisingly, it involves waiting.
>
> > I would like to offer one more counsel to those who find themselves devoid of the presence of God. It is this: wait on God. Wait, silent and still. Wait attentive and responsive. Learn that trust proceeds faith ... Trust is confidence in the character of God. Firmly and deliberately you say, "I do not understand what God is doing or even where God is, but I know that He is out to do me good." This is trust. This is how to wait.
>
> If we are stuck and cannot go forward in our prayers, let's not go backward by blaming God or jumping to action too soon. Let's stay in neutral if we must, grounded in the assurance that God is for us and not against us—that he is working. Let's wait expectantly before him in an attitude of heart prayer, convinced his will is good and perfect for us and for our times.[4]

Finally, one messenger's testimony summarizes the challenges, the importance of trusting God, and remembering truth in cross-cultural ministry:

---

3 Tripp, *New Morning Mercies*, 571.

4 Lamp, *Journey with Me*, 174, quoting Richard J. Foster, *Celebration of Discipline*.

On most days life here feels overwhelming. There is a constant barrage of unwanted comments, stares, and sideways glances with whispers. Not to mention a feeling of inadequacy with the language and culture. On top of that there are the constant attacks of the enemy telling me that I don't belong here and that it would be so much easier to be somewhere else and that I am completely unable to do this work or to thrive here. I feel like I am falling behind. In my heart of hearts, I know that all of the sacrifice is worth it because He is worth it and none of this is about me or my abilities. From one day to the next though, it can feel like the enemy is right about me and about this. That it would be much easier to throw in the towel … The moments [come] where I have to decide which voices to listen to. Do I get depressed and listen to my fickle feelings and the enemy's lies? Or do I go to the Scriptures and renew my mind with Truth from my Father, who loves me even in my unbelief.

REFLECTION

Name some biblical characters who struggled. Describe how they chose to walk through their trial rather than choose an easier route.

What helps you be joyful when facing trials?

How have you developed a theology of suffering?

What are the benefits and challenges of waiting on God?

RESPONSE

Read John 12:23–33. Meditate on verses 27–28. Write out your reflections on this passage and what you are learning from Jesus.

PRAYER

Lord, thank you for sustaining grace. You give strength to the weary. I like easy. I dislike hard. But nothing is too difficult for you. It is your power that is at work in me, the same power that raised Jesus from the dead! May I follow you no matter how you lead me, knowing you will give me strength for the journey. Amen.

RESOURCES

https://emilypfreeman.com/podcast/192/ _____
(Hold on to Hope)

https://www.theheartlandconnect.com/god-does-not-always-deliver-article-tim-knutson/ _____

https://www.instagram.com/liturgiesforalifeabroad/ _____

https://justbetweenus.org/overcoming-adversity/waiting-on-god/when-god-has-you-waiting/ _____

https://velvetashes.com/a-liturgy-for-staying/. _____

https://send.org/Blog/staying-sent-well _____

Denise Beck and Sarah Hilkemann, *Yet We Still Hope: Stories of Courage from Women Serving Around the World* (Velvet Ashes Publishing, 2022)

Nik and Gegg Lewis Ripken, *The Insanity of God: A True Story of Faith Resurrected* (Nashville: B & H Publishing Group, 2013).

PART TWO

Staying Well When Others Go—Grace Needed

Introduction

In our pre-departure orientation, I (Eva) teach a workshop on the inevitable change inherent in cross-cultural ministry. I begin the session by creating a timeline on a large whiteboard. I add initials under the dates as I recount the comings and goings of my overseas team. Over the span of ten years, we experienced fifteen changes, not including the normal ebb and flow of home assignment (disruptive enough on its own).

While Sue speaks about the transience of cross-cultural life in an earlier chapter, we feel this specific issue warrants its own section, especially for those who stay when others go.

People leave places and things all the time. Members leave churches. Employees leave jobs. We change gyms. We move houses. We cross state lines. We resign from associations, clubs, and ministries. So, if transient behavior is common, then why are we so devastated when someone leaves a team? Why such potential for damage left in the wake? Why the hurt feelings and the sense of betrayal?

The level of hurt and disappointment seems commensurate with the level of closeness or conflict in the group. If a sporadic church attender leaves, no one really misses them. When the difficult member moves on, everyone breathes a sigh of relief. But if the endeared Sunday school teacher resigns, her loss affects everyone.

Typically, a deep sense of commitment, camaraderie, and friendship develops on a global team. Because of the lack of immediate and extended family, these relationships often become surrogates. They may vacation together, worship weekly, celebrate holidays and birthdays—all those things one would most likely do with family if they lived nearby. Workers quickly learn to rely on one another for vital needs—fellowship, accountability, fun, perspective, help with practical matters, and many more. The team becomes a primary factor in their ability to have grit for the long haul.

The cost and time needed to get a messenger of the gospel overseas factor into this as well. Most field workers go through rigorous screening, training, donor development, speaking, and perhaps counseling before they even reach foreign soil. Then they devote one to three years to learning a new language and how to function in their new culture. Only after all this are they ready to actually do what they came to do. This investment contributes to the difficulty of just picking up and leaving.

This being the case, losing a missionary teammate is akin to losing an associate pastor if you're the pastor, a spouse if you are married, or at least, a dear friend. It disrupts the equilibrium of life, vacates ministry roles, and forces unwanted change.

Sue and I offer this handbook because we believe that this specific transition can help us grow stronger and healthier—developing grit—instead of deflating and depleting us.

During my years as a member care provider and Sue's as a leader and coach, we have identified some common reactions from those who say goodbye to exiting teammates. These reactions may not be exhaustive, but are based on our extensive observations and experiences. Following these common reactions, we suggest some responses or ways that those who stay, or stayers, can readjust and move forward.

When I collected testimonies for this section, I received far more suggestions for adjusting and moving forward than for dealing with the emotions of staying behind. I attribute this to the fact that we typically want to forge ahead rather than feel uncomfortable. But we encourage you to work through the reactions first. Hopefully, this will allow you to find solutions from a place of health without being clouded by hurt, unforgiveness, or judgment.

At the beginning of each chapter, you will find testimonies we garnered from global workers. These real-life experiences flesh out the reactions and responses described in each chapter.

We realize our workbook cannot address every situation and unique circumstance surrounding the frequent changes in teams and among teammates. So much nuance exists in every situation of a person leaving. However, some similarities do exist. Find the one(s) that you can relate to and start there. Feel free to make this your own and use this guidebook in whatever way you find most helpful.

Chapter 11

I Feel Betrayed and Let Down
Hurt and Disappointment

When you're hurting, you can't really see outside yourself.

—J. B.

I wrestled with feeling abandoned by teammates, God, and sometimes field leadership. I felt like things were such a mess that we couldn't possibly accomplish anything good. I felt stuck because I felt like it was my responsibility to hold the crumbling pieces together. I felt a heavy burden to carry on, like all of the loss my teammates [who left] had gone though would be for nothing if I didn't continue what we started.

I felt betrayed, not that a couple left due to their pregnancy, but that they gave a two-week short notice.

I often feel like we are constantly just trainers to the new folks and then get them trained just to watch them leave shortly after.

It's hard not to always take their departure personally.

They're hurting as they go just because it's hard. Even if they wanted out, it's still hard. They're hurting and they can only see their side of it. I'm hurting and I can only see my side of it. This was really helpful for me to think, "They have this hurt too, I never considered that," because I was only thinking about my side of it.

[I feel] lots of emotions (anger, sadness, loss, bitterness, betrayal) about them leaving in the way they did.

I tend to feel really betrayed even though I know it has nothing to do with me. It just hurts.

I felt hurt by the lack of communication. I found out a few weeks after arriving on the field that my boss was leaving, and she hadn't told me. She didn't need my approval, but I would have appreciated being told.

I certainly felt betrayal and anger after my [missionary kid high school] graduation, and for many years afterward. I thought I had deep friendships—perhaps even lifelong— and yet so many of my friends seemed that they "couldn't wait" to leave and didn't seem to have any regret about the end of our friendship … I guess I would say that those feelings morphed into "prolonged hurt" though I still recognize a reluctance to develop friendships with new colleagues I sense may leave.

After our teammate's stabbing incident, he and his family returned to the US for treatment and healing. While I knew in my heart they needed to leave, I experienced hurt. We had known them since seminary days and dreamed of working together. Our children loved each other, too. I was disappointed that our ideal team had disintegrated after only a few months.

Later, when we sensed our own imminent departure, we hesitated to talk to our teammates because we didn't want to hurt them or let them down. We knew they desired us to consult them regarding our thought process and decision-making steps, but we assumed they wouldn't listen objectively. We feared they would try to persuade us to remain on the field. And even if we consulted them, should we share everything? Whatever course of action we took, it would probably hurt them. They might think we abandoned them or gave up.

I wonder if one of the Old Testament spies felt similarly. Caleb, along with Joshua and ten others, explored the land of Canaan for forty days at the request of Moses, the leader of the Israelites (Num 13:17–33). While there, they discovered that the benefits of a fruitful land could not be obtained without overcoming the obstacles of powerful people and heavily fortified cities (vv. 27–28).

But Caleb was not put off by the size of the enemy, the magnitude of the task, or the strength of their cities. He, like many cross-cultural workers, chose to forge ahead with enthusiasm to fulfill God's command. His words describe his commitment: "We should go up and take possession of the land, for we can certainly do it" (v. 30).

Ten of the men immediately shut down Caleb's positive faith: "'We can't attack those people; they are stronger than we are.' And they spread among the Israelites a bad report about the land they had explored" (vv. 31–32).

In essence, Caleb's teammates quit. They refused to complete the task. They up and left. And this meant Caleb (along with Joshua) had to endure the consequences along with those who lacked faith or disobeyed.

I realize that Caleb's situation doesn't mirror everything that gospel messengers experience, but I can imagine he felt similar feelings. Just when he wanted to plow ahead, the people he needed to help get the job done bailed on him. In his shoes, I would have felt let down and hurt. Perhaps more than hurt. Certainly frustrated. Maybe even angry.

Whenever a teammate or other expat leaves the mission field, those remaining commonly experience hurt or feel abandoned. They're left holding the bag saying, "Thanks a lot! Now what?" Small teams may feel even more isolated and alone. Stayers may think the goer broke a promise. *What about all those hours we spent in excited discussion and strategic planning? How in the world will I carry out our mission without you?*

If you are the one staying behind, you may have tried to persuade your teammates to remain and thought you were making progress. Maybe they didn't let you know their plans and blindsided you with their announcement. You thought you deserved at least a conversation or an opportunity to give input. Either way, you feel betrayed and abandoned. *I thought we were better friends than this. Did you even think of me when you were making this decision? About my situation, my feelings?*

The truth is, no matter how strong the argument—we need you here, the job isn't finished, no one else can do it like you do, your language is excellent, you have good relationships with national friends, your financial support is good—if God leads, it doesn't matter. No argument will be persuasive enough; they need to follow him.

Most messengers are volunteers. While they have joined an organization and need to go through a formal process of resignation, they are free agents. The sending agency does not tie people down, chain them to the floor, or force them to stay. When they have made their decision, those that remain also face a choice. Stayers can accept their departure, bless them, and adjust, or they can give in to hurt and self-pity. And someday the time will also likely come when the stayers are the ones deciding to leave.

The degree of our hurt may also depend on our degree of closeness, why the goers leave, and what they leave behind, such as a hole in the team, messes to clean up, or incomplete projects. If you find your hurt has become overwhelming and restricts your ability to move forward, please get help. Share with someone, perhaps pay for a professional debrief or a counseling session. Take responsibility for your emotional health as you do your physical health. Others may not know how deeply the departure of another affects you unless you say something.

REFLECTION

Read and reflect on Psalm 55 and 2 Samuel 15–20. Journal and pray about what God is saying to you.

What might be some of the underlying issues behind your hurt?

If you feel the other party broke a promise or lied to you, how might you reframe this to give them the benefit of the doubt?

How can you continue to show love and not let their leaving taint your opinion of them?

How can you listen objectively and let them process, even if it means you will lose them?

How can you discuss their decision without making your input manipulative?

RESPONSE

Name your hurt and/or disappointment. Ask God to help you release it.

When you are ready, symbolically lay it down. Let God heal your hurt.

PRAYER

Lord God, I admit that I'm hurt and disappointed. I realize this situation has left me reeling. I feel like Caleb. You, Lord, understand betrayal. You understand when others let me down. I cast my hurt on you, Lord, and ask you to sustain me. Heal my heart that I might continue loving and serving you. Amen.

RESOURCES

http://hiveresources.com/wphives1/ps-55-two-things-to-do-when-youre-betrayed-by-a-friend/ _____

https://trotters41.com/2013/02/08/revolving-door-revolving-heart-looking-back-on-a-year-in-asia-part-5/ _____

https://velvetashes.com/the-transient-community-of-a-life-overseas/ _____

https://velvetashes.com/staying-healthy-amidst-change/ _____

https://missionarycare.com/pdfs/Missionaries-Those-Who-Stay.pdf _____

https://www.mmct.org/ _____
(Mobile Member Care Toolbox—debriefing tools)

Elizabeth and Jonathan Trotter, *Serving Well: Help for the Wannabe, Newbie, or Weary Cross-Cultural Christian Worker* (Eugene: Resource Publications, 2019).

Chapter 12

We Were Going to Change the World Together
Unmet Expectations

While they tend to tolerate a degree of disappointment with their unsaved national friends, missionaries look at each other and tend to expect certain behavior from each other as co-workers. There is also pressure to conform to these expectations.

—SUE EENIGENBURG

Right from the beginning, nothing went the way I thought it would go. For starters I was shocked that our new teammates had bottled up expectations for us. On the way from the train station to their home in a rickety old taxi, James pelted us with his own exciting dreams for us: they were so glad we were there; it was so wonderful to have another married couple on the team; he could imagine that soon we would be team leaders and they would move on; we would lead the church planting project; we would eventually become focus group leaders; Lowell was uniquely gifted to fill this role; I was a joy to have around; they were finally freed up to pursue a burden they had for the people in another state; wasn't God good?[1]

When my leader told me over breakfast that he would be leaving to take on a role in another location, though not surprised, I was crushed. The announcement shook me like I would have never imagined. His giftings were going to be missed, and I felt it was going to impact my work greatly. As I think back now, I realize that I was sad because of my expectations of working long term with this family. I had dreams that I wanted to realize with this family.

I [Sue] expected to stay on the field until retirement. I expected my teammates to stay that long too. Being a child of missionaries with Wycliffe Bible Translators gave me the example of longevity, at least to the point of completing a New Testament translation. That process took my parents twenty-five years (they went on to do a second one) so I grew up with an expectation of long-term missions and determined to follow suit when I signed up.

I expected folks to get along. I expected understanding. When a new couple arrived, I expected them to pitch in, attend meetings, and contribute to the work. I expected them to step in where needed, such as planning team retreats and leading children's programs.

---

1 Eenigenburg and Bliss, *Expectations and Burnout*, 36.

And of course, they would stay as long as necessary to get the job done. I expected folks to ask for my input in decision-making. I expected acceptable reasons to quit. If they decided to go, I expected them to say goodbye appropriately and leave well. But I did not expect to say goodbye to so many teammates, friends, and other expats. I never wrote these expectations on a piece of paper. I just knew when my assumptions weren't met.

And so, when a teammate told us they planned to leave the team, I was devastated. *Who was going to do all those things I had been sure they were going to do? What about our wonderful strategy? This wasn't fair. We were going to change the world together.*

I imagine Abram had expectations of his nephew Lot since he had no children of his own. Or perhaps Lot expected Uncle Abram, his closest relative, to care for him since his own father had died. Uncle and nephew formed a father-son relationship. Love, loyalty, and inheritance bound them together as family, with all the expectations of blood relations (Gen 11:31–12:5).

As their wealth increased and conflicts arose between their herdsmen, I wonder if they realized their unrealistic expectations of living and working together. I respect Abram's response. As family, he didn't want dispute to come between them. Better to separate and take over different spheres of influence than clash and fight (Gen 13:1–13). As the elder, Abram could have legitimately chosen first and instructed his nephew where to go. But instead, he gave the choice to Lot.

However, despite Abram's loyalty and kindness to his nephew, God communicated that Lot would not be Abram's heir. Abram then turned his expectation of an heir to his servant, Eliezer of Damascus (Gen 15:2). But even that belied God's plan. God would give Abram a son from his own body despite his old age (Gen 18:10). Abram had to release his expectations to God's overarching plan.

Many messengers do not realize the expectations they put on their teammates. Since it is commonly known that conflict among teammates results in workers leaving the field, might it be "worthwhile to ask, 'How many of these problems are caused by unmet, unstated and possibly unrecognized expectations?'"[2]

As we addressed earlier, change happens despite our plans, strategies, training, and even our prayers. Changing one's mind is a human trait. Yet our teammates' change of mind still catches us off guard.

Through my experiences with the revolving door of exiting teammates, I learned to normalize change. Despite my attempts to stop it, change will happen. The coming and going of teammates characterizes the missionary life.

When I transferred my expectations from my teammates' behavior and my well-devised strategies to my heavenly Father, I was not so upset and upended by their sudden or slow decisions. I let go of trying to control the outcome, convince them to stay, persuade them of all the thousands of reasons we needed them, or even trying to guilt them into my plan for their lives. I could trust God that he would plant his church and build his kingdom his way, in his timing, with his players.

Accepting that our sovereign God will build his church frees me from the burden to make it happen or the sense of failure when it doesn't. I like to envision God leaning over a map of the world, seeing every village and every household. In his supreme wisdom and omnipotence, he knows exactly who needs to be where and when in order for them to hear of the saving grace of Jesus. He directs willing workers to one country so that they will learn

---

2 Eenigenburg and Bliss, 110.

a particular language. Then he moves them to a new city so they'll strategically meet the right people whom he is wooing to himself. After a certain amount of time, he directs them to yet another country or even sends them back to their passport country to minister to other missionaries or speakers of that language they learned—or to traditional jobs in their own culture. He sees the whole plan and the big picture, and nothing, not even the cost of sending a large family overseas, exceeds the budget or the time needed to save one soul.

Last, God uses everything I endure for my growth—the changes, the dashed expectations, the hurt, and the disappointment. Could it be that God is so concerned about me, my maturity, and my journey that he would send some teammates for only a short period of time because I need to learn something from them? Can I see their presence as a gift and a way for them and myself to grow and mature, not as simply a means to complete my ministry plan?

REFLECTION

Reflect on the following passages. What do these verses tell you about your expectations of change?

Hebrews 13:5–8

Jeremiah 29:11–13

Philippians 1:6

Proverbs 3:1–8

What are or were your expectations of your teammates?

In what ways have your teammates not met your expectations?

How can you adjust any unrealistic expectations?

If you feel your expectations have been dashed and you never want to expect anything ever again, how can you rebuild faith in others?

RESPONSE

Sue often suggests to audiences that they have a funeral for their expectations. Why not do that? After you have identified your dashed expectations in relation to your teammates leaving, plan a memorial service.

What would you say by way of a eulogy to your expectations?

PRAYER

Lord God, my expectations get in the way so often. In fact, I usually don't even realize I have them until I fail to achieve them. I view my teammates as family, making it tough to see them leave before our vision has been implemented. Our partnering together had such potential. I had high hopes for our future together. I lay my expectations to rest and trust that you will pick up the remaining pieces and build something beautiful from them. Amen.

RESOURCES

https://velvetashes.com/staying-healthy-amidst-change/ _____

https://www.seebeyond.cc/four-ways-to-uncover-expectations _____

https://screamsinthedesert.wordpress.com/2017/11/03/a-crown-a-boat-and-four-graves/ _____

Chapter 13

I'm Sad and Grieving
Loss and Grief

Loss strips us of the props we rely on for our well-being. It knocks us off our feet and puts us on our backs. In the experience of loss, we come to the end of ourselves. But in coming to the end of ourselves, we can also come to the beginning of a vital relationship with God.

—GERALD L. SITTSER

I felt some feelings of anger, weariness, and sadness as we saw a death to our dream.

All workers need to mourn the loss well and in a healthy way together.

It felt like a death, yet they are still alive. It felt like death, but no time to grieve.

My soul is worn and frayed with the many goodbyes I've had.

One big emotion I also feel is fear. Things feel shaky when a leader leaves or another person leaving is a huge shock. Reminding myself of Scripture with God as my rock has helped me so much. It stabilizes me when I feel so unstable.

One of my dearest memories is my son crying in the back seat as I parked the car and me crying as well. My good friend was his good friend's mom. With their leaving, we both felt a huge gap, but crying together helped. I think we were both surprised the other one was hurting so badly.

My teenage son doesn't want to go on furlough because he knows everything will change while he's gone. He's actually asked me if I can leave him here for eight months.

This month we said goodbye to three teammates. We are so grateful for their time here and bless them with what God has for each of them. We also feel the sadness and loss deeply. Sometimes it's hard to be the "stayers," watching our team grow and shrink over so many years. We are asking God to help us to "run with endurance the race He has set before us."

I remember when a couple left our field and one of the hardest things for me was figuring out how to help our new [national] sisters in Christ grieve well their loss while grieving my own. I'm not sure what is needed to help both to grieve well, but sometimes one person's departure can affect a church plant when all the experts are looked at as people getting ready to leave.

Talk openly about how it makes you feel. Express grief when you feel it. Don't try to keep everything the same as it was. Expect and embrace the changes. Don't be jealous if the conversation is focused on the leaving unit for a time. Recognize that some teammates may need more time to find a healthy way forward while others can move forward rather quickly. Neither is a wrong response, just different.

In second grade, my good friend returned to her passport country because her father died tragically in a plane crash. Then another close friend left after sixth grade so her father could continue his education. Because I attended a missionary kid school, every year I said hello to new teachers and goodbye to others as well as to classmates taking their turn for home assignment. At age eighteen, I left the place of my birth and moved to my passport country for college. I would not see my parents and younger sister until I completed my bachelor's degree. Ten years later, my husband and I said goodbye to family and friends to head overseas ourselves. During our first term, I lost a baby to miscarriage. During our second term, two families left our team due to medical and emotional health issues. Over the course of our time overseas, I experienced over fifteen changes in my team structure and in my wider circle of friends—including the deaths of two co-workers.

The Apostle Paul understands our losses and resulting grief:

> When Paul had finished speaking, he knelt down with all of them and prayed. They all wept as they embraced him and kissed him. What grieved them most was his statement that they would never see his face again. Then they accompanied him to the ship. After we had torn ourselves away from them, we put out to sea and sailed straight to Kos. (Acts 20:36–21:1)

Notice the poignant words in this text: embraced, kissed, grieved, never see again, accompanied, torn away. Paul experienced the same kinds of goodbyes we do every time we take our family with our tower of suitcases and bags to the airport or watch our teammates' and friends' planes disappear into the clouds.

I find the same sense of sadness in two of Jesus's disciples, Cleopas and his companion. After his tragic death on the cross and having all hopes of a new earthly kingdom dashed, they took a walk together on the Emmaus Road, discussing all that had happened (Luke 24:13–14). I imagine their conversation sounded much like any global messenger after the departure of a teammate (especially a leader)—full of sadness, grief, anxiety, confusion, and all they would miss.

> While they were talking and debating these things, Jesus himself approached and began to accompany them (but their eyes were kept from recognizing him). Then he said to them, "What are these matters you are discussing so intently as you walk along?" And they stood still, looking sad. (Luke 24:15–17 NET)

Sometimes, we just have to stand still, looking sad. The Bible teaches us how to mourn and many passages speak of lament (Ps 77:1–9). A few weeks ago, I (Sue) attended a webinar about lamenting. I had never "officially" lamented before and as I listened, I thought I had nothing to lament. Then I remembered how much I hated wearing masks because of COVID-19. My lament began. And it continued. Words poured out and emotions bubbled up that I didn't even know I had as I gave myself time to acknowledge and grieve this sadness.

Let's stand still in sadness when others leave. We won't stay in this place forever. But we need to remain here for a while because sadness is a necessary part of grieving well.

Therapists tell us we also need comfort during this stage of grief. And many people experience a lack of support in their grieving process. Comfort means "being there with understanding and love, not trying to change or fix things. … Comfort validates grief and gives permission for the grieving process or mourning to take place."[1]

We erroneously think that we simply need to remind others of the things they should be grateful for in an attempt to encourage them. Encouragement has its place, but first we need consolation. We comfort and console one another by standing still together. "It's okay. That's horrible. I'm so sorry. I am sad with you. That sounds really hard."

Jesus knew this as he stood with the men on the road to Emmaus. Please don't fail to recognize who stands with us in our grief—Jesus himself! He knows our sorrow and comforts us with his presence.

Jesus also experienced his own set of losses. He left heaven to become like us (Phil 2:6–8). His earthly father died and his cousin was brutally beheaded (Matt 14:9–10). He possessed no home (Matt 9:58), no paying job (Luke 8:1–3), and his friend betrayed him (Luke 22:4–6).

Jesus did not gloss over his losses but instead grieved them. He spent time in solitude following his cousin's murder (Matt 14:10–13), wept when his friend Lazarus died (John 11:35), and expressed his own deep sorrow (Luke 22:41–44) before his death. The prophet Isaiah describes Jesus as acquainted with deepest grief (Isa 53:3).

While Jesus gives us permission to mourn and we know we have hope in eternity, we still hurt. Author Carolyn Custis James writes:

> When Paul said not "to grieve like … [those] who have no hope" (1 Thessalonians 4:13), he was reassuring us that the sorrow we experience in this world is mingled with the solid hope that sorrow won't have the last word. Somewhere along the line, however, his words have also come to mean that, in some sense, we sorrow *less* than others. Somehow, because of our hope, we are supposed to rise above our losses. … I think, instead, perhaps the difference between

---

1   van Reken and Pollock, *Third Culture Kids, 3rd Edition*, 314, 94.

how we and the world sorrow is that we sorrow *more*, not less, and in our sorrowing we are entering in some mysterious way into God's sorrow.[2]

Member care providers, counselors, and many books state that life is filled with ordinary losses from small to large. A friend moves away. A parent dies. A job changes. A favorite plate shatters. Children grow up and move out. The freedoms of the single life evaporate with the joys of marriage. Movement becomes restricted by a decline in health. Losses come with each change in life stage and is unavoidable with sin's effect on our world.

These normal life losses follow us into our overseas life and compound when we encounter a new set of losses. The missionary also has the loss of identity and language ability and very often the loss of dreams, ideals, and expectations. But the loss of teammates might be one of the greatest losses endured by those who labor on the mission field. We mourn every time one of these dear friends goes on furlough or follows God to their next assignment—even when we understand why they have to go. And we lament when the departure of the one we care about is due to sin, especially when it results in their walking away from God. All of these losses—big and small—must be grieved or they will accumulate and become overwhelming, possibly contributing to burnout or depression.

As a stayer, you have experienced great loss. So, what do you do? Grieve. Mourn. Grieving will be unique to everyone. Some may move past the loss of a teammate fairly quickly. However, we do caution that you not avoid the grieving process thinking that it's best to just move on. Even if you only take a day or two, spend time mourning. Or take time when the waves of sadness wash over you, even if only briefly. Don't stuff the grief down, deny it, or explain it away. Please don't spiritualize it. As Christians in ministry, we so want to find the silver lining, the element of praise, the thing to be grateful for. That is all good and necessary, and you can get to that place, but only after you have taken some time to mourn.

Connie Befus perfectly expresses the goal of our grieving: "Mourning our losses allows us to let go. Only then do we have the emotional space to open ourselves to new people, new experiences—and joy."[3]

If you don't mourn adequately for your departing teammates, you will forfeit space to open yourselves to the next teammates. You may become callous and bitter, to the point you no longer want to get to know anyone.

I propose a *spiritual discipline of mourning*—a way to mourn losses as a normal rhythm of life—so that they do not accumulate and become too heavy to bear:

- *Acknowledge losses.* Name them, no matter how big or small, out loud, in writing, to a friend, or simply in prayer. Secondarily, what else have you lost? For instance: In losing our teammates, we lost the hosts for our Sunday gathering, the group clown, the language expert, and the gifted evangelist.

- *Feel and release emotions appropriately.* As you look over your list, allow yourself to feel whatever emotions surface. Cry if needed. If you feel anger, that's okay. Recognize your feelings without judging them. Then, find an appropriate way to release them—weep, lament, journal, chop wood, knead bread. Once, when particularly angry, I found a private forested area and threw rocks at the trees as hard as I could. With each throw, I articulated the loss, the hurt, and the disappointment.

---

2 James, *Half the Church*, 142.

3 Befus, *Sojourner's Workbook*, 33.

- *Meditate on Scriptures* relating to grief, lament, and comfort in grief. Let God comfort and heal your heart.

- *Practice good self-care.* Grieving can be exhausting. Get adequate rest, perhaps more than you usually do. Do more life-giving activities. Have fun. Laugh if you can.

- *Let go or say goodbye* in some way. For example: Make a collage to remember the teammates. Print out and frame some photos if the memories are happy. If not, take your loss list, tear it up, flush it, or toss it into the waves. One worker took the shards of her painful loss list and created a beautiful mosaic depicting God's healing.

Repeat these steps regularly. Address your losses daily, weekly, or at least monthly. We offer you a worksheet to help with this in Appendix Four. We urge you not to wait until you take your home assignment or experience burn out.

REFLECTION

Reflect on the following passages. Journal your thoughts to God on this subject.

Matthew 14:1–14

John 11:1–44

Luke 22:41–44

What losses have come with the departure of your teammate(s)?

What other losses (big and small) have you experienced?

Reflect on why that particular thing is a loss for you.

How can you mourn your losses as part of your regular rhythm of disciplines?

How can you comfort others with your presence? Even virtually?

RESPONSE

Practice the spiritual discipline of mourning described above as it relates to the leaving of your friend or teammate. Choose a life-giving activity and schedule or plan a time to do it soon.

PRAYER

Lord Jesus, it comforts me to know that you understand loss, and you showed your sadness by weeping. I am tempted to make light of my losses because so many experience sorrow to a much greater degree. However, this is my life, my lot, and I take responsibility for doing business with the grief in my soul. I cast my cares on you, Lord, and receive your comfort and grace. Amen.

RESOURCES

https://velvetashes.com/when-staying-equals-transition/ _____

https://trotters41.com/2016/06/01/7-tips-for-stayers-and-goers-velvet-ashes/ ___

https://evaburkholder.com/2021/08/28/grieving-losses-never-ends/ _____

https://evaburkholder.com/2020/05/16/stand-still-and-be-sad/ _____

https://evaburkholder.com/2022/09/07/true-comfort-soothes-and-strengthens/

https://globaltrellis.com/shop/how-to-handle-all-the-loss-you-experience/   ___

https://globaltrellis.com/author/katieb/   _____
(Katie Brown is the Grief Specialist and blogs quarterly about grief and loss.)

https://www.alifeoverseas.com/an-empty-ocean-and-the-10-things-we-must-
remember-about-grief/   _____

Alicia Boyce, Heather Fallis, and Tamika Rybinski, *Liturgies & Laments for the Sojourner Volume One* (Guin: Vinehouse Publishing, 2023).

Kate Motaung, *Letters to Grief* (Middletown: Independently published, 2020).

Chapter 14

I Invested So Much and So Few Are Left
Rights and Scarcity

The missionary has to give up having his own way. He has to give up having any rights. He has, in the words of Jesus, to "deny himself." He has to give up himself.

—Mabel Williamson

Sometimes the people that leave create a heavier workload for those who stay behind.

People left after a short term and delegated their organization's work to us, but never returned. We are now holding up that work as well.

Great. They're gone. Now we have to fill in their job on top of our own. Sigh.

It's hard not to have the mindset that "I can use you for my purposes."

As a single, I can be tempted to want to make sure that I will have relationships in the future. Instead of living in a scarcity mindset, I need to move to investing in whoever God puts in front of me, and trust that he will bring me the community I need when I need it.

I can still remember when our leaders left and all of us were overwhelmed with all the holes in ministry to fill and feeling the weight of the expectations of those who were impacted by their ministry.

When my supervisor left, many ministries had to be stopped because we did not have the staff or the skills to continue them. This was hard for our team because all of these ministries seemed "essential." But our wise new leaders realized that the workload was not possible with the current team and made the hard decision to put some of the ministries on hold. I believe this gave the team more life and more freedom to continue on in our skill sets.

We prayed so long for more hands to lighten the load. Finally, my team welcomed a new family to our field. Our entire team spent hours and hours helping them find a home, purchase furniture, and start their language study. On top of this were the intangibles expended, like explaining cultural differences, listening to their concerns and fears, strategizing about the ministry, and creating space for their unique skills and talents. We instructed them from the storehouse of knowledge we had gained by learning what worked and what didn't. We wanted to spare them the pain of our mistakes. And then, after all we had invested, after all our time and energy spent, they announced their intention to leave one year later. And once again, we didn't have enough workers.

I felt I had a right to know their plans. I had a right to know they were thinking of leaving—and they didn't even tell me. I had a right to be consulted. I had a right to have a say in their decision. I felt like Lady Catherine de Bourgh in *Pride and Prejudice* who insisted on finding out if her nephew has made an offer of marriage to Elizabeth Bennet, "I am almost the nearest relation he has in the world, and am entitled to know all his dearest concerns."[1]

Can you relate? If you are the team leader, perhaps you feel you have the right to tell your teammates they can or cannot go. Maybe you wonder how you will ever get another to replace them.

Living on this planet makes us keenly aware we have limited resources. Even Jesus said that the "workers are few" (Matt 9:37). With only so many hands to go around, when we finally get more colleagues and teammates, we tend to cling to them for fear we will lose them. This scarcity mindset leads to comparison, competition, and a me-first attitude. We begin to hoard our personnel and fear that their leaving means we will go without. This fear further encourages us to control and seek a say in decision making. We can even convince ourselves this is our right.

Jesus speaks to this kind of mindset in a familiar narrative in the Gospels:

> When Jesus looked up and saw a great crowd coming toward him, he said to Philip, "Where shall we buy bread for these people to eat?" He asked this only to test him, for he already had in mind what he was going to do.
>
> Philip answered him, "It would take more than half a year's wages to buy enough bread for each one to have a bite!"
>
> Another of his disciples, Andrew, Simon Peter's brother, spoke up, "Here is a boy with five small barley loaves and two small fish, but how far will they go among so many?" (John 6:5–9)

I think Philip expressed the feelings of many a messenger of the gospel: "It would take more than we have on hand. How are we going to get more workers? We don't have enough to hire someone to fill in, even temporarily. The resources are too few." And perhaps Andrew says it best: "How far will they go among so many?" (v. 9).

When I, like Andrew, view my life and ministry through a scarcity mindset, I become stingy with my time, resources, talents, and co-workers. I try to assert myself to get my share, my rightful place on the team, and my say in the plans. Or I shrink back and disappear because others have already taken the seats at the table.

But Jesus tells us to sit down and give thanks; to use what we have. He will feed us. He will provide. He will take our resources and multiply them as he already has the end goal in mind. He reminds us: "I am the bread of life. Whoever comes to me will never go hungry, and whoever believes in me will never be thirsty" (John 6:35). In Jesus, there is enough bread to go around. What looks like scarcity becomes abundant multiplication.

---

1 Austen, *Pride and Prejudice*, 273.

When I view my life and ministry through Jesus's lens of abundance, I can release my selfish rights. Because in actuality, the only rights I have are spiritual rights, and these are given to me by God through the blood of Jesus—spiritual blessings, sonship, access to the Father, the indwelling Holy Spirit, freedom from sin, and future inheritance (Rom 8:14–17; Gal 4:6–7).

There's an old mission manual by Mabel Williamson entitled, *Have We No Rights?* It's not a popular book as you can imagine. According to Williamson, gospel messengers typically prepare to "eat bitterness," a Chinese idiom for "suffering hardship."[2] Missionaries know they will have to suffer for Jesus. They expect the struggles of language learning, separation from family, doing without electricity, or ants in the cereal. But they often don't prepare to "eat loss." Eating loss—"suffering the infringement of one's rights"—raises the bar to another level.[3] Williamson says:

> It takes a little while to get your palate and your digestion used to Chinese food, of course, but that was no harder than I had expected. Another thing, however ... that I had never thought about came up to make trouble. I had to "eat loss"! I found that I couldn't stand up for my rights—that I couldn't even *have* any rights. I found that I had to give them up, every one, and that was the hardest thing of all. ...
>
> On the mission field it is not the enduring of hardships, the lack of comforts, and the roughness of the life that make the missionary cringe and falter. It is something far less romantic and far more real. It is something that will hit you right down where you live. The missionary has to give up having his own way. He has to give up having any rights. He has, in the words of Jesus, to "deny himself." He has to give up *himself.*[4]

When we hear the news that someone plans to leave the field, our reaction might be rooted in a sense of entitlement. Especially if we have invested a lot, we feel we deserve a return on that investment. Williamson reminds us that a team, friendships, or even a community are not rights owed to us.

Only God has the right to move people around as he wills. Ultimately, he controls all, including the spiritual harvest. He knows what he needs to build his kingdom in all parts of the world. If I can play a part—even a small one—in preparing someone to continue to build the kingdom, then I have done my job. I may no longer reap the benefits of my teammate's skills and contributions, but I know the kingdom will advance. My focus becomes that which will promote God's agenda globally, not just in the tiny corner where I serve.

Gratitude is an antidote to scarcity and entitlement. When we thank God for what we have, who he has sent our way, and what resources we enjoy, we can pick up and move ahead. When we rejoice over his works in our midst, we can let go of our right to more workers while we keep praying for more.

If I operate from a scarcity mindset, I will moan the loss of yet another set of hands. But if I remember God owns everything and works with abundance, then I can release my teammate into God's greater work. I rejoice that another has received training to serve in a new area and I had a part in that.

---

2 Williamson, *Have We No Rights?*, 8.

3 Williamson, 8.

4 Williamson, 8–9.

In essence, Jesus tells us we have enough resources to go around and thus we can encourage our teammates in their desire to serve somewhere else. We can have faith that God is in charge and will get the task done. We can celebrate their wins even if we think we have lost. We can say with Elizabeth "Blessed are you among women, and blessed is the child you will bear!" (Luke 1:42). We can agree with her son, John the Baptist, who releases his disciples to follow Jesus (more on this later).

REFLECTION

Reflect on the following passages. What might God be saying to you about your rights and scarcity mindset?

Matthew 6:25–35

Luke 14:25–35

Ephesians 3:16

What rights have you had to give up when a teammate leaves?

Has a scarcity mindset affected your use of your gifts? How?

In your situation, what would it look like to deny yourself?

How might you put the needs and desires of the one leaving before your own?

What would it look like to operate from a multiplication mindset?

RESPONSE

After reflection, write out what you can be grateful for currently.

Ask God to provide out of his abundance.

PRAYER

Lord, Son of David, help me. I come to you because only you have the words of life (John 5:68) and an unlimited supply of resources. Help me stop striving for my share of the goods, clinging to my teammates, competing to get ahead, or shrinking back in fear. Help me instead to confidently trust that you are enough. I put my trust in you to determine the appropriate return for my investment. Amen.

RESOURCES

https://www.enlivenpublishing.com/2013/12/03/break-the-scarcity-mindset-with-this-revelation/   _____

https://www.christianitytoday.com/women-leaders/2016/august/stop-leading-from-scarcity-mindset.html   _____

https://evaburkholder.com/2019/08/22/enough-bread/   _____

Chapter 15

It's All My Fault, Yet What a Relief
Conflict and Guilt

It is perfectly appropriate to feel relieved at the same time you are feeling devastated. It doesn't mean you haven't loved fully, or cared for the person to the best of your ability.

—RABBI EARL A. GROLLMAN

When I said goodbye to them at the airport, I felt we could have done a lot of things better. There was this side of guilt and there was this side of "Whew! That's not my issue anymore, my responsibility" and it was a relief.

[It's] literally twenty years from the date that we came, and we have no team and no church planting work. We've had a lot of people come through in those years and done the cycle many, many times, and that's sort of where the guilt comes in. We're the common denominator in all this. If only we were different or did things differently. What are we doing wrong that people come and then go and don't stay?

There was a lot of frustration and anger when we were misrepresented and spoken ill of publicly when the whole issue was a complete misunderstanding. We felt like we were not heard, and neither did our church acknowledge any understanding of the situation. I would also add we were simply in pain from the whole incident.

We raised our families differently, had different interests, different philosophies of ministry. It was just too much to try to continue this work.

I sometimes feel guilty like, "If I'd had them over more, they wouldn't have left." I know it's a lie, but it still comes to mind.

There are also situations where missionaries are "taken off the field" for sinful situations. This is hard to work through because they are immediately gone. As the people who knew and loved them, the lack of closure in this type of situation is difficult.

We need open communication with the people who have chosen to leave. And not to shy away from the hard conversations because it may help with the processing of feelings as they leave.

Serve others even when it is hard emotionally (makes me think of Jesus washing the disciples' feet). How can I best serve them before they go knowing that I did all I could in the time I had with these missionary friends?

Ask their permission to ask hard questions. This way it can come across as "I want this to go well for you and also for me." Try to show concern.

Sometimes, the blame for a missionary's departure is laid at my feet. But as with most things, the fault never lies totally with one party, even if there is some truth in the accusations. "You dropped the ball. We were hurting, and you did not come to our aid. You did not ask how I was doing or if I needed help. As our member care providers, you are the main ones to look out for us and you failed. We would have stayed if you had been better leaders or given us the support we needed. Hence, we are going to look for another agency that will take better care of us."

Could I have done better? Certainly. Did I drop the ball? Yes. Could I carry the guilt of this member's leaving? Yes, if I let myself.

Perhaps you know you played a part in the departure of a valued co-worker. Perhaps you were embroiled in a conflict. Perhaps you failed them in some way. How do you reconcile this and move on? How does your team heal from a time of intense conflict?

Consider the example of the two feuding women in Philippi:

I plead with Euodia and I plead with Syntyche to be of the same mind in the Lord. Yes, and I ask you, my true companion, help these women since they have contended at my side in the cause of the gospel, along with Clement and the rest of my co-workers, whose names are in the book of life. (Phil 4:2–3)

Rather than see Euodia and Syntyche as *arguing* teammates, I choose to see them simply as teammates who dealt with ordinary situations of conflict, just like we all do. These female co-workers labored with Paul from the "first day" (Phil 1:5) that they birthed the church in a beachside prayer meeting (Acts 16). Somewhere along the way, they ministered with Paul to spread the gospel and make disciples.

Because Paul mentions them by name, they must have played a prominent role in the church, making it especially crucial that they work out their differences. Other translations describe Paul's admonition in verse two as "live in harmony" (NASB), "come to an agreement" (CEB), "iron out their differences and make up" (MSG).

Being of the same mind doesn't refer to preferences, such as politics or lifestyle choices. It doesn't mean we have to agree on the team meeting format, parenting styles, or sabbath day activities. Differences in these areas may actually benefit the body of Christ by ensuring all types of people receive care and all methods are employed in discipleship and preaching the gospel.

But what about agreement on the fine points of theological matters? Do we have to agree on how we interpret every verse of the Bible or whose podcast we follow? Paul spoke to this when he called out the Corinthians for quarreling over which spiritual leader they followed—him or Apollos (1 Cor 3:3–5). Saying that we are students of Calvin or Piper or Shirer is not our goal here. Rather, we find a clue to Paul's intent earlier in his letter where he says:

> Do nothing out of selfish ambition or vain conceit. Rather, in humility value others above yourselves, not looking to your own interests but each of you to the interests of the others. In your relationships with one another, have the same mindset as Christ Jesus. (Phil 2:3–5)

Being of the same mind means we have Christ's mind—we are Christlike. He set aside his own desires and rights and became a servant (Phil 2:6–8). Paul doesn't ask for uniformity, just unity. He wants us to have "the same attitude of mind toward each other that Christ Jesus had so that with one mind and one voice you [we] may glorify the God and Father of our Lord Jesus Christ" (Rom 15:5–6).

I am of the same mind with my team when I think of their needs before my own, when I work at living in peace, when I put on love above all things, when I can agree to disagree—agreeably.

When we feel like we didn't do enough or could have tried harder to prevent attrition, guilt can be a common reaction. And yet, we may also feel relief that certain teammates have left. We may justify our feeling with thoughts like: *They're difficult, hard to get along with, are not team players, don't adhere to the team strategy, or just want to do their own thing.* And then we feel guilty for feeling relieved. Frankly, it's easier to let these folks go than try to convince them to stay and work things out. The issues seem insurmountable and the effort too great to try to work together.

If you feel guilty, can you accept God's forgiveness for yourself? You cannot do everything perfectly or fulfill everyone's expectations or desires. Give yourself grace to fail and try again. Remember, too, that people leave for multi-layered reasons. While you may feel you are the sole cause of their departure, in reality, you are probably only one piece of their decision-making puzzle.

Try to gain perspective, keep learning, and continue growing. (We'll address forgiveness further in a later chapter.)

When conflict, abuse, manipulation, or unhealthy relationships exist, seek mediation and counseling as soon as possible. Talk to trusted leaders, pastors, and friends. Try to understand the goer's side, but do not submit yourselves to continued dysfunction. Initiate an exit interview practice so that the goer can express concerns and the agency or team can do better next time. We offer a sample exit interview in Appendix Five.

When a teammate leaves due to conflict, the stayers may experience a huge sense of relief and succumb to the temptation to "get on with what's important." However, we strongly suggest staying teammates pause for a time of evaluating, processing, grieving, and forgiving in order to heal and rebuild. Conflicts have two sides, and the health of those remaining depends on facing their parts in the strife and growing from the struggle.

Evaluate what happened and determine if anything could have been conducted or handled differently. Was the orientation inadequate? Were their talents and skills not utilized? How might the team have served them better? What can we learn from this?

Sometimes the departure of a teammate is due to sin. Those left behind need to heal before moving on. We recommend attending a counseling or debriefing program or meeting with a licensed counselor for as long as it takes. Processing with professionals in a monitored setting helps eliminate gossip and contains knowledge of the events to necessary parties.

While we tend to put the blame on the departing member, conflict can reveal deficiencies in ourselves that need attention—ways that we contributed to the dysfunction or reasons we allowed it to continue. If we can at some point evaluate ourselves, our reactions, our attitudes, and our hearts, we can grow from this hurt.

Situations also exist in which the healthy teammate goes because they recognize the unhealthiness of the team. In this case, closing one's eyes to the concerns and admonitions of the goer may result in further damage and more teammates leaving. Addressing a dysfunctional team is beyond the scope of this book, but please don't ignore our entreaty to consider, evaluate, get help, and heal—now.

REFLECTION

Reflect on the following passages:

Philippians 2:3–8

Philippians 4:1–6

How might you need to "work it out" with a fellow laborer?

What are some life skills, leadership skills, or communication skills that you might learn or learn about more so that you do not repeat this with others?

What will your relationship with your departing teammate look like going forward?

How can you show humility?

Have you listened—really listened—to the other side? (This doesn't mean you have to agree, only that you seek to understand.) Without interruption? Without defensiveness? Without justifying?

RESPONSE

Prayerfully consider and identify what part of the conflict you can take responsibility for and what part is not your responsibility.

Ask the Lord to show you how you can pursue an outcome that will lead to unity—not necessarily uniformity. Then do what the Holy Spirits prompts you to do.

PRAYER

Lord God, in my frequent attempt to avoid conflict, I either keep my mouth shut or push the differing ones away and cut off relationship with them. Sometimes I don't seek to understand their side or why they think as they do. I don't go the extra mile to reach over and hear them out, and then I get offended when someone disagrees with me. I take it personally rather than realize we can still be friends even if we don't see eye to eye. Teach me to put on the mind of Christ and think of their needs above my own. Lord, I may not be able to resolve this conflict, but help me acknowledge where I failed, learn from it, forgive, and keep moving forward. Amen.

RESOURCES

https://evaburkholder.com/2018/02/19/the-mindset-of-christ/ _____

https://evaburkholder.com/2018/03/19/help-them-be-christlike/ _____

https://peacepursuit.org/ _____

https://globaltrellis.com/annual-debrief-course/ _____

Laura Mae Gardner and Lois Dodds offer good resources at
https://www.heartstreamresources.org/shop _____

Peter Scazzero, *Emotionally Healthy Spirituality: It's Impossible to Be Spiritually Mature, While Remaining Emotionally Immature* (Grand Rapids: Zondervan Press, 2017).

Chapter 16

Wait, You're Leaving Because of That?
Judging Motives

> *Being judgmental is not about how quickly you form opinions.*
> *It's how certain you are of them.*
>
> —ADAM GRANT

I find it difficult to make the choice to go or stay because of the inevitable judgment from other missionaries. It sometimes feels like bullying from other missionaries who do missions differently than you.

Something I struggle with is giving people the benefit of the doubt and pushing in and asking them questions.

What is hard is when you don't know why someone left, especially when they gave no clues.

During a coup d'état, each mission family followed God's leading, whether to stay or go. Most left. Then we were all judged by those mission families who weren't present in country when the decisions were made. That hurt.

When you can, ask them, "When the nationals ask me why you are leaving, what do you want me to say?" Give them time to process my questions as well.

I don't know how to process a teammate leaving when you don't know the reason and they have cut off communication.

I went away [from our conversation] with a sentence about why he's leaving and why she's leaving in my head and I felt like they are not good reasons to leave. If they had said "this" I would have been like, "Okay that makes sense" but these two things that they said, I don't think that's really a good reason to leave. We could work on that here or I could show you that's not true. What they actually went to do was not the reason they gave to leave.

Don't speculate as to why the goer left; accept their departure; learn from the reasons for the goer's departure and try not to repeat that with other teammates in the future. We wondered for several months if God was leading us to leave because the visa issue had become so impossible. We tried hard, going month by month on temporary visas. Then a national colleague went rogue, and our teammate was stabbed, and our house was broken into. Those things made us lean toward leaving, of course. But it was the visa that was the ultimate issue, and the government confirmed that. I think the other issues were definitely God saying it's time to go. And certainly, had we not left, who knows if we would've recovered or been of any use.

Our team gathered for our weekly time of worship, prayer, and business. During their sharing time, our teammates dropped the bombshell. "We feel led to leave."

As we listened to their reasons for this sudden change in plans, their thought process remained unclear. Something to do with not being a ministry fit and needing to serve their extended family at home. To tell the truth, I don't really remember their reason. I just know that it didn't sound great to me. It didn't really make sense. *They couldn't leave because of that!*

In the absence of clear information from them, I filled in the blanks with my own: *They couldn't make it. They don't really like it here. Their family's not adjusting well. I don't think they're stating the real reason.*

Basically, I judged them. I didn't believe they were justified in their decision to leave. I had a list of acceptable (or unavoidable) reasons for leaving the mission field and theirs did not fit. Of course, I hadn't written these reasons down anywhere. I just *knew* them.

I wonder if this is how the Apostle Paul felt when Mark, Barnabas's cousin (Col 4:10), suddenly left at the second stop of their missionary journey (Acts 13:13). We can surmise his hurt and disappointment because of his reaction two years later when Barnabas suggested they invite Mark to join the next journey. Paul objected so strongly that the two partners split up (Acts 15:36–41). Paul felt Mark had "deserted them" (v. 38). Other verses using this same Greek word are translated "turn away" (Heb 3:12), "abandon" (1 Tim 4:1), "withdraw" (Acts 22:29). Scripture doesn't give us the details, but I think Paul would have used a less intense word if Mark had cited an acceptable or unavoidable reason.

Some scholars think that Mark left because he longed for home or didn't adequately count the cost. Others believe he seriously objected to something Paul did. Whatever the reason, Paul called it desertion. And he refused to give Mark a second chance. Barnabas disagreed. And sadly, the missionary dream team dissolved.

I propose that Paul judged Mark's motives because Paul did not allow for the possibility of change or maturity in Mark. One strike and he was out. Paul did not want to trust him again. Since we don't know the details, we cannot say if Paul exhibited wisdom or stubbornness in contrast to Barnabas's willingness to take a chance on Mark. Thankfully, if we read to the end of the narrative, we learn that at some point, Mark joined Paul, and they ended on a happy note, reconciled (2 Tim 4:11; 1 Pet 5:13).

Why do gospel messengers, like Mark, leave their place of service? Or their role? Or their agency? The most common explanations I have heard in my experience as a member care provider mirror those of a recent survey by Andrea Sears at *The Missions Experience*: retirement, personal problems, children and family issues, team conflicts, financial problems, disagreement with leadership, personal dissatisfaction with work, unsuccessful cultural and language adjustment.[1]

Some reasons remain out of a person's control and thus feel justifiable. For instance, immigration denies their visa or asks them to not return. Perhaps health issues prohibit life in their host country and they need medical treatment elsewhere. Children's mental health or educational needs may extend beyond the resources of their current context. Perhaps they experienced a traumatic hostage situation or arrest. Or maybe their recruitment to a leadership role necessitates a geographical move.

However, we must acknowledge that even these obstacles do not stop some who desperately want to stay. For example: Anastasia struggles with mold toxicity and needs a special diet, yet she remains in her place of service. She desires this so much that she will move homes as often as necessary, spend extra time making her required meals from scratch, and wear a special mask whenever she goes out.

Benito and Sadie had already started a business when their visa was denied. But feeling led to keep pursuing, they took the government to court. Every year they spent three months in country, three months out, while waiting for their case to make it through the court system. They finally won after fifteen years.

Let's also recognize that acceptable reasons can also justify a desire to leave: Judith secretly desired to leave her country of service because she felt like she was simply surviving instead of thriving in her life and ministry. She wished the government would deny her visa, or she'd get sick, or something else major would happen so she'd have to leave without telling her partners and teammates how she really felt.

Gary was so riddled with fear that he spent many nights lying awake wondering if he and his family would be subject to attack. When the local government called him into immigration and told him to pack his bags, he was relieved that now he had grounds to leave that he was not ashamed of.

Janet experienced many difficulties in the country, both emotional and physical, and wished God would give her the go-ahead to leave.

These examples show us that sometimes the stated reason for leaving is not the actual or only motivation. Everyone makes their decision based on very personal factors, values, and desires that the whole team cannot possibly know or totally understand. The book, *Worth Keeping*, describes the various reasons:

> Some reasons are explained in the missionary's prayer letter (called "stated reasons"), while revealing additional reasons to his/her close friends/family ("personal reasons"), and may even believe in another set of reasons deep in his/her heart ("secret reasons"). The team or field leader may identify "leader's reasons" but only a subset may go on file ("recorded reasons"), the sending base director may believe in another array of reasons ("believed reasons") and in the mission's journal "socially accepted reasons" may be published, and the missionary's professional counsellor may identify further reasons, while the "true reasons" may still be

---

1 Sears, "Overview of Survey and Methodology."

a combination of all of these—or even be different again. In fact, in most cases it is not one reason alone but often a whole range of reasons that all contribute to the decision.[2]

In truth, many people cannot verbalize or admit the real reason for their departure. Sometimes, they actually don't know or lack the self-awareness to know their root motivation. Or they cannot share it because they fear others will judge them. Perhaps this explains why some resort to playing the *God card*. When we question them further, asking for more specifics, they say, "God has told us to leave." End of discussion. One cannot argue further. If God said so, then who can differ? What else can we say?

Thus, we judge. Why do we tend to judge our teammates' reasons for going? Perhaps we feel stronger or more resilient than the one who leaves. After all, we may have felt the same as our departing teammates and yet we carry on. Maybe we, like the examples above, can find a way around their excuse. Maybe we secretly want to quit and need a reason to persevere. If they leave, why should we stay?

But I think we also judge because we want to understand. When something threatens our control or doesn't make sense according to our standards and thought processes, we seek to comprehend. When our colleagues give a justification that doesn't sound right to us, we look for other explanations to fill in the blanks. In doing so, we sometimes succumb to judgmental conclusions.

We try to understand why a family would undergo all the time, money, energy, and stress of quitting their jobs, joining an agency, raising support, traveling overseas, setting up a home, and learning a foreign language only to reverse the whole process one year later.

Emily P. Freeman, in her book *The Next Right Thing*, says:

> Our Western minds are trained to go down the path of explaining. We think if we can understand it, then we can control it. …We are conditioned to believe the only reason we should do things is if we know why, where we are headed, and for what purpose. No wonder we have trouble making decisions. If we don't have clear answers or sure things, then taking a big step feels like a risk at best and a wasteful mistake at worst. If I understand it, then I can control it.[3]

My own mother questioned our decision when we left Indonesia. She wanted to make sense of what seemed, to her, an early departure. When we cannot control another's decision, we endeavor to at least understand it. We desire to figure everything out, to have all the pros and cons listed, and for the reasons to make sense (to us).

What are you going to do next? Do you have a new job lined up? These common and understandable questions don't always have good answers, or any answers at all. The ones leaving just know in their hearts that the time has come to say goodbye. But that doesn't seem clear enough for those who don't want their teammates to leave or will miss them and their contribution. In order to accept this huge disruption to their life, the departing teammates must have clear next steps. But they don't. Or at least not anything that the stayer will accept or understand.

It does help to know why. But sometimes we are not given this privilege. We simply need to accept that God controls all. Would we want our teammates to trust us when we reveal how God leads us? Give your teammates the benefit of the doubt and trust that God has a reason

---

2 Hay, *Worth Keeping*, 12.

3 Freeman, *The Next Right Thing*, 16.

and will be glorified. In those instances when the decision-making process appears dubious at best, we can still trust that God will lead. Ultimately, they must answer to the Lord for their decision, as must we for our reactions.

What does God say about judging motives? The Greek word *krino* means "to pronounce judgment, to subject to censure, finding fault with this or that in others." Matthew instructs us to look at ourselves first (Matt 7:1–5).

When we communicate judgment, either by our words or by our raised eyebrows, silence, or crossed arms, our teammates may find it hard to confide in us honestly. Where they might have shared the fears and motives behind their actions, instead they retreat inward and protect themselves. If we truly want an honest dialogue, an opportunity to influence their decision-making, or just to listen and be there for them in the process we need to listen without judgment. Even still, we may not receive the honesty we desire and can only let it go.

I wonder how many times I let someone's departure taint my opinion of them for a long time as Paul did with Mark. My husband and I have matured since we left Indonesia twenty years ago. We now recognize the ways that we might have made the transition a little easier for our teammates. I would be heartbroken if we were judged forever by that one decision.

Ultimately each one of us must make our decisions before the Lord, listening to his voice, and acting as we feel we must for the sake of our lives, our testimony, our children, our marriages, and our ministry (and whatever else is relevant).

REFLECTION

Reflect on the following passages. What is the Holy Spirit saying to you about your particular situation?

Matthew 7:1–5

Romans 14:1–13

James 4:11–12

List some of the reasons you consider legitimate for someone to leave the mission field or a ministry.

List some of your unacceptable reasons for someone to leave.

Compare your lists. Pray about these. Meditate on them. What would God say about them?

How might you approach your teammates to create a safe space for sharing?

Over what might you be trying to maintain control?

What is your reason for staying— your true, deep down, heart reason?

RESPONSE

Write your judgmental thoughts on a piece of paper. Then wad it up and throw it away.

Locate a list of the New Testament "one another" commands. How might focusing on these (rather than the above list) help you stay out of the realm of judging?

PRAYER

Father God, I don't understand my teammates' reasons for leaving. To be totally honest, I could give the same justification and hop on a plane, too. I confess that I have judged their motives. Please forgive me. Help me to release their reasons, their departure, and all my judgment into your hands. Thank you that they will still serve you, no matter where they end up. Amen.

RESOURCES

https://thingspaulandluke.wordpress.com/2012/11/21/why-did-mark-leave-paul/

https://themissionsexperience.weebly.com/   _____

res3_152_link_1292428260.pdf   _____
(worldevangelicals.org) page 14

Laura Mae Gardner, _Healthy, Resilient, and Effective in Cross-Cultural Ministry_ (Condeo Press, 2015).

Chapter 17

I Will Overlook and Pardon Them
Forbear and Forgive

Forgiveness is healing the hurts we don't deserve. Forgiveness means you can stop paying for your offenses.

—Pastor Edward Banghart

When others are in crisis, I cannot expect them to be understanding or sensitive to me. I must forbear any slights or oversights because they are in survival mode.

Forgiveness is essential!!!

As stayers, be intentional to not put a guilt trip on the goers.

At the time we left, I was quite self-focused on my family and when the government gave us ten days to "get out and not come back," I was in organization mode. It never occurred to me how our leaving affected the team we left behind. I can see now how that must have been a tremendous jolt. I mean, we had worked hard to recruit all of them because we enjoyed them and valued their input to the work. I wish we could have talked through this years ago (maybe they tried and I couldn't hear them). But I'm so sorry for my self-centeredness and insensitivity to what all of them were experiencing too.

I realize that we may not have given full consideration to how our decision would affect everyone around us and for that I am sorry. I wonder if the geographical distance contributed to that in any way? We were in our passport country and were wrestling with things every day, trying to figure out what would be next. I think if we had been with our team, they would have at least had an inkling that this was something we were wrestling with and maybe would have had more opportunities for input, or at least time to prepare. That was one of the hardest decisions we've ever made and I think of it often. Love them as they leave instead of judging them or trying to convince them to stay. Keep in touch after they leave (to the extent that's appropriate with whatever level of relationship you had before).

You should not have said that, my conscience nagged me as I headed home from our team meeting. Why did I open my mouth and express my opinion so freely? I was sure that my offhand comment hurt my teammate. Since we committed to keeping short accounts on our team, I called her to apologize as soon as I got home. "I'm not sure if you heard what I said during our meeting, and I'm sorry if my words offended you. I was wrong to quickly blurt out my thoughts without first assessing how they might make you feel. Please forgive me."

Relationships in a cross-cultural setting range from casual acquaintances to thick-as-blood family and everywhere in between. We know that our deepest wounds come from those we love the most—those we've pinned our hopes on, who reciprocate our love, and those we expect will treat us well. Thus, when teammates let us down, move away, quit the ministry, or follow God to do something new, we can struggle to forgive them.

Jesus tells a parable about a man who struggled with unforgiveness in Matthew 18:21–35. The story answers the Apostle Peter's question about how many times he should forgive someone who sins against him. Peter thinks seven times is generous. Jesus's answer surprises him, "I tell you, not seven times, but seventy-seven times" (v. 22).

The story goes like this: Once upon a time, a king decided to balance his financial records. He called to account a man who owed him millions of dollars and threatened him with jail time. Because the debtor obviously could not repay what he owed, he begged for mercy. The king took pity on him, forgave his debt, and released him from his obligations.

Immediately this newly debt-free man encountered a colleague who owed him a few dollars. With a lapse in memory of his own recent good fortune, he demanded payment. He wanted his measly coins so badly that he grabbed the man by the throat and began to choke him. Despite the poor man's pleas for patience, he ordered the man thrown into prison.

Unfortunately for our man with the short-term memory, some other colleagues witnessed this violent exchange with dismay. They then reported his horrible actions to the king who called him back to his office. After reprimanding him for his hypocritical behavior, he reinstated the debt and threw him in jail.

Jesus then states the point of the story: "This is how my heavenly Father will treat each of you unless you forgive your brother or sister from your heart" (v. 35).

Jesus realized this issue would be so important and so difficult for his followers that he included it in the prayer he taught them to pray, the Lord's Prayer (Matt 6:9–13). According to Jesus's model, we first acknowledge our Father and praise him (v. 9). Then we make our requests in the framework of his will admitting our dependence on him for daily provision (vv. 10–11). Finally, when we are in the right frame of mind, we address our relationships, first with God himself ("forgive us our debts"), and then with others ("as we have also forgiven our debtors") (v. 12).

I find it interesting that in the only prayer that Jesus modeled, he includes this aspect of relationship—forgiveness—and not love or service, for instance. Perhaps he knew forgiving others would be one of the hardest things we undertake. In fact, Pastor Edward Banghart calls forgiveness a miracle of grace.[1]

1　I am indebted to the teaching of Edward Banghart, founding pastor of Montclair Community Church in Upper Montclair, New Jersey. With his permission, I use his material from three taped sermons: *"Honest Forgiveness: Healing the Hurts You Don't Deserve"; "Guilty of Hurt in the First Degree"; "Forgiveness: The Gift of the Magic Eyes."* Updated versions of these sermons are included in the resources of this chapter.

The *imago Dei* in each of us longs for a world full of justice and goodness. So when we do not receive what is due (or what we believe is due) to us and all is not fair, we naturally want to right all wrongs.

But before we home in on forgiveness, Banghart points out another antidote we must consider for the hurts and pains we experience: forbearance. While forgiveness is a miracle, forbearance is a mercy we extend to others. We forbear slights, small offenses, and superficial pains.

We find this not-often-talked-about concept throughout Scripture. And we must understand how it differs from forgiveness. According to my friend and author Carol Dowsett, "Forgiveness happens usually after we have been offended, after the wound has festered and needs to be healed. Forbearance happens before. It is a shield that keeps the hurt from embedding."[2] Banghart says that if we don't distinguish between forbearance and forgiveness, "we will either live in a constant state of crisis or we will cheapen the miracle of forgiveness."[3]

In Scripture to forbear means "to bear with or endure another's opinions and actions."[4] "Bear with each other and forgive one another if any of you has a grievance against someone" (Col 3:13). "Be completely humble and gentle; be patient, bearing with one another in love" (Eph 4:2). "A person's wisdom yields patience; it is to one's glory to overlook an offense" (Prov 19:11). According to pastor and author Dan Miller:

> Forbearance is applied primarily in spaces where we encounter believers who bore, annoy, irritate, frustrate, intimidate, exasperate, or just plain make our lives hard. Invariably, when Christian brothers and sisters bore, annoy, irritate, frustrate, intimidate, or exasperate us, such visceral responses are rooted in our own sinful passions. Forbearance reigns [*sic*] in those passions. It expresses enduring love for people our flesh wants to fight against or flee from. Forbearance is love in work boots.[5]

Applied to our topic, we know teammates will do all that Miller so eloquently described. Their leaving will also produce some of these visceral responses. Can we simply forbear with one another, choosing not to let their choices annoy or exasperate us and allow them to follow the Lord?

However, forbearance may not be enough. According to Banghart, the miracle of forgiveness is necessary when we have experienced a personal, unfair, or deep pain that we cannot forget.[6] These kinds of wounds are typically results of disloyalty, betrayal, and violation.

Forgiveness doesn't mean we deny the pain, forget the offense, or tolerate the sin. We must honestly acknowledge the wrongdoing. But to forgive means we don't hold it against our offender, judge, punish, or use it to manipulate or control them. And that requires a miracle only God can give because only he can truly forgive sin.

---

2 Dowsett, "Forbearance: A Greater Grace."

3 From personal notes on Pastor Edward Banghart's taped sermon, "Honest Forgiveness: Healing the Hurts You Don't Deserve." Used with permission.

4 "G430—*anechō*—Strong's Greek Lexicon (KJV)." Blue Letter Bible. Accessed 19 Oct, 2021. https://www.blueletterbible.org/lexicon/g430/kjv/tr/0-1/.

5 Miller, "Forbear with One Another."

6 If your heart wounds or soul are bleeding, that is beyond the scope of this book. That requires attending to by professional therapists.

Therefore, when God gives us a revelation of our own desperate need for forgiveness, we can then offer that same forgiveness to others. We must first accept that Jesus willingly offered his own body and blood in exchange for our debt of sin (Heb 9:12, 14). He did not merely pardon us (for that would mean we would be let off the hook without paying for our wrongdoing). Instead, he wrote "paid in full" over the ledger sheet of our offenses.

Because of Jesus's mercy (not getting what we deserve) and grace (getting what we don't deserve), we who believe in this substitution are forgiven by God and cleansed of all sin (Heb 10:10, 22). Therefore, when we realize how God has forgiven us, we can see our offender through the eyes of understanding. And we can forgive them—repeatedly (Luke 17:3–5). May God give us who have been forgiven this kind of vision.

Remember, this is a process. We start by making the decision to forgive. Then we reaffirm it over and over, choosing to release the offender from their indebtedness to us. Seventy-seven times means that every time the stab of hurt comes back, we take out the ledger of offenses and erase the debit column.

Forgiving our teammates means they are free to stop paying for their offenses toward us. It means we don't demand a prescribed repentance or arbitrate how they make amends. Just as we owe God nothing, we can release our teammates from what we feel they owe us.

When you're left holding the ministry bag, it may feel impossible to forbear and forgive. Especially when they promised to help get the business started, or plant the church, or take care of the finances. Now they're gone and you're left with the task you never wanted to do. Or you agreed to start a business only if they helped you. Perhaps the parting was contentious, with hurtful words hurled before they left. How could they do this to you?

Can you wish your teammates well (Rom 12:21)? If not, and you instead wish them harm or want them to suffer as much as they made you suffer, then you need to start or keep pursuing forbearance and forgiveness.

Just as Jesus released you from the debt you owe him, release your teammates from their debt. Do they deserve it? Maybe not. Does it still hurt? Probably yes. Could it have been handled differently without so much pain? Perhaps. Nevertheless, Jesus asks us to forgive.

REFLECTION

Reflect on the following passages. What is the Holy Spirit saying to you?

Matthew 18:21–35

Colossians 3:13

Hebrews 9:12, 14

Hebrews 10:10, 22

What offenses of your teammates might you need to forebear?

How have your teammates shown you forbearance?

What types of hurts have you experienced that require the miracle of forgiveness?

What sins of yours did Christ pay for on the cross?

What sins of others against you has Christ paid for on the cross?

RESPONSE

Consider your situation with your departing teammates. Write out an IOU. In the debit column, write the things that they owe you. After praying about this and when you are ready, write "Paid in Full" across it. Rip up the IOU.

PRAYER

Precious Jesus, thank you for taking the penalty for my sin upon yourself. Thank you for giving me complete forgiveness and cleansing in exchange. Help me examine my heart and understand my feelings. Where I am annoyed or offended, help me to forbear. But for those areas of deep hurt and pain, please give me the miracle of forgiveness toward my offender. As you no longer require me to pay what I owe, help me to erase what they owe me. Amen.

RESOURCES

https://www.youtube.com/watch?v=UHmjLbPuvc4 _____
"Love May Be Hazardous to Your Health" by Edward Banghart

https://www.youtube.com/watch?v=e9LeFF_1qqE _____
"Healing a Wounded Spirit" by Edward Banghart

https://www.youtube.com/watch?v=ip4qWzAvmoc _____
"The Gift of Magic Eyes" by Edward Banghart

Tim Keller, *Forgive: Why Should I and How Can I?* (New York: Viking, 2022).

Chapter 18

I'm Still Meant to Be Here
Remember Your Commission

> Remember where you started, remember where you're headed, think of how great it will be to get there, and keep going.
>
> —RALPH MARSTON

I have surely struggled at times with doubting my significance. I have had seasons of suffering a loss of a sense of purpose to my remaining on the field as so few have come to Christ. My staying has come from a hope that God has a purpose in my being his representative here that may or may not be seen in my generation. There is no promise that I will see the fruits of my labors according to my earthly expectations. I do, on the other hand, have the promise that "in this world you will have trouble, but take heart, I have overcome the world" (John 16:33).

He is in control, and he will work it out for his good and glory. I am called to be obedient to what he calls me, and trust in him that he is leading them to obedience too.

A missionary family was leaving the country after only four years of work. They seemed happy to be leaving and stated firmly, "We have put our time in and now we will go back to our life in the USA. Missions is over for us." I was floored by the idea that missions would be over because sharing the gospel is to always be a part of who we are as believers, but maybe their job as a full-time financially supported missionary was over. The attitude floored me, but at the same time it made me very cautious that by God's grace, I would learn from their calloused words and never let my heart go down that road.

My husband and I made our preparations to return to the field after our home assignment in the States. On the political scene, Al-Qaeda cells erupted daily in our majority-Muslim host country. The strategies of these extremists became table discussions among our family and friends. They asked us again and again, "Aren't you afraid to go back there?"

Each time, I answered, "No, because I am sure of my calling. I know that God wants me there."

That certainty enabled me to persevere. But a few years later, I wasn't so brave as I helplessly watched a steady queue of helicopters airlift tourists, expatriates, and local people to the safety of a neighboring island during four days of rioting on Lombok Island, Indonesia. At that moment, I wanted to abandon it all, jump on one of those copters, and fly to the US. Nothing causes us to question our reason for staying like seeing others go.

Perhaps the most dramatic example of calling in Scripture is the conversion of Paul—the about-face of one who previously hated Jesus, persecuted Christians, and tried to squash the movement of the church (Acts 9). When he saw the light on the road to Damascus and heard the voice of Jesus, Paul believed. He realized that he was the chief of sinners and put his faith in Jesus whom he previously hated. God calls Paul to himself.

But then we see God gives him a commission, a particular task, a *raison d'être*, if you will. Paul must go to the Gentiles and testify to what he has seen and heard (Gal 1:15–16). This is the mission Jesus gave to Paul:

> Now get up and stand on your feet. I have appeared to you to appoint you as a servant and as a witness of what you have seen and will see of me. ... I am sending you to them to open their eyes and turn them from darkness to light, and from the power of Satan to God, so that they may receive forgiveness of sins and a place among those who are sanctified by faith in me. (Acts 26:16–18)

This mission kept Paul through all kinds of suffering, persecution, jail, beatings, and desertion by others. Paul never wavered from what God told him to do although he did sometimes change course or adjust plans as he heard the voice of the Spirit directing him.

Sue addressed this concept of calling in chapter one. However, we feel it bears further examination specifically as it relates to the revolving door of teammates. For our purposes in this section, we need to know why we are doing what we're doing—and be convinced enough of it to continue doing it even if others leave.

According to Merriam-Webster, a calling is "a strong inner impulse toward a particular course of action especially when accompanied by conviction of divine influence."[1] In our global worker world, we use this word to describe our conviction that we are following God.

However, I believe that we often confuse our calling with our commission. The Bible uses calling to refer to our invitation to salvation, not our specific vocation or task. The Greek word for "calling" is *klesis* and means "the divine invitation to embrace salvation of God."[2] For example:

> I pray that the eyes of your heart may be enlightened in order that you may know the hope to which he has *called* you, the riches of his glorious inheritance in his holy people. (Eph 1:18)
>
> As a prisoner for the Lord, then, I urge you to live a life worthy of the *calling* you have received. There is one body and one Spirit, just as you were called to one hope when you were *called*. (Eph 4:1, 4)
>
> I press on toward the goal to win the prize for which God has *called* me heavenward in Christ Jesus. (Phil 3:14)
>
> With this in mind, we constantly pray for you, that our God may make you worthy of his *calling*, and that by his power he may bring to fruition your every desire for goodness and your every deed prompted by faith. (2 Thess 1:11)

---

1 https://www.merriam-webster.com/dictionary/calling.

2 "G2821—*klēsis*," *Strong's Greek Lexicon* (NIV). Blue Letter Bible.

Because of this biblical definition of calling, I prefer instead to use other words like vocation, task, commission, or mission, when talking about the "good works" God created us to do (Eph 2:10). Scripture also uses a variety of words to convey this concept. I've highlighted examples in the Scriptures below:

> What is more, he was *chosen* by the churches to accompany us as we carry the offering, which we administer in order to honor the Lord himself and to show our eagerness to help. (2 Cor 8:19)
>
> He *appointed* twelve that they might be with him and that he might send them out to preach. (Mark 3:14)
>
> While they were worshiping the Lord and fasting, the Holy Spirit said, "*Set apart* for me Barnabas and Saul for the work to which I have called them." (Acts 13:2)
>
> I am *sending* you to them to open their eyes and turn them from darkness to light, and from the power of Satan to God. (Acts 26:17–18)

Furthermore, let's not complicate the issue by heaping on more layers with words like faithfulness, perseverance, loyalty, and trustworthiness.

Does being faithful to our calling mean we must remain at our post all our lives, the same post that God gave us twenty years ago? What does it mean to persevere when the biblical concept of perseverance means sticking with the faith, not staying on the job (3 John 1:3–5)? How do perseverance, endurance, and loyalty play into our calling and how do we determine if we should stay when others leave?

First, remain faithful and loyal to God, living a life that leans steadfastly on him. Cultivate a relationship of abiding in him, listening to his voice, and enjoying his presence and the riches of your glorious inheritance.

Then do what God has asked *you* to do. Complete the task. Be a trustworthy servant by obeying and fulfilling that task for as long as he directs you. But make sure you don't stay longer out of loyalty or a false sense of faithfulness or stubbornness.

It could be argued that mission work can only really be done in length (as Sue pointed out earlier). Therefore, it feels like anyone who leaves the field after three or five years has not been faithful. In actuality, the Lord of the Harvest determines when the task is complete. Therefore, each one individually must hear God and determine his or her specific path.

So, return to your commission, your vision, your purpose. Remind yourself why you stay. What have you been appointed to do? What were you set apart for? Has that changed? If not, then persevere despite the actions of your teammates. Stay the course. Keep going.

If your vision has leaked, dwindled, or taken a hit, ask God to reaffirm it. Ask him for fresh assurance for why you remain. And resist the temptation to judge your departing colleagues as unfaithful. They are struggling enough with their decision as it is.

The author of Hebrews tells us to hold firmly to our faith (4:14) and unswervingly to our hope (10:23), not "hold fast to your job as a missionary." Hold fast to *your* mission and let your teammates follow Christ.

This topic also presses into how we individually discern God's will. Because ultimately, isn't that the question we all ask, "What is God's will?" Is God really the one saying, "Follow me?" Can we accept God might use a restless spirit or a personality that desires change to direct someone? Or that depression or anxiety might necessitate leaving the field for treatment just as cancer would?

If you aren't sure of your task, then this may be a good time to reexamine your mission and vision and perhaps to consider some ways you have misconstrued or confused true calling with commission. When we no longer confuse calling and commission, we can persevere in staying for as long as God leads us, and, at the same time, let our teammates go.

REFLECTION

Reflect on the following passages. Journal what God might be saying to you.

Acts 22:14–21

Acts 26:15–23

Jeremiah 1:4–10

What is your current commission? Has it changed? If so, how?

If it seems impossible to fulfill God's commission because your teammate has left, ask God to provide the means, personnel, and resources.

Ask God to remind you anew of your foundational overarching calling to him.

Ask God to solidify your unique commission and why you stay.

RESPONSE

After prayer and reflection, write out your mission and vision statement. Work on it so that it is succinct and easy to memorize. Post it where you can refer to it often.

PRAYER

Father God, I am most grateful for the reminder that my true calling is to you and you alone. You have invited me to be a member of your kingdom and call me heavenward. Second, you have asked me to build your kingdom. This will be my lifelong commission wherever I live in the world. But right now I need assurance that I walk in your will regarding my individual tasks at my location. I want to know that I am doing what you have asked me to do. Please confirm my task or show me what may need to change so that I can persevere faithfully in all that you have asked me to do. Amen.

RESOURCES

http://www.thecallingjourney.com   _____

https://evaburkholder.com/2019/07/31/persevere-in-your-calling/   _____

Dr. Rick Kronk, *Not Called: Recovering the Biblical Framework of Divine Guidance* (Wipf & Stock, 2022).

Chapter 19

I Affirm and Bless Them as They Go
Speak Well Of

> *If you think well of others, you will also speak well of others and to others. From the abundance of the heart the mouth speaks. If your heart is full of love, you will speak of love.*
>
> —MOTHER TERESA

Share how they have taught, mentored, or blessed you.

Affirm their contribution to the work there. Bless the goers. Offer practical help.

Have an acknowledgment/celebration/occasion for others to share what they appreciate about the Goer.

The stayers can help the goers by celebrating with them before they leave. Remembering with them. We were able to take a few days away together and just be together. It was a very special time. Bittersweet for sure.

One teammate who left gave each of us who stayed a photo book of special memories. Our whole family still looks at it eight years later! It was such a meaningful way to say goodbye, and also to remember. One teammate wrote a long letter as she left, taking time to express appreciation for each member of our family and how she valued each one of us. Another family took special time to just be together with our family before they left. They also make it a priority to host us whenever we are in their area.

I wanted to communicate to them that they will be missed, that they are valuable, that I cared about them and it really mattered to me that they were here and they were leaving (but I also didn't think about how those same words might make them feel pressured).

We hosted four families and one single person as they left the field. They sold all their belongings, turned off their electric, water, phones, and came to stay with our family. The families leaving were then able to take the last few weeks to properly say goodbye, spend time with those they had deep relationships with and not have to worry about house-type issues. Of course, I got a good bit of extra moments with them. But it was a way to serve them and help them finish well. It gave me a sense of closure in that I did all I could to help.

When our son's classmate left to return to the USA, the boys put together (with mom's help of course) a Shutterfly book of pictures—different birthdays, school trips, sporting events, memories they had together—and then each boy wrote a handwritten letter that we pasted in the back empty pages of the book. It was a sweet surprise to give him. Each boy could say something nice, plus then the parents were happy that their kids had something happy to take with them.

Bless them. Help them leave well according to their and your needs. Help ensure handovers and tying up loose ends. Spend time together grieving, talking. Help them make a list of meaningful ways to say goodbye. Leaders help stayers move forward—planning and dreaming and hoping. Don't forget the children. Plan what and how to communicate with them. Have an exit interview.

I don't recall when I first met Lori. One day, she and her husband showed up at our church. They wanted to be our friends, so my husband and I started hanging out with them, sharing our stories and doing life together. Little did I know at the time what a blessing I would receive from Lori.

I used to walk by Lori's place of employment on my way home from my work. If I had time, I stopped in to see her, though she never demanded it of me. She always greeted me with her famous smile, a hug, even a kiss on the cheek. She introduced me to her colleagues, and soon I discovered the fan-club Lori had around her. I watched her share Jesus in a natural way by simply loving others.

Sometimes, we ate our lunches together and prayed. We shared about our week, our children, our plans. I always felt like she cared just as much about me and my life as I did about hers. She never complained but spoke freely of how God sustained her during times of illness and her hope for life eternal. She smiled and laughed, and I always felt better after being with her.

Lori enriched my life. She showed me how to be more pleasant, more friendly, more positive, and non-demanding, to love others and greet them cheerfully, to rejoice in suffering. Lori taught me to be a friend because she was one to me.

When I told Lori that we were moving away to join our current ministry, Lori gave me the greatest gift any friend can give. She graciously let me go. No strings attached. No pleas to get me to stay. No heaping on guilt. Through Lori, I learned what blessing another person looks like.

Long before I met Lori, I had many failed attempts at blessing others. Whenever a teammate left, I tried to put on a happy face. We typically gave them a gift, wrote some encouraging words in a book or card, had a party, and sent them on their way. While I went through the motions, I don't think I truly blessed them—particularly as Scripture defines it—every time.

When our time to leave arrived, my teammates blessed us. Their memory book still sits on a shelf in my office. The *tikar* (woven mat) they gave us adorned my bedroom floor for many years. While difficult for them, they sent us off as best as they knew how.

Elizabeth, Mary of Nazareth's older cousin and the mother of John the Baptist models how to bless others. Scripture doesn't say if Elizabeth knew of Mary's pregnancy before she showed up at her cousin's home. Because of the lack of quick communication in those days, I presume she didn't.

According to author Osheta Moore, the listeners of this account would have expected conflict between Elizabeth and Mary, a sort of competition, if you will, between women. Elizabeth, the elder would have expected and deserved the place of "first birth."[1]

But in a very counter-cultural way, the Spirit enables Elizabeth to instead respond with blessing, "Blessed are you among women, and blessed is the child you will bear!" (Luke 1:42). The word used here for blessed, *eulogeo,* is from the root words *eu* (to be well off) and *logeo* (speech) and means "to express a good attitude or to speak well of something or someone."[2] The English word *eulogy* derives from this root word.

I have written and delivered several eulogies, both in person and on my blog. The most difficult was my eulogy for Lori a few years after I moved away. I extolled her strengths, contributions, achievements, and why she meant so much to me. I praised and honored her. And according to Scripture, I blessed her because I spoke well of her.

When Elizabeth called Mary "blessed," she was speaking well of her, praising her, and testifying that Mary had received a gracious favor from God—the distinction of giving birth to God's Son.

After Mary received Elizabeth's empowering words of blessing, she turned around and wrote one of the most courageous and famous songs of praise to God (Luke 1:46–55). How beautiful to realize that our speaking well of our teammates might overflow in their songs of praise!

How can we speak well of our teammates when they leave? Some would say this depends upon the manner of their departure. But does God tell us to only bless those that treat us well?

When we *eulogeo* someone else, we don't ask God to make their life easy or give them material blessings. Rather, we praise them and speak well of them as we are also commanded to do of our enemies and of those who curse us (Luke 6:28).

I suggest that to speak well of a departing teammate, we focus on what we might say in their eulogy. In what ways were they meaningful to us? What are their good characteristics, helpful skills, pleasing traits? How have they helped the work? How is our life enhanced by knowing them? What are we grateful for from our time of serving together? If you walked where they tread right now, what would you like to hear?

Dwell on these things rather than on the ways they have hurt you or the reason for their departure. Then affirm them. Authors Ruth Van Reken, David C. Pollock, and Michael V. Pollock suggest an approach called R.A.F.T. for saying healthy goodbyes which includes an intentional step of affirmation (the A in R.A.F.T.) before a goodbye.[3] This is when we seek to affirm one another and communicate those things we will regret later if they are not expressed.

---

1 Sermon by Osheta Moore, Woodland Hills Church, St. Paul, MN. December 13, 2020.

2 Bill Klein, Greek Thoughts.

3 Building a R.A.F.T. (Reconciliation, Affirmation, Farewell, and Think Destination) is an approach to saying healthy goodbyes developed by Ruth Van Reken, David Pollock, and Michael V. Pollock in their book, *Third Culture Kids 3rd Edition: Growing up Among Worlds*, 240–46. For more on R.A.F.T., see the last chapter of this book.

Perhaps you feel you are insincere or giving a false impression, even lying in giving affirmation. Perhaps not much good comes to mind when you think about the goer. Ask God to give you at least one positive thing that you can tell them as they prepare to leave. Don't tell them all the ways you have been hurt or their mistakes. Chances are they already feel guilty or bad about leaving. They may feel like quitters. Remember that you do not know exactly how they feel (even if they have expressed something to you), and they are not responsible to you.

If you still feel hurt, disappointed, sad, or unforgiving, work through those emotions using the previous chapters in this guide. Ask God to help you get to the point where you can truly say "God bless you."

REFLECTION

Reflect on the following passages and meditate on the various ways that we bless others.

John 12:13

Galatians 3:9

1 Corinthians 14:16 (*eulogeo* is translated as "praising")

Mathew 14:19 (*eulogeo* is translated as "prayed or gave thanks")

According to this definition, what would it look like to bless your teammates as they leave?

How can you celebrate them and their contribution to the work? How can you pray for them?

RESPONSE

After further meditation and prayer, prepare some statements you can make to speak well of your departing friends/teammates.

Choose a time and place when you will share them.

PRAYER

Father God, show me how my colleagues have enriched my life so that I might sincerely bless them. Give me practical ideas of how I might encourage them so that we both can offer a song of praise to you. Enable me by your Spirit to speak well of others, especially those who harm me. Amen.

RESOURCES

http://www.biblefood.com/blessings.html   _____

https://pioneernt.com/2011/01/25/word-study-89-bless-blessed-blessing/   _____

https://evaburkholder.com/2020/03/20/speak-well-of/   _____

https://screamsinthedesert.wordpress.com/2020/06/25/living-eulogies/   _____

Chapter 20

I'll Let Them Go
Relinquish and Release

> *Some people believe holding on and hanging in there are signs of great strength. However, there are times when it takes much more strength to know when to let go and then do it.*
>
> —ANN LANDERS

After eleven years living in a "revolving door" city, I accepted that many friendships are for a season and there is richness in each relationship, even if it isn't going to last lifelong.

Release them, apologize, make it equally easy for them to stay or leave.

It wasn't really a wrestling. It was more of a letting go of people we loved and letting them go. It was a goodbye. It was very sad, like the tearing away of a part of ourselves. But it didn't change our commitment to stay. (Honestly, maybe part of that was pride! We were the stayers, not the leavers!)

By God's grace, talk together, maintain relationships, and keep them involved in participation as appropriate or available. Some workers mourn when people leave and then cut off communication or relationship. The relationships should be maintained, albeit most likely at a diminished level. Trust them to be following God if they are leaving without a blowup. Don't try to guilt them into staying. Listen to their story. Let them know they will be missed.

The stayers can "absolve" the goers of any guilt for "leaving the stayers behind." Let them go. Bless them in their going. Rejoice with them.

My daughter never went to the airport to say goodbye. As soon as she was old enough to express her opinion, it was a resounding NO to a goodbye airport run. So, we gave her space. Let her quietly say her goodbyes at our home to whatever visitors, groups, or family members may be leaving. It was not until she was fourteen years old that the subject of going to the airport for a goodbye came up. She asked, "How do you do it?" She wanted to know the plan, the steps, the how-to—getting them checked in, giving them a snack, filling out exit paperwork, making a line, and hugging each person as they walked into the immigration line to leave and finally waving goodbye to the last person in line as the doors closed. Once she heard the process and could picture herself in the different activities, it was a go. She went. She said goodbye. She laughed as she hugged different people, had a tear with one or two and then as we walked back to the car she calmly said, "That wasn't as bad as I thought it would be. I still don't like it, but I can do that." Isn't that how it should be?

God has definitely used their time here. This eternal perspective (nothing is wasted) has helped me pour into teacher after teacher who I know won't be here forever. And of course, sometimes God surprises us and they stay!

"I'm joining another team," she reported.

My heart sank. "Not again! Lord, why are we losing yet another one?" This time, the revolving door hit me more intensely since she was my mentee, my disciple, so to speak. After investing many hours into her, I watched her move out of my life. How does a leader let go of those into whom they've poured their heart and soul?

John the Baptist shows us how. The angel promised his father Zechariah that his son would "be filled with the Holy Spirit even before he is born" (Luke 1:15) and would "make ready a people prepared for the Lord" (Luke 1:17). Zechariah himself said, "And you, my child, will be called a prophet of the Most High; for you will go on before the Lord to prepare the way for him" (Luke 1:76). We also know that John "grew and became strong in spirit; and he lived in the wilderness until he appeared publicly to Israel" (Luke 1:80). No wonder John had a successful ministry with disciples and crowds of followers. Even if some found him crazy, they listened. By our current standards, John deserved an important place in the church.

One day, some of John's disciples—his inner circle, in whom he had invested time, energy, perhaps even funds—up and left him for another celebrity. Standing with two of his disciples as Jesus passed by, John said, "Look, the Lamb of God!" Immediately, the two disciples left John and followed Jesus (John 1:35–37). Just like that! Without a going-away party, thank you card, memory album, explanations, or expressions of appreciation to John for all the time and energy he had put into training, teaching, and loving them. Certainly no time to construct a R.A.F.T.[1]

To top it off, Jesus accepted these new disciples without a word of acknowledgment to John. He didn't even try to convince them to stay with John or seem to care that he might steal John's sheep.

---

1 Van Reken, Pollock, and Pollock, 240–46.

John's other disciples struggled with the attrition of their group. They came to John and said, "Rabbi, that man who was with you … —the one you testified about—look, he is baptizing, and *everyone is going to him*" (John 3:26, emphasis added). In other words, "He's taking our people. We're losing followers. This isn't fair."

How did John handle this? He knew who Jesus was—the Lamb of God, the Messiah, the Savior of the world, the real star. I believe John learned this from his parents, especially his mother, who spoke well of Mary and blessed her younger cousin. Surely, the Holy Spirit also empowered John to understand his unique role. Therefore, John purposely pointed his disciples to Jesus and prepared them to follow Jesus, not himself.

Not only did John know Jesus's identity, he also knew his place as only the preparer, the voice pointing to Jesus. "I am not the Messiah but am sent ahead of him" (John 3:28). John called himself the "friend who attends the bridegroom"—the best man (v. 29). Any wedding centers on the groom. He gets the bride. The best man's job is to wait for and listen for the groom and is "full of joy when he hears the bridegroom's voice" (v. 29).

Thus, when John heard Jesus's voice, he rejoiced and responded with these telling words: "He must become greater; I must become less" (v. 30). While we aren't privy to John's growth process (perhaps he struggled with his superior cousin for a time), we see his amazing conclusion. He didn't try to convince his disciples to stay with him. He didn't give ten reasons why they had such a good thing going and could do so much more together. John knew when to bow out. He had prepared the way for Jesus and now the time had come to fade from the scene. He could rejoice that his disciples had left him to follow the Messiah.

The fisherman Zebedee had a similar experience. "Without delay he [Jesus] called them [James and John] and they left their father Zebedee in the boat with the hired men and followed him" (Mark 1:20). Talk about leaving someone holding the bag. *Thanks a lot, guys! I raised you, invested in you, trained you, hoping you would help me run this business and take over one day.* What was Zebedee supposed to do? Add to this the cultural importance of honoring one's father by caring for him and following in his footsteps. While leaving the group to follow someone who simply says, "Come, follow me," feels rash, unwise, or simply dumb, remember who they followed—Jesus (Mark 1:17).

Letting go of one's teammates takes great humility, especially for leaders. They invest in teaching, discipling, listening, advising, praying with (and drinking cups of coffee and tea with) those they love and serve. They see potential in their disciples and want them to mature and effectively serve Jesus. But deep down, they may want a return on their investment. They'd like the members to stay and help. They'd like some credit for any success. They'd like to keep influencing them. They want the team to function their way.

Taking time to identify the root of reluctance to let go can be enlightening and freeing. Sometimes, our angst isn't about what we think it is. My counselor husband often says, "It's not about this, it's about that." We may think on the surface that our reluctance to release a teammate stems from our need for their assistance with the task. However, some careful thought and self-reflection (and with the help of the Holy Spirit) may reveal that the real struggle lies in realizing our children will miss their playmates or that we are losing control, we feel we've wasted our time, or we've undergone one too many losses lately.

Like John the Baptist did with his disciples, can you let your teammates go? Can you release them to serve Jesus, no matter where they end up? When you think that your teammates have not heard God accurately, can you still trust God to provide for you?

As messengers of the Gospel, we know Jesus promises to build his church (Matt 16:18) and God alone makes it grow. This promise helps ease the pain of releasing our teammates to their next chapter of service. We each play a part in preparing the soil, planting seeds, or watering them (1 Cor 3:6–7). It may take years to see a harvest, and we may be long gone, but we had a role in the whole process. This helps us believe that our departing teammates have also played their parts.

Remember, you can't see all the plans and movements of the Lord. While it may not make sense to you now, God knows what he's doing. Their departure has not upset his strategy. Unlike us, he doesn't wring his hands wondering what he's going to do now that one or several of his servants have gone missing in action (according to you). He continues his work with or without our teammates (or us, for that matter). Our goal, then, becomes what one gospel messenger shared:

> I remember reaching out to my team leader about how hard it was to keep losing so many people. He said, "We aren't losing anyone. We are sending them off to serve from here. Our prayer is to send them off better for having been here."

We may never see or reap the full benefit of the time and energy we invest in our teammates but letting them go frees us from clinging too tightly. We intentionally trust God to use his people wherever he desires. Letting go comes easier when we focus on building God's kingdom and accept that God directs the process.

REFLECTION

Reflect on the following passages. Journal what God might be saying to you.

John 3:22–30

Acts 13:25

John 13:16

Who might you be struggling to let go of? In what ways?

Why do you struggle? What is the real reason or reasons you cannot let them go?

What do you expect from your investment in them? What might be God's perspective on your investment?

What plans of the Lord can you see in this loss of teammates?

RESPONSE

Write out all the ways that your departing teammates have benefited or contributed to your life. Write out all the ways that you have contributed to (taught, discipled, served) your departing teammates.

Talk to God about this list. Thank God for the opportunity you have had to influence them, which may then influence a new ministry or location.

Release your teammates into God's hands.

PRAYER

Father, forgive me for holding too tightly to my teammates. Teach me to release them, as John did. May I point them to you so that when they hear your voice, I can say, "Go, follow Jesus. He is the Lamb of God. He is the one who has eternal life." Show me when I should bow out and fade from the scene. Help me to rejoice that my friends follow you no matter where they choose to serve. Amen.

RESOURCES

https://evaburkholder.com/2014/01/21/let-go-and-release/   _____

https://evaburkholder.com/2013/02/23/letting-go/   _____

https://screamsinthedesert.wordpress.com/2020/10/27/hands-off-my-alabaster-jar /

Chapter 21

I'll Concentrate on My Responsibilities
Readjust

Never do anything of importance that others can do or will do when there is so much of importance to do that others cannot and will not do.

—DAWSON TROTMAN

If there are any gaps left in the team, decide who will fill them.

Regroup, meet as the "new" team. Find ways to readjust together, bond, dream about new things. Pray.

Some might need counseling help, grief counseling, and also time to go for an extended retreat to reflect upon life to rediscover passion in God and what God wants the people to do as stayers.

Debrief the experience and allow for grief and mourning of losing a teammate. Schedule times of grieving, processing, and regrouping together.

Delegate the tasks they were doing. Acknowledge the loss as it comes up. Even if it was a hard or tense departure, don't just ignore it.

Keep close to God. "I can do all things through Christ who strengthens me."

Talk about the loss and readjust the team. Make sure the remaining members fill the gaps that have been left by those who go. Reevaluate the team, its covenant, etc. Also recruit new workers to fill any need.

Take time to do a group debrief, share stories and experiences you had together, cry with one another.

Pray. Share feelings with others about the loss and plan for the future ministries without that person.

Encourage each to seek wisdom and strength in the Bible.

When we felt lost without the lead missionary, God raised up nationals to help us!

Give permission and time to remember. Talk about the people we miss. Connect with them together. Grieve together. And then also give permission to keep going without the people who have left, in some ways to let go of them.

They should be careful to spend time together and distribute the ministry responsibilities evenly among those who remain. They should remember with love and understanding those who have made the decision to leave so that if any who are staying later need to actually go, they will know that it is okay, and their decision will be accepted.

After our team of eleven had become four, our regional leader sat down with us to regroup. A new team leader had to be chosen and responsibilities adjusted. I remember taking some time to simply sit around a pool and rest. Some difficult conversations ensued as our best friends became our leaders as well as our peers. We decided we could not proceed with some plans that had been in the works. We had to focus on what we, four people, could realistically do.

You do not need to take on all the responsibilities that your departing teammate leaves behind. Moses delegated some of his responsibilities because he could not do it all alone (Exod 18:17–23). But what if no one remains to delegate to? What if your only teammates just left and you do not have the skills nor the inclination to pick up their tasks?

We offer four suggestions. First, begin by determining the difference between responsibilities and concerns. Author Paul David Tripp shares a helpful distinction in his book *Instruments in the Redeemer's Hands.* Concerns, he says, are "things that concern me but are beyond my ability and thus not my responsibility."[1] In these matters, I trust God. Responsibilities, on the other hand, are the "things that God has called me to do that I cannot pass on to anyone else. The only proper response is to seek to understand and to faithfully obey."[2]

---

1 Tripp, *Instruments in the Redeemer's Hands*, 250.

2 Tripp, 250.

As teammates leave, the stayers must regroup and prayerfully determine their responsibilities and concerns. Clear biblical responsibilities include things like loving your spouse, parenting, maturing in Christ, and being his ambassador. Other responsibilities may be determined by your vocation and team covenant, such as learning a language, church planting, or teaching Scripture.

Concerns may be the need for a Sunday school teacher or an accountant, but they may not fall under your responsibility. We need to learn the difference and obey accordingly. Some tasks may go undone until God supplies another teammate or an alternate solution. Don't become a workaholic by thinking you have to do everything now that your teammates have left.

Second, plan times for debriefing. Debriefs provide a space for someone to talk while a neutral party listens. I suggest an unstructured personal debrief as well as one for the team. Telling your side of the story in a personal debrief gives you time to process, gain clarity, listen to God's voice, and (hopefully) move forward. In this non-judgmental, personal debrief setting, you can talk through any unresolved issues with the departing team member that you need to confront or forgive. This should be a safe place to express feelings of anger, grief, resentment, guilt, and relief.

In addition, gather your remaining team together and conduct a group debrief. You may want to ask an outside party to sit in and moderate your discussion, especially if you expect expressions of raw and intense emotion. Let each person share their feelings about the departure of their teammate. Leaders should also refrain from explaining their actions or decisions. Don't judge responses or feelings and don't give advice or solve problems. Share. Listen. And pray for each other.

After everyone has shared their feelings, the facilitator might then ask questions such as, "How did the fact that they left (or were asked to leave) impact you? How does it affect the team? What will you miss about them? As a team, what can we do differently in the future? What did we learn from this? Collectively as a team, what things did we do that we need to ask forgiveness for?" See Appendix Six for a sample team debrief when losing a teammate.

Third, regroup. Meet to problem solve after conducting debriefs. Who will take on what responsibilities? Which tasks or ministry will you put on hold for the time being? Who might you recruit to join the work? One missionary described what this might look like:

> Talk about it. Host a get-together meal for remaining stayers after the goer has left. Consider texting ahead of time about the meal's purpose so the stayers arrive in the right mindset and ready to minister to one another/be ministered to. It is better to be intentional, assuming that people need debriefing versus assuming that all is well. Debrief the loss of coworkers. Reassess the makeup, best contribution, and vision of the team in light of the change in personnel.

Finally, don't forget your soul care routines. With the stress of extra responsibilities and concerns, determining which is which, and finding solutions, you need to care for your soul now more than ever. While this may be the last thing you feel you have time for, pace yourself. Create margin. Don't try to do it all yourself. And ask for help from your leadership.

REFLECTION

Reflect on the following passages. Journal what God might be saying to you.

1 Thessalonians 1:3

Mark 6:31–32

1 Samuel 23:17

Psalm 103:13–14

List your responsibilities. List your concerns.

What concerns have you placed in the area of responsibility?

What tasks have you taken on that the goers left behind? Who else might fulfill these roles?

What would it look like if those tasks were put aside for the time being?

Look around your current community. Who might you reach out to for new friendships?

RESPONSE

Talk to God about your concerns. Ask him to help you release control of tasks that are not your responsibility.

Trust God to be faithful to supply your need and provide the resources you need if the work stops or there is no one to help. Trust him for the timing of his provision.

PRAYER

Father God, sustainer and provider of all things, readjustment takes so much energy, especially when I don't choose it. Help me determine my true responsibilities while I place my concerns in your care. Please provide new hands to do those tasks which must be done to build your kingdom in our part of the world. Teach me to see the work through your eyes so that I might let go of things that cannot get done. Use this time of upheaval and change to bring about a result that glorifies you and propels us forward. Amen.

RESOURCES

https://kellyminter.com/2019/03/11/moses-and-the-mutual-benefit-of-delegating-responsibility/   _____

https://praetorianproject.org/wp-content/uploads/sites/12/2021/02/Clarifying-Responsibility-Tripp.pdf   _____

http://storage.cloversites.com/countryacresbaptistchurch/documents/Burning%20Brightly%20without%20Burning%20Out%207%2028%2013.pdf   _____

https://velvetashes.com/a-liturgy-for-staying/   _____

http://www.thecultureblend.com/the-transition-that-never-ends-the-ongoing-cycle-of-expat-stayers-goers-and-newbies/   _____

http://www.thecultureblend.com/going-nowhere-ten-tips-for-expat-stayers-who-want-to-stay-well/   _____

Chapter 22

I'll Invest and Nest Here
Stay Awhile

This view of the present makes us aware of the wonder of life itself, gives us a keen awareness of the world around us, and deepens our appreciation for each moment as it comes to us.

—JERRY SITTSER

My apartment was decorated by the last people who lived here and it's just not me. After adding lots of plants, it feels more like home, but I really need to take the time to put up pictures and make the little changes that will make it my nest. It's worth the time.[1]

After being here for a few years and living with the second hand "goodies" left by our predecessor, I met a new friend who immediately painted her walls, had beautiful throw pillows made, bought a comfortable bed, and filled her home with flowering plants. She told me she was in it for the long haul and this was going to be her home. That shifted something in me, giving me permission to make my home a place our family enjoyed. It is about investing in sustainability![2]

After many people coming and going, I got really hesitant to put any effort into new members. But I know that God has a reason to have them here, for however long. So if they are here, I need to be there for them, even if it seems like I don't get anything out of them. God has his plans and purposes.

Be thankful for the amazing individuals we are blessed to know and serve with while living in another culture.

Choose to reach out and build new relationships, even when it means we have to do so every single year.

---

1 Lydia's comment on Stallings, "Build Your CABIN."

2 Comment on Stallings "Build Your CABIN."

Don't check out but keep investing in each other.

I had to learn to be aware of my own feelings when I started feeling that I didn't want to get close to someone because they might leave soon or earlier than me. When I was able to identify that, I had to intentionally decide to build the relationship without fear of losing them but rejoicing that I have another friend.

We lived in a place where so many people came and went that it was tempting not to make friendships with new people.

Build relationships with local people, so you're not putting the burden of all your emotional needs on the other expats. But also recognize the other stayers may need to process and vent with you in ways their local friends can't understand. Build genuine relationships with expats and locals, not fake surface-level relationships. Take time to grieve together but then find ways to move forward and give each other the freedom to change and grow and not be stuck in the ways the goers always used to do things.

For me it was hot showers that helped keep us there for the long haul. I find that if I am honest with myself about what will help keep me going and give me life so I can give out to others, I can usually figure out what that one or two things are. Then I go ahead and "indulge" in that. But for me the important thing is that I still hold even these things that I truly need, with an open hand. As long as I can honestly say, "Jesus, if you asked me to give this up today in order to continue to follow you, I will do it in a heartbeat because following what you want is far more important to me than this thing that I need," that is the line in the sand.

Living in a rural community without walls or a compound, where people are literally going to bed hungry next door, we had a hard time with this. Plus the pressure that it meant we "couldn't take it" if we started bringing up anything but the basics. Even though we have to fly everything up (which makes it even harder to "justify"), this year we started bringing up a variety of storable (even fun) food items, bought a fridge, and double gas burner and gas bottles, expanded our solar capabilities, and flew up a motorcycle. I even started wearing loose pants around the house on the evenings and weekends and even in front of the guard walking from the house to the cook house. And finally had seat cushions covered for our wood "couches."

Brought an espresso machine to my context where they are virtually non-existent (or collect dust at restaurants) and it has dramatically changed my outlook on life here. Feels a sense of normal. Small luxury but big impact.

I sweated a lot in Indonesia. Cement brick and tile floors attempted to retain some semblance of coolness. Occasionally, a breeze that helped a tad flowed through the house. Since local folks did not have air conditioning, we determined to make a go of it without this commodity. We would adapt and bear it with the rest of the nation.

This strategy worked for the first few years when we lived at a higher altitude, which made the temperature a bit cooler and the nights bearable. But everything changed when we moved to the coast where the hot sticky air continued after the sun's rays stopped beating down. Even after a shower, lying still on 100% cotton sheets, with multiple fans moving air over our almost naked bodies, we still baked. Neither my husband nor I wanted to be touched. It became apparent fairly quickly that we (and our marriage) could not survive this for long. We finally broke down and purchased an air conditioning unit for our bedroom. A few years later, we also put one in the main living area of our house.

At each adjustment after a teammate left or a crisis zapped our energy, we found ourselves needing more and more ways to ease the normal difficulties of life. If you want to remain overseas, you gotta do what you gotta do to stay awhile. Settling into the moment is necessary, if you want to stay well, especially when others leave.

I failed miserably at this. I hardly ever lived in the present. Instead, I looked backward and longed for what had been: *Our team was so much better last year. We'll never have fun now that she's gone. We had such a good thing going. I miss her encouragement immensely.*

Other times I lived for some future event or transition: *They're leaving next week. New teammates will come next year. We're going on home assignment in six months. When we've said our last goodbye, then I can hunker down and get to work.*

However, God calls us to focus on today. God has redeemed our past and takes care of the future. He is with us *now.*

> And my God will meet all your needs according to the riches of his glory in Christ Jesus. (Phil 4:19)
>
> Then the LORD said to Moses, "I will rain down bread from heaven for you. The people are to go out each day and gather enough for that day. In this way I will test them and see whether they will follow my instructions. (Exod 16:4)
>
> Give us today our daily bread. (Matt 6:11)
>
> Therefore do not worry about tomorrow, for tomorrow will worry about itself. Each day has enough trouble of its own. (Matt 6:34)
>
> Why, you do not even know what will happen tomorrow. What is your life? You are a mist that appears for a little while and then vanishes. (Jas 4:14)

In her article, "Build Your CABIN," Patty Stallings introduced two very helpful ways to stay awhile: investing in community and nesting. I share them with her permission:

> Invest in your community. It can seem like those who are leaving have all the best adventures. But look around. There are opportunities and relationships that only the "stayers" get to experience—and they are waiting for you *because* you stayed. Find the treasures hidden in the deep places. Enjoy the vista reserved for those who stayed on *this* particular trail just a little longer.[3]

It is typical and understandable to hesitate to make new friends. After all, so many have left you already. And new team members will most likely leave you in the future. However, despite the fear of losing yet another friend, take the risk to engage again—and again.

---

3 Stallings, "Build Your CABIN."

Take your eyes off your departing teammates, dashed expectations, and "what ifs" and say hello to the next one that arrives or to the existing people around you. Search for new people to pray with, hang out with, invite over for dinner, or take on an outing. Expand your circle of friends to include some new ones. Don't be afraid to initiate. Be present to the people in your life right now.

Consider your local friends. They probably expect that as a guest in their country, you will leave. Yet we desire for them to befriend us. If you want those in your host country to be your friend, it helps if you intend to stay. Jerry Jones at *The Culture Blend* suggests you "reboot your sense of wonder":

> Learn the history of your host culture. Study the art, the architecture, the current events. Learn a song, a dance, a poem, a story. Take a trip, eat something painfully local. Go back to the adventure but do it all fully aware that you need to do a load of whites before you go to bed. … What are three things that you used to be excited about but haven't thought of for a long time?[4]

Keep working on learning the language so that you can really dig in. Be the tourist. Visit fun sites. Meet people. Take walks. Talk to the mothers in the playground. Hang out with the men drinking coffee in the bar. Attend local festivals and events. Discover their favorite types of music, literature, famous heroes, legends, and leaders. Focus in on one segment of society—women, children, the marginalized—and find out how they are treated in that context.

Practice your life-giving activity in your new community. Do you paint? Learn a local art technique. Do you run? Enter a marathon. Do you like to do macramé (as I do)? Find a shop that sells supplies and locate other artisans. If you find refreshment in baking, join a cooking class. If you love music, take voice lessons.

Intentionally seek and pray for community—an international church, local neighbors, or expats from different companies or countries. Engage, yet again.

Besides investing in community, Stallings offers another helpful tactic:

> Nest. Make *your* home your home. Buy a plant. Spend a little extra on the comfortable pillow. Brighten up your place with floral curtains or striped rugs or funky lamps or abundant bookshelves—whatever says, "This is where I dwell. This is *my* cabin!"[5]

That all sounds wonderful, you say, but what about Jesus? He had no place to lay his head (Matt 8:19–22; Luke 9:57–62). He didn't even have a den like the foxes or a nest like the birds. He told his followers to leave behind the cares of this world. He didn't accumulate stuff. And what about the other saints of old? They lived as strangers and foreigners on earth, longing for a better country, a heavenly home (Heb 11:13–16). Shouldn't we be more concerned about our heavenly home than our earthly one?

These biblical truths keep some global workers from allowing themselves to nest, to own at least one home. (I grew up with both a village home and a base home.) They might feel they need to give up comforts for Jesus. But if some comforts ease our adjustment to cross-cultural living, how do we determine which ones are okay and which are not? (As a kid, I joked that an electric toaster was extravagant, whereas my parents' over-the-burner toaster was the real deal.)

---

4 Jones, "Going Nowhere: Ten tips for expat Stayers who want to stay well."

5 Ellie's response to Stallings, "Build Your CABIN."

Consider that Jesus had a physical home the first thirty years of his life. He only gave that up to pursue his teaching and preaching ministry. Jesus traveled on foot for three years but that was unique for him, not prescriptive for all of us. Your ministry doesn't need to mirror anyone else's.

Some of us truly don't need or care much about our surroundings. Some enjoy a minimalist lifestyle, content to carry what fits in a backpack. Others thrive in a full home experience. Aesthetic surroundings and a feeling of beauty inspire them and bring life.

But we all need some kind of a roof over our heads. We need to care for our physical bodies and our emotional souls. We cannot minister to others if we are physically or emotionally starved.

Know yourself. What do you need in order to flourish? It might not be air conditioning but find what optimizes your service. Perhaps the yard, a location, or a certain activity can provide energy and life for your soul. Build the nest that will enable you to have grit and stay well.

In other words, create a place that you can settle into and make your own. Because our home often reflects our values, this can be a source of conflict. What one messenger finds necessary, another deems extravagant. Don't let that stop you.

From the earliest days of missionary endeavors, workers have asked, "What kind of home should we have? Should it mirror the local style and economic level or can we make it comfortable for our lifestyle?" Of course, you will have to make this work for you and find your own answers, but here are some that have guided me:

- Choose within your financial means.
- Follow agency guidelines, where applicable.
- Consider your occupation and the reason you chose this country and live accordingly.
- Determine what aspects of the local lifestyle you can live with easily. Whatever local customs you can adopt readily, do so. Such will help bond you to your host culture.
- Identify what aspects of home life you simply must accept. Ask God for strength and grace to endure.
- Finally, choose what features you have freedom to adjust so that you may enhance your longevity. Build these into your nest so that you may endure more joyfully.

For me and my husband, the air conditioning became our point of departure from the culture. We also discovered we needed to create a place of beauty, a refuge. Over time, we purchased better furniture, art work, new cushions and pillows to make our home fun and lovely for us. We built a *berugak* (a bamboo and thatched-roof platform for sitting outside) in our yard. We remodeled our garage for a cool office space. I planted frangipani bushes (because I love them) even though Indonesians consider them funeral flowers. Other teammates put less money than we did into their home, and some spent even more.

Bottom line—do what you need to do to stay awhile. Be a little bit foreign. Be a little bit strange.

REFLECTION

Reflect on the following passages and journal your thoughts to God on this subject.

Psalm 23

Matthew 6:9–13

James 4:13–16

How can you be present to your current reality?

What benefits do you have because of your current situation?

What practical step(s) will you take to invest in and develop relationships in your community?

Do you feel at home where you live? Why or why not?

What can you do to make your home more your nest, a place you want to remain in?

RESPONSE

Make a mental or physical list of all that you have now—currently (relationships, home, family, work).

Thank God for all that you have and are experiencing this moment.

Choose one activity you can begin to do to invest in your community and/or build your nest.

PRAYER

Lord Jesus, since you did not have any place to lay your head, sometimes I feel guilty for enjoying my nest so much. But you remind me that comparing myself to others is unhelpful (especially when our commission differs). Show me what I need for my own soul care. Show me when I am simply escaping or indulging, rather than truly creating a way to be resilient and stay well. Amen.

RESOURCES

https://www.instagram.com/p/CZzFrlxrQwm/?utm_medium=copy_link _____
(A Liturgy for When People Leave)

https://velvetashes.com/a-cord-of-three-strands/ _____

https://www.takingroute.net/taking-route/couches-on-helicopters-supporting-families-living-abroad _____

https://bit.ly/TakingRouteNewsletter_Issue026 _____
(Something Old, Something New, Something Borrowed, Something You)

https://www.globalcrossroadsconsulting.com/post/building-a-dock-a-resource-for-the-stayer _____

PART THREE

Deciding to Stay or Go—
Grit *and* Grace Needed

Introduction

We (Sue) had an opportunity to leave during our second term overseas. Leadership in our US office asked us to return to the US and help mobilize for Christar. It was a shock. We felt like we were just getting started and excited about opportunities coming our way. After spending all this time learning Arabic and building relationships, why would we want to leave? But we also knew the leadership wasn't asking us these questions about relocating lightly. We wanted to honor them and follow God's leading. We looked at the needs of our kids, the needs on the field, the needs at the office, and basically the pros and cons equaled each other. We didn't want to leave with the open door of ministry before us. So, we said no. But it wasn't a clear path forward nor an easy decision.

Eight years later when the government declared my husband's visa unrenewable, we thought about fighting it within the legal system of our host country. We had to consider not only what we should do but how what we did would affect our national brothers and sisters and our co-workers. We left because of the loss of the visa. It was a situation outside of our control.

Two years later in our second country of service, we faced yet another choice. We tried to balance the ministry to our family with ministry outside of our home. We faced the significant needs of our kids and our community ministry and noted how God was at work in both spheres. We had long (very long) discussions about what to do. Stay? Go? We made lists. We talked as a family. Discussion dragged on and on because we hesitated to make a wrong decision. We finally decided to leave to serve at our US office. We still wondered if it was the right decision, but did the best we could with what we knew.

Ultimately, choosing what to do causes stress no matter what the outcome. Deciding to leave a field is distressing, but leaving ministry, even more so. Because of such life-changing ramifications, making the decision when we feel healthy and stable must be a priority. This isn't always possible, but we can strive towards it. Carey Nieuwhof, in his article "Is It Time to Quit Ministry?" wrote, "I know when I'm in a not-very-good-place emotionally, I'm far more likely to make poor decisions. Abandoning a calling has the potential to be a long-term poor decision."[1]

When I (Eva) told my mother we planned to leave Indonesia, she asked me, "Is the job finished?" My mother was a Bible translator. She enjoyed a defined role with an obvious end. She worked twenty-five years to translate the New Testament into a formerly unwritten language.

But I was a church planter. I lived in a foreign country to bring light to a dark place. I sought to prepare the soil for the good news, and perhaps plant a few seeds. My best job description was simply to present Jesus. When is that ever "finished"?

And one could also argue that even when the New Testament is finally printed, what about discipleship? A church? Is the worker's job done when ten believers attend worship? Twenty-five? One hundred? In the end, my mother stayed after translating the first New Testament to help complete another. Only declining health convinced her to leave.

After eleven years as cross-cultural servants, my husband and I left for our home assignment knowing we needed to make a huge decision. We consulted our sending church

---

1 Nieuwhof, "Is it Time to Quit Ministry? How to Tell If Your Time As a Pastor is Over."

leaders, talked to a counselor, prayed, journaled, and searched Scripture. And in the end, God graciously directed each of us at different times, in different ways, to the same verse: "I have called you back from the ends of the earth, saying, 'You are my servant. For I have chosen you and will not throw you away'" (Isa 41:9 NLT).

Some might think that we left because of all the crises and stresses we endured. They did play a part in our decision in that those painful events revealed the need for deep emotional healing in my husband and in our marriage. We tried many of the tools and techniques Sue beautifully described in part one of this book. We also received help from professionals. As God touched childhood wounds and trauma, we both became more aware of our giftedness and could make our decision from a healthier place. I accepted I married a man who thrived under frequent change and was now mature enough to admit it. And so, we made the heart-wrenching decision to say goodbye, even with a vague future ahead of us.

We (both Sue and Eva) have been the ones to leave, and we've been the ones to stay and say goodbye to those who leave. Sometimes, leaving became the obvious thing for others to do so we could anticipate the change. Yet other times, the news came out of the blue, leaving us shocked. We've had teammates who were forced to leave and others who chose to leave. Some reasons we understood. Others we didn't.

We've also had our share of team conflict. Some distressing team meetings left me (Sue) feeling like I wanted to leave. Or I wanted others to leave. But, as we muddled together through those difficult times, deeper friendships emerged. Commitment to vision increased and lifelong friendships established. Forged in a crucible of fire, refined relationships lead to resilience. Sometimes, not always. Other times, relationships didn't deepen. They just diverged.

Saying goodbye will always be tough, but the pain can be eased through good communication—open wrestling (not physical), working through facets of the decision together, giving and receiving input, and affirming gifts and contributions. Pray together. Trust and love one another enough to let go or hang on. Use discernment to lovingly encourage one another, whatever the outcome.

Some missionaries have dreamed of serving overseas since childhood. They've sat through a gazillion missions conferences, read missionary biographies, and studied cross-cultural ministry in college. Their church backs them, an agency welcomes them, others join their support team, and they feel ready to arrive before they get on a plane.

Others feel the call later in life. This was the case for me (Sue). We had been married eight years, had one child and then two more by the time we arrived overseas. I felt like a late bloomer and slightly intimidated when I interacted with others who had wanted to minister across cultures since early childhood.

Whether deciding early or late in life, some of us have stayed and some of us have left. God has designed each one of us differently. Some go through harrowing difficulties and stay. Others go through far less serious challenges and leave. And vice versa.

Steve and Barb served across cultures through some harrowing difficulties for thirty years. Steve wrote about some of their challenges and their response:

> Summer came and with it, an increase in the fighting. Every night we heard several bombs explode, often followed by the firing of machine guns. Then the dogs would bark. We had trouble getting enough sleep. There was still nothing in the newspapers to tell us what was happening, but there were often soldiers in full battle dress with loaded rifles on street corners.

The situation was clearly becoming more and more dangerous. An American soldier in our city was killed when he tried to start his booby-trapped car. I started looking under my car for bombs each time I got in. Things were going from bad to worse. It never occurred to us, however, that we should leave. We had been called and would not leave until He called us away, as He did some thirty years later.

Steve encouraged us when the local police called Don in for questioning. Steve said, "Being imprisoned is frightening. But once you've experienced it, it isn't as scary." Going through the process of not knowing if Don would be coming home made me want to find a safe place—like my parents' home, where I always felt secure.

The first time Don went in for questioning, he didn't get home until very late. I paced and prayed, trying to figure out how I would handle telling the kids and packing our things if he was imprisoned or deported. The fear and uncertainty made me want to run away. When things got hard, the gut reaction of fear and wanting to leave for some place safer typically followed. But by God's grace, I didn't.

My desire to run away differs from purposefully deciding whether to leave or stay. If bombings had increased, if our family's safety had been jeopardized, if direct threats had been made, I might have decided that leaving was the best course of action.

However, not everyone has the same response. One messenger wrote, "We stayed because we did not want to avoid hardship. We knew going into ministry would bring hardship and hard people to deal with."

I don't think anyone can say with absolute certainty, "This is the will of God for you" to those considering staying or going. But we can have opinions, offer our experience, and ask questions to help people process the decision.

God leads people to do different things. Consider Paul throughout the book of Acts as he responded to challenging times and persecutions. Sometimes he stayed. Sometimes he left. Sometimes he wanted to go, but the Holy Spirit directed him not to. Because Paul experienced challenges whether he stayed or went, we know that choosing the easiest route did not motivate him. Likewise, each person must seek God, desire to do his will, and decide.

Almost everyone who leaves the field states that God is leading them. But sometimes we can convince ourselves of God's will, even to the extent of committing sins of defiance and disobedience. For instance, "I feel God is leading me to divorce my spouse and marry another." "I need more money for ministry so I can be creative in how I present my ministry success numbers."

We don't believe that deciding to leave the field or go somewhere else represents a sin or disobedience issue. But we propose that sometimes when someone declares that God has led them elsewhere, they may be trying to convince themselves because they really want to go. When someone says, "God is leading me this way," no one can really argue with that. Who wants to fight against God?

On this cautionary note, let's sincerely question ourselves (not others) and examine our motives as we prayerfully decide whether to go or stay. In this section, we want to help you reflect on your decision-making process. What questions will help you discern God's leading? What resources will benefit you as you consider next steps?

Take your time in this section. Relax. Do the exercises. Ponder the passages. Look up the resources. Answer the questions without rushing through them. Use the time to reflect and process. Then discuss your answers with a trusted friend or transition coach.

We're asking God to help you use this time to think through next steps as you pursue him and seek his will.

We pray for you as Paul did for the Thessalonians: "May the Lord direct your hearts into God's love and Christ's perseverance" (2 Thess 3:5).

Chapter 23

What Is My Calling?
The Foundation

> *Calling is not only a matter of being and doing what we are but also of becoming what we are not yet but are called by God to be.*
>
> —Os Guinness

What does it mean to be "called"? I (Eva) addressed this in part two as a necessary fuel to stay when everyone else goes. While we have communicated that believers are first called to God through salvation, we understand missionaries use this word to explain why they choose to serve cross-culturally or with the sense that they are doing what God has told them to do.

Since you are reading this book, we assume that you have already been led to cross-cultural ministry, are contemplating it, or support someone who has. Now you may be sensing that this direction has changed or are trying to assist someone else in the throes of confusion.

When we (Sue) felt led to missions, we heard no audible voice. While willing to go, I just never thought I would. I didn't fit the "missionary image" I had in my mind. However, in my husband's first year of seminary, we considered if God was inviting us to serve overseas. We decided he was, and we said yes. We didn't have a specific destination; we only recognized the need of the least-reached presented to us. We considered the possibility that we could help share the gospel in dark corners of the world. We thought we could. God kept opening doors and confirming his will, and we obeyed. While the specific tasks of our mission have changed over the years, the basic calling remains.

My (Eva's) missionary story corresponds with Sue's in that overseas ministry was not my first choice. While studying for a degree in Christian education, I met my husband. I knew at the time we dated that he desired to serve cross-culturally. Since I am a third culture kid (missionary kid specifically), I understood what that meant. But I had deliberately chosen to not pursue missions as my default path. As I sought God's will for my marriage, I accepted that serving overseas would accompany my decision to marry. When we said, "I do" for life, I also declared, "I will be a global worker for life." When my husband began to speak about leaving, I needed God to clearly confirm through Scripture and other means that he was giving me a new direction apart from merely following my husband.

Some spouses with similar calling stories never fully embrace cross-cultural ministry and so when the challenges come, they can be more prone to believe the lies laid out in the first section and leave too soon. But all messengers of the Gospel can face this same temptation. And when tempted, they point to their call for the resolve and fortitude to stay when they contemplate leaving.

Tom, working in southeast Asia, wrote:

We were under intense pressure to leave the work and stop living in the mountains due to kidnapping and, eventually, regular killing attempts/threats. Although we did evacuate from time to time, we always returned and saw the completion of our work after twenty-eight years. Commitment to the call. This is not merely a job. Souls are at stake. The glory of God is paramount. Prayer, fasting, and surrender of our own wills is paramount. We cannot do the will of God if we have any will of our own.

Do calls change, or more so, circumstances? Often, workers join an agency or a team with what they consider a shared vision. Maybe they find out their goals differ, or maybe their vision evolves. As their identity and giftings mature, they may need to switch to a new commission. They also need to determine if they use their calling to cover up their stubbornness or fear of looking like a failure.

My (Sue's) picture of a missionary and my niche in missions look quite different. I still feel called and I stay true to that calling. But what it looks like now differs from what I imagined at the beginning of our career. I (Eva) remain called to build God's kingdom, but in my passport country and not overseas.

As you consider your next steps, reflect on your calling.

REFLECTION

Reflect on the following passages, underlining what you are called to. How does what you want to do compare to what God calls you to? What are ways your calling will affect your decision to leave or stay?

God is faithful, who has called you into fellowship with his Son, Jesus Christ our Lord. (1 Cor 1:9)

You, my brothers and sisters, were called to be free. But do not use your freedom to indulge the flesh; rather, serve one another humbly in love. (Gal 5:13)

And we know that in all things God works for the good of those who love him, who have been called according to his purpose. For those God foreknew he also predestined to be conformed to the image of his Son, that he might be the firstborn among many brothers and sisters. And those he predestined, he also called; those he called, he also justified; those he justified, he also glorified. (Rom 8:28–30)

Let the peace of Christ rule in your hearts, since as members of one body you were called to peace. And be thankful. (Col 3:15)

Fight the good fight of the faith. Take hold of the eternal life to which you were called when you made your good confession in the presence of many witnesses. (1 Tim 6:12)

But you are a chosen people, a royal priesthood, a holy nation, God's special possession, that you may declare the praises of him who called you out of darkness into his wonderful light. (1 Pet 2:9)

But how is it to your credit if you receive a beating for doing wrong and endure it? But if you suffer for doing good and you endure it, this is commendable before God. To this you were called, because Christ suffered for you, leaving you an example, that you should follow in his steps. (1 Pet 2:20–21)

See what great love the Father has lavished on us, that we should be called children of God! And that is what we are! The reason the world does not know us is that it did not know him. (1 John 3:1)

RESPONSE

Describe your call (commission) to cross-cultural ministry and what it means to you today.

Who will you talk with about what you're learning about calling?

PRAYER

You have called me. You have shown grace to me. I pray you will make me worthy of your calling. I am reminded of Paul's prayer in 2 Thessalonians 1:11–12 that by your power, you would bring to fruition my every desire for goodness and every deed that is prompted by faith. I pray this so that the name of Jesus will be glorified in me according to your grace. Amen.

FOR FURTHER REFLECTION

1 Corinthians 1:26–31:

Brothers and sisters, think of what you were when you were called. Not many of you were wise by human standards; not many were influential; not many were of noble birth. But God chose the foolish things of the world to shame the wise; God chose the weak things of the world to shame the strong. God chose the lowly things of this world and the despised things— and the things that are not—to nullify the things that are, so that no one may boast before him. It is because of him that you are in Christ Jesus, who has become for us wisdom from God—that is, our righteousness, holiness and redemption. Therefore, as it is written: "Let the one who boasts boast in the Lord."

Meditate on the above passage and write out what you notice about calling.

RESOURCES

https://www.abwe.org/blog/how-know-if-god-calling-you-missions-10-point-checklist-0 _____

https://scnd.org/story/5-myths-of-the-missionary-call _____

https://www.takingroute.net/taking-route/2016/12/05/time-go-home-know __

Tony Horsfall and Debbie Hawker, *Resilience in Life and Faith: Finding Your Strength in God* (Abington: The Bible Reading Fellowship, 2019).

Parker J. Palmer, *Let Your Life Speak: Listening to the Voice of Vocation* (San Francisco: Josey-Bass, 2000).

Chapter 24

What Are The Pros and Cons of Staying? Of Leaving?
Weighing the Reasons

> *God knows that the process of seeking Him is as important as the answer He might give to any question. As you take steps of faith and learn to recognize His leading, you grow spiritually and strengthen your relationship with Him. It is not always a simple process, but in the end, it's worth it.*
>
> —FAITH ENG AND EVANGELINE VERGO

As we consider staying or leaving, thinking through pros and cons is a good way to determine the benefits and downsides of our options and help us make decisions. Yet sometimes God asks us to do the opposite of what seems rational. And that's the rub.

Consider the following biblical examples: Jesus said, "For whoever wants to save their life will lose it, but whoever loses their life for me will find it" (Matt 16:25). Delineating pros and cons of marching around a city for seven days to win a battle makes little sense from a human perspective (Josh 6). The Apostle Paul determines to go to Jerusalem, though others plead with him through the Spirit not to go (Acts 21). Paul also writes about how a great door for effective work has opened for him, along with many who oppose him (1 Cor 16:9). And God leads Paul and his companions in a different direction than they originally plan. I don't know how or why the Holy Spirit keeps them from preaching in Asia or how the Spirit of Jesus doesn't allow them to go to Bithynia. But God closes those doors to open another and they conclude God is leading them to go preach the gospel in Macedonia. They look at their circumstances, assess their situation, and heed God's call (Acts 16:6–10).

Remember that neither couples nor single people have to make the decision in isolation. Invite teammates, counselors, or leaders to help in the process. Depending on their ages, parents can ask their kids to weigh in since leaving or staying affects them as well. Others may help us think through things more objectively and thoroughly.

As you begin to think through your pros and cons for decision-making, keep in mind one drawback suggested by Emily P. Freeman, in her podcast, *The Next Right Thing*:

> But a pro con list has at least one major flaw. It assumes every line item weighs an equal amount, and we all know they don't. A list could have ten cons on it and only one pro. But if that one pro is your family or your health or your safety and well-being, well, then that one item on the pro list outweighs all the items on the con list. Another major flaw with the pro con list, we tend to make them only when we're feeling desperate.[1]

---

1 Freeman, "03: Make the Most Important List."

Freeman suggests that as we make our pro con list, we also ask ourselves two questions that tap into our heart longings. As you consider your life overseas, "What has been life-giving?" and "What has been life-draining?"[2] In addition, my (Sue's) husband has created his own system of applying a number value to each item on his pro/con list. This way he can add up the weight of each list for a more accurate assessment.

So, as you list the pros and cons of staying or leaving, remember that this tool is just one factor of many to consider. Not everything rests on this method. Remember to keep praying and seeking God as you wrestle through the decision-making process.

REFLECTION

Write out the pros of staying. Write out the cons of staying.

Write out the pros of leaving. Write out the cons of leaving.

What has been life-giving?

What has been life-draining?

RESPONSE

Share your list of pros and cons with a trusted friend or advisor. Ask for their input and pray together as you look to God for guidance.

PRAYER

Lord, I desire to do your will, but I am not sure what to do. As I think through pros and cons, please direct my steps. Guide me as I walk by faith in you. Thank you that you know the way. I'm so thankful that you invite me to come to you and ask for wisdom. I do this with confidence that you will give it in your timing as I wait on you. Even though hard, I commit to waiting on you and seeking to do your will. Amen.

---

2 Freeman, "03: Make the Most Important List."

FOR FURTHER REFLECTION

Acts 21:3–15:

After sighting Cyprus and passing to the south of it, we sailed on to Syria. We landed at Tyre, where our ship was to unload its cargo. We sought out the disciples there and stayed with them seven days. Through the Spirit they urged Paul not to go on to Jerusalem. When it was time to leave, we left and continued on our way. All of them, including wives and children, accompanied us out of the city, and there on the beach we knelt to pray. After saying goodbye to each other, we went aboard the ship, and they returned home.

We continued our voyage from Tyre and landed at Ptolemais, where we greeted the brothers and sisters and stayed with them for a day. Leaving the next day, we reached Caesarea and stayed at the house of Philip the evangelist, one of the Seven. He had four unmarried daughters who prophesied.

After we had been there a number of days, a prophet named Agabus came down from Judea. Coming over to us, he took Paul's belt, tied his own hands and feet with it and said, "The Holy Spirit says, 'In this way the Jewish leaders in Jerusalem will bind the owner of this belt and will hand him over to the Gentiles.'"

When we heard this, we and the people there pleaded with Paul not to go up to Jerusalem. Then Paul answered, "Why are you weeping and breaking my heart? I am ready not only to be bound, but also to die in Jerusalem for the name of the Lord Jesus." When he would not be dissuaded, we gave up and said, "The Lord's will be done."

After this, we started on our way up to Jerusalem.

Read and reflect on Acts 21:3–15. Take time to ponder Paul's decision to go despite others' protests and pleading.

What would have been his list of pros and cons?

Write out what you think led Paul to make the decision he did.

RESOURCES

https://thinkinsights.net/strategy/pros-and-cons-decision-making/   _____

https://idea-sandbox.com/blog/three-simple-decision-making-tools/   _____

https://jeffsimmons.org/2017/01/03/spiritual-discernment/   _____

https://emilypfreeman.com/podcast/03-make-important-list/   _____

https://thirdculturethriving.libsyn.com/should-i-stay-or-should-i-go   _____

Chapter 25

Why Do I Want to Transition?
Determining Desires

> *No matter what my future holds, I want to be characterized as someone who stayed well and lived fully. I do not want to forget the changes, the progress, and the good I have seen in the places I have lived. I do not want my body to be living in one place while my mind and heart are far away. If I move again, I want it to be because God called me to a new location and not because I failed to stay well.*
>
> —Emily Smith

As we've discussed earlier, cross-cultural workers transition in their locations and ministries for many reasons, none of which are simple. Some changes are forced. These transitions are unwanted and often do not give time for preparation. But in a way, they are clearer because the decision is out of our control, and we move forward confidently (even if sadly) knowing God wills us to leave. These kinds of moves are decided for us and few question our motives for leaving.

Other transitions come about through requests from others. Most of the time, our motives for these transitions are considered acceptable (but not always) and our team can release us to our new role.

Then there are the transitions we initiate ourselves. In these cases, our reasons can come across as vague, nebulous, or unacceptable. This may be the toughest type of transition because we ask those left behind to trust us and accept our decision. It could be that our area is now "reached," and we want to move to a people group that hasn't heard the gospel. Perhaps we've discovered another area of ministry where our gifts can be more strategically useful.

As we consider making a move, we must think through the whys of transitioning and determine our underlying motivation. Which reasons matter most and why? Why exactly do we want to stay or go? Are any of our reasons for leaving solvable? What changes might make a difference? This exercise requires honesty and a willingness to admit our heart's true desires, even if it feels unacceptable or unspiritual.

When I (Sue) felt like leaving, I considered two major factors. First, I weighed the wellbeing of my family and my ministry within the home. Then I looked at the effectiveness—or lack thereof—of my ministry in the community. In one country, family life was going well, but ministry didn't seem fruitful. We stayed. In another country, the ministry seemed fruitful, but our family struggled. We left.

When considering transition, we must note the difference between our goals and desires. Confusion between these two things can affect our decision to leave or stay. Derek Johnson teaches our members that goals involve what we can control, such as our own emotions, actions, and thoughts. Desires, on the other hand, include those aspects I wish and hope to achieve but cannot control, things like others' emotions, actions, and thoughts. Derek says that unmet goals are misplaced desires and can lead to anger.

Perhaps you may have confused a goal with a desire. Taking the time to differentiate a goal from a desire might help you make your decision about transition.

REFLECTION

Consider which category your reason for leaving falls under (forced, unwanted, requested, self-initiated, etc.). How might identifying this help your process?

Write out some of your goals and desires. Note where you may have confused a goal with a desire.

What role might fear of judgment play in your reasons for wanting to transition?

RESPONSE

Why are you thinking about transition? List the reasons. No editing. Write them down as they come to mind.

Review your list. Does anything surprise you or bring clarity? Find someone to help you process your reasons for transitioning.

PRAYER

Lord, you are the God who never changes. Change seems constant for me! You see my confusion because you know everything about me. You know me better than I know myself. As I think about moving, help me think clearly. Please direct my steps. May I be honest with myself and others. Help me as I think through the differences in my goals and desires. Guide me to someone who might help me talk things through. My heart's desire is to do your will. Amen.

FOR FURTHER REFLECTION

Acts 18:1–4, 18–20, 24–28:

After this, Paul left Athens and went to Corinth. There he met a Jew named Aquila, a native of Pontus, who had recently come from Italy with his wife Priscilla, because Claudius had ordered all Jews to leave Rome. Paul went to see them, and because he was a tentmaker as they were, he stayed and worked with them. Every Sabbath he reasoned in the synagogue, trying to persuade Jews and Greeks.

Paul stayed on in Corinth for some time. Then he left the brothers and sisters and sailed for Syria, accompanied by Priscilla and Aquila. Before he sailed, he had his hair cut off at Cenchreae because of a vow he had taken. They arrived at Ephesus, where Paul left Priscilla and Aquila. He himself went into the synagogue and reasoned with the Jews.

Meanwhile a Jew named Apollos, a native of Alexandria, came to Ephesus. He was a learned man, with a thorough knowledge of the Scriptures. He had been instructed in the way of the Lord, and he spoke with great fervor and taught about Jesus accurately, though he knew only the baptism of John. He began to speak boldly in the synagogue. When Priscilla and Aquila heard him, they invited him to their home and explained to him the way of God more adequately.

When Apollos wanted to go to Achaia, the brothers and sisters encouraged him and wrote to the disciples there to welcome him. When he arrived, he was a great help to those who by grace had believed. For he vigorously refuted his Jewish opponents in public debate, proving from the Scriptures that Jesus was the Messiah.

Reflect on Priscilla and Aquila from Acts 18. How many transitions did they have? What do you think they learned through their moves?

RESOURCES

https://www.thewaybetween.org/blog/2019/4/2/rk1uiq9kze2wvr8tiitd5gzrtl0cir

https://www.thewaybetween.org/blog/2019/3/28/career-changing- _____
decision-making-grid

https://globaltrellis.com/how-to-handle-loss-at-the-hand-of-your-organization/ __

https://globaltrellis.com/5-key-questions-that-help-you-assess-staying-or-
leaving-the-field/ _____

https://globaltrellis.com/processing-transition-aka-learning-to-trust/ _____

Chapter 26

Who Should I Talk to and When?
Necessary Conversations

> *The best way to determine whether you should stay or go is to get a circle of people around you who love you enough to tell you the truth.*
>
> —CAREY NIEUWHOF

Making decisions apart from the counsel of others is considered unwise. "Plans fail for lack of counsel, but with many advisers they succeed" (Prov 15:22). "Listen to advice and accept discipline, and at the end you will be counted among the wise" (Prov 19:20). "Surely you need guidance to wage war, and victory is won through many advisers" (Prov 24:6). We encourage you to seek the advice of others. You don't have to follow their counsel but hearing different perspectives and more objective opinions contributes to a more coherent decision.

Many organizations do not have a good discernment matrix specifying who needs to be included in the decision-making process. Having such guidelines may have helped prevent some of the hurt I (Eva) created among my team by not including them more in my decision. Knowing who to talk to and when can be challenging. Our agency recommends workers discuss plans with both field and sending church leadership at least six months before the anticipated departure to allow for good closure. These discussions address concerns that give cause for considering moving on and help ensure that the sending church and organizational leadership stay in touch with each other and involved in the discussion.

If I feel hesitant about discussing my desire to transition with another person, I first consider what holds me back. Is it fear of judgment? Are my leaders going to try to talk me into staying? Have I tried to talk with them before and they brushed me off? Am I afraid they'll find me wimpish? Will they give me advice that doesn't fit my plans? Who can I invite into the process?

As you examine your list of teammates, supporters, pastoral staff of churches, member care personnel, and other cross-cultural workers, find those who could be a help to you. Determine not to stop after one attempt at getting the help you need. When you have serious physical health issues, you eagerly go for a second and sometimes third opinion. You know you need expertise. Likewise, when making decisions about leaving or staying, seek help to avoid faulty decision-making.

One young gospel messenger told me she almost left at the end of her first year in cross-cultural ministry. Frustrated, unable to find her niche, and certain she contributed nothing, she wanted to pack her bags. But she stayed because she had a coach—someone to talk through her frustrations with. Those conversations helped her gain clarity and gave her a safe place to unpack issues. She also gained skills to handle the challenges coming her way.

This missionary had the foresight to be proactive in getting the help she needed so that she could flourish. She could then make wiser decisions from a healthy place.

When I asked a member care specialist about things she did to help people determine whether leaving or staying would be best for them, she wrote:

> I believe that debriefing or just some "listening sessions" are helpful. Processing with an objective person who has served long-term overseas often helps them to hear their own heart for what God is speaking to them. They normally already know and just need permission to leave or encouragement to stay the course. (Even though it may be difficult either way.) Validating their feelings is important and so healing.

As you seek someone to discuss what you are thinking about in terms of staying or going, choose someone who is dedicated to listening without judgment and, if you can, without stake in the game. Don't give up until you find people who can listen well and help you process your experience so that your decision is the best one for you and reflects God's purposes for you.

Talking with teammates about this decision and the timing of the talk is critical. I offer two "if onlys" for improving team conversations about leaving or staying:

If only teammates thinking about leaving would talk about it with their team *before* already making the decision to go. Processing a huge decision like this on our own doesn't seem wise. Talking about our feelings, doubts and fears with others who know us, and our situation is oftentimes a better way. Too many times, people announce their plans to leave, catching teammates off guard, and leaving them on their own to process what happened.

If only teammates would not use the threat to leave as a way to get people to understand how serious the issue is or to pressure them to do what they want. Threatening to leave is akin to a marriage where one partner uses the "D" word (divorce) frequently as a threat. Going to this extreme amid challenges devalues the other person and leaves them nowhere to go or no positive way to move forward. Using the "I won't stay unless" in teams escalates the issue to the extent that being able to work things through seems hopeless and erodes team trust.

Communicating in a timely way with the team is important. Talking with trusted individuals can help us think through issues and ultimately make wise decisions.

REFLECTION

Who have you already talked to and how was it beneficial?

Have you talked with someone but found it unhelpful? What would have made it a more helpful conversation?

Are you putting off any of these conversations? If so, why?

What are your primary advisors telling you?

RESPONSE

Make a list of possible people to talk with. Think about who would be most helpful and why?

Choose one of these people to talk with. Give them a heads up. Set up an appointment. Start your conversation by sharing what you need from them.

PRAYER

Lord, I need help making this decision. Please lead me to the right ones with whom to talk. I ask you for the resources I need so that I can make a wise decision. May I hold my heart open so that your will becomes the most important thing to me. My opinions and desires, what other people think I should say or do, all may be helpful. Help me to listen and have discernment. I ultimately look to you to guide my steps and establish the work of my hands for your glory. Amen.

FOR FURTHER REFLECTION

2 Chronicles 10:1–16:

Rehoboam went to Shechem, for all Israel had gone there to make him king. When Jeroboam son of Nebat heard this (he was in Egypt, where he had fled from King Solomon), he returned from Egypt. So they sent for Jeroboam, and he and all Israel went to Rehoboam and said to him: "Your father put a heavy yoke on us, but now lighten the harsh labor and the heavy yoke he put on us, and we will serve you."

Rehoboam answered, "Come back to me in three days." So the people went away.

Then King Rehoboam consulted the elders who had served his father Solomon during his lifetime. "How would you advise me to answer these people?" he asked.

They replied, "If you will be kind to these people and please them and give them a favorable answer, they will always be your servants."

But Rehoboam rejected the advice the elders gave him and consulted the young men who had grown up with him and were serving him. He asked them, "What is your advice? How should we answer these people who say to me, 'Lighten the yoke your father put on us'?"

The young men who had grown up with him replied, "The people have said to you, 'Your father put a heavy yoke on us, but make our yoke lighter.' Now tell them, 'My little finger is thicker than my father's waist. My father laid on you a heavy yoke; I will make it even heavier. My father scourged you with whips; I will scourge you with scorpions.'"

Three days later Jeroboam and all the people returned to Rehoboam, as the king had said, "Come back to me in three days." The king answered them harshly. Rejecting the advice of the elders, he followed the advice of the young men and said, "My father made your yoke heavy; I will make it even heavier. My father scourged you with whips; I will scourge you with scorpions." So the king did not listen to the people, for this turn of events was from God, to fulfill the word the Lord had spoken to Jeroboam son of Nebat through Ahijah the Shilonite.

When all Israel saw that the king refused to listen to them, they answered the king:

> "What share do we have in David,
> what part in Jesse's son?
> To your tents, Israel!
> Look after your own house, David!"

So all the Israelites went home.

Reflect on 2 Chronicles 10:1–16. What do you learn about giving or getting advice? How does one decide which advice to follow?

RESOURCES

https://careynieuwhof.com/is-it-time-to-quit-ministry-how-to-tell-if-your-time-as-a-pastor-is-over/   _____

https://ministry127.com/missions/6-questions-to-ask-before-leaving-the-mission-field   _____

https://missionexus.org/is-it-time-how-to-know-when-its-time-to-leave-the-field

https://themissionsexperience.weebly.com/blog/archives/11-2018   _____
(Family Factors)

https://globaltrellis.com/sjc/ (Global Trellis, Sabbatical Journey Course)   _____

Chapter 27

What Part Do My Relationships Play in This Decision?
Resolution and Reconciliation

> *When we avoid difficult conversations, we trade short-term discomfort for long-term dysfunction.*
>
> —PETER BROMBERG

Relationships remain among the top six reasons people leave the mission field.[1] Missionaries come better prepared to deal with people from a different culture than with teammates. I asked a member care provider the main reasons that missionaries seek help. She wrote:

> So often it is the relationships among their team. We often feel we have more grace for the people group to which we are called than the ones we serve with. Leaders/systems are on this list—having people in the system who are dictating rules and regulations to people serving in places they have never served in is difficult. Sometimes the system does not listen to the real needs on the ground.

People would do well to examine their relationships before deciding to go or stay. Sometimes unhealthy relationships begin to feel normal, and we get used to harmful cycles of relating to one another.

On my team, I (Sue) had several confrontations which wiped out my emotional energy. I didn't want to go to the team meeting where I had to talk with a member about an unwise dating relationship. I remember crying in the shower and telling God, "I can't do this." But I did. Though uncomfortable, the end result benefited both our teammate and the team.

Other meeting outcomes weren't so positive, leading to the departure of teammates. When a teammate leaves without attempting to repair relationships, even more damage ensues. We have already spoken about the importance of forgiveness in an earlier chapter. Work through that again if hurt from teammates inhibits your decision-making process. Make amends where you can by admitting your mistakes and showing appropriate remorse. Don't make excuses but instead ask for forgiveness for your part in the problem. We encourage you to not leave because of team conflict if you can do anything about it.

---

1 Thompson, "Is Conflict with Teammates Really the Top Reason for Missionaries Leaving the Field?" "The most important non-acceptable reason as perceived by leaders of mission agencies (and some sending churches) for why missionaries from the US stopped working with their agencies twenty years ago is problems with peer missionaries."

According to Eric Willis, certified Christian conciliator and coach, "Reconciliation is the spiritual willingness to allow God his transformative work" in us and in the other party.[2] We maintain an open heart to have conversations and accept their apologies. Even if our teammate never seeks further relationship with us, we remain willing and ready to receive them should the opportunity arise.

Ronald L. Koteskey writes, "The single most helpful earthly resource for combating stress is social support—feeling comfortable sharing with others and then actually sharing with others who are positive and supportive."[3] When missionaries fail to develop these relationships, they become weaker. How sad when teammates, who should provide social support and stress relief, become the stressors themselves.

That said, we recognize that in some instances leaving may be the only option or pursuing further relationship may be unwise. So, before you decide to transition, consider your relationships.

REFLECTION

What has caused tension with your teammates?

How has confrontation and forgiveness been demonstrated on your team?

How do you know if bitterness and unforgiveness are still issues?

What does reconciliation look like on your team?

RESPONSE

Describe your team stressors and examine how much of an influence they are on your desire to leave.

---

2 Willis, *Sacred Conflict*, 69–70.

3 Koteskey, "What Missionaries Ought to know about Relationships."

Who might you need to forgive, make amends, or reconcile with? Decide what steps you will take.

PRAYER

Lord, you have forgiven me so much. I don't want bitterness to be an issue in my heart or the hearts of my teammates. Help me to love others well. Help me always remember your grace in my life and may that grace flow from me to others. Show me what steps I can take to make amends with those I have hurt. Open my heart to be ready to receive those who have wronged me. Amen.

FOR FURTHER REFLECTION

1 Corinthians 12:12–27:
Just as a body, though one, has many parts, but all its many parts form one body, so it is with Christ. For we were all baptized by one Spirit so as to form one body—whether Jews or Gentiles, slave or free—and we were all given the one Spirit to drink. Even so the body is not made up of one part but of many.

Now if the foot should say, "Because I am not a hand, I do not belong to the body," it would not for that reason stop being part of the body. And if the ear should say, "Because I am not an eye, I do not belong to the body," it would not for that reason stop being part of the body. If the whole body were an eye, where would the sense of hearing be? If the whole body were an ear, where would the sense of smell be? But in fact God has placed the parts in the body, every one of them, just as he wanted them to be. If they were all one part, where would the body be? As it is, there are many parts, but one body.

The eye cannot say to the hand, "I don't need you!" And the head cannot say to the feet, "I don't need you!" On the contrary, those parts of the body that seem to be weaker are indispensable, and the parts that we think are less honorable we treat with special honor. And the parts that are unpresentable are treated with special modesty, while our presentable parts need no special treatment. But God has put the body together, giving greater honor to the parts that lacked it, so that there should be no division in the body, but that its parts should have equal concern for each other. If one part suffers, every part suffers with it; if one part is honored, every part rejoices with it.

Now you are the body of Christ, and each one of you is a part of it.

Reflect on 1 Corinthians 12.12–27. What do you learn about body life? What does it mean to be a member of this one body? Why are different parts needed? How can this passage influence team relationships?

RESOURCES

https://www.abwe.org/blog/single-reason-most-missionaries-don-t-last-field-and-how-fix-it _____

https://www.alifeoverseas.com/is-conflict-with-teammates-really-the-top-reason-for-missionaries-leaving-the-field/ _____

http://home.snu.edu/~hculbert/tough.html _____
(Tough Times: The breakup of a team of career missionaries)

http://home.snu.edu/~hculbert/cases.htm#using _____
(Use this as a case study.)

https://www.missionarycare.com/relationships.html _____

https://themissionsexperience.weebly.com/blog/archives/01-2020 _____
(Team Factors)

Chapter 28

What Would I Do If I Weren't Afraid?
Facing Fear

> *Anything I've ever done that ultimately was worthwhile ...*
> *initially scared me to death.*
>
> —BETTY BENDER

We planned to be in our home country for six months. We normally visited during the summer so our kids could stay in our host country's school system. But this time we wanted an extended home assignment so our kids could witness that school and work exist in America, too. Not just vacation and travel.

While in the States I (Sue) had CMV (cytomegalovirus) that zapped my energy. I didn't have the capability to travel and keep up my normal workload. We ended up staying for an extra six months until I grew strong enough to move back overseas.

I remember feeling guilty. It was my fault we couldn't get back overseas as planned and I didn't know how long it would take to regain my strength. I read an article that stated 75 percent of marriages with a spouse dealing with a long-term illness ended in divorce. I read that to my husband. He said, "Let's be part of the 25 percent, OK?"

On those days it felt I would never feel stronger, I feared that my role in our family and our mission might diminish. I remember asking, "Who would I be if I wasn't a missionary?" Trying to figure out how I would move forward scared me.

But staying because I fear leaving is not a good reason to stay. Staying might simply be the more comfortable choice in the face of the unknown. And leaving because I fear staying is not a good reason to leave. I can become stymied by a lot of what ifs that may never come to be. Be intentional to reflect on your fears of staying or leaving. Fear is a factor to consider but shouldn't be the deciding vote.

In an article entitled "Fear in Decision Making: How This F Word Messes You Up" the author summarizes three things fear does to us when we try to make a decision:

- Fear can lead us to overthink a decision, factoring in variables you have no way to predict. This can lead to analysis paralysis and often crazy decisions.

- Fear can cause us to put off or avoid some decisions, which often results in lost options and worse decisions, not better.

- Fear can reduce the number of decisions you make so that over time your decision-making abilities do not improve. Every decision is unnecessarily hard and often comes with poor results.[1]

---

1 McDaniel, "Fear in Decision Making."

- On the other hand, John Piper points out, "Peace and calm are not the only factors in determining what one ought to do."[2] We also need obedience, walking by faith, and not letting fear keep us from pursuing and doing God's will.

For some, the unknown is exciting. For others, it is scary. For those who find it more frightening than exciting, we offer encouragement from the story of Barak and Deborah. "Then Deborah said to Barak, 'Go! This is the day the LORD has given Sisera into your hands. Has not the LORD gone ahead of you?'" (Jud 4:14).

Knowing God never leads me where he hasn't been always makes me braver.

REFLECTION

What about the unknown is scary to you?

How can you not succumb to those fears?

How might your fear rush or delay your decision-making?

What would you do if you were not afraid?

RESPONSE

Write out the major fears you face in making a decision.

Choose an area of fear and talk to your mentor, advisor, or friend about your concerns.

---

2 Piper, "Should I Ever Take an Action I Don't Have 'Peace' About?"

PRAYER

My Lord, my refuge. When things happen that are obviously out of my control, I so often respond in fear. As I come to know you more, may faith instead be my response. Thank you for going ahead of me, for knowing the way. You are my King. Amen.

FOR FURTHER REFLECTION

Psalm 46:
God is our refuge and strength,
an ever-present help in trouble.
Therefore we will not fear, though the earth give way
and the mountains fall into the heart of the sea,
though its waters roar and foam
and the mountains quake with their surging.

There is a river whose streams make glad the city of God,
the holy place where the Most High dwells.
God is within her, she will not fall;
God will help her at break of day.
Nations are in uproar, kingdoms fall;
he lifts his voice, the earth melts.

The LORD Almighty is with us;
the God of Jacob is our fortress.

Come and see what the LORD has done,
the desolations he has brought on the earth.
He makes wars cease
to the ends of the earth.
He breaks the bow and shatters the spear;
he burns the shields with fire.
He says, "Be still, and know that I am God;
I will be exalted among the nations,
I will be exalted in the earth."

The LORD Almighty is with us;
the God of Jacob is our fortress.

Reflect on Psalm 46. What does it say about God? How does knowing God as our refuge affect us? Write out your own paraphrase of the psalm and insert some of your challenging circumstances while remembering who God is.

RESOURCES

https://www.paultripp.com/wednesdays-word/posts/afraid-of-the-unknown

https://screamsinthedesert.wordpress.com/2019/02/08/fear-based-courage/

https://www.desiringgod.org/topics/fear-and-anxiety#the-root-of-our-anxiety

https://evaburkholder.com/2013/02/01/bollards/

David C. Benner, *Surrender to Love: Discovering the Heart of Christian Spirituality* (Downers Grove: InterVarsity Press, 2003), chapter 2.

Bob Goff, *Dream Big: Know What You Want, Why You Want It, and What You're Going to Do About It* (Nashville: Nelson Books, 2020).

Chapter 29

What Do I Know About Myself That Affects This Decision?
Self-Awareness

> *Practiced consistently, this simple method [of asking others' opinions of your strengths] will show you within a fairly short period of time, maybe two or three years, where your strengths lie—and this is the most important thing to know.*
>
> —PETER DRUCKER

My (Eva's) husband waited eagerly to hear the results of the assessments he had just taken at the request of our agency. The coach summed up his results. "According to this test, you should not be a church planter." Suddenly, so many things made sense. He responded, "No wonder I've felt so out of place."

Learning and accepting that he was not an evangelist by gifting set him free to pursue what he was gifted to do—discipling, teaching, counseling, and encouraging.

To thrive in ministry, we need to know so much more about ourselves than what we do in the beginning of our career. We need to ask ourselves along the way, what we really want. I (Sue) want to be useful. I want to be led and empowered by God. I am called to serve God, and I want to do so faithfully and joyfully. I (Eva) want to help women and men flourish to use their gifts to their full ability. I want to make the Bible practical and applicable for daily life.

How do we become more aware of who we are? We implement instruments like CliftonStrengths® or GRIP-Birkman® assessments. We find our Enneagram® number. We listen to feedback. We identify our passions and what brings us joy. We try new things. We read about life stage traits. With time, we discover how we are wired; what we have the capacity to do, and what we probably shouldn't do.

I (Sue) appreciate learning my teammate's passions and skills through the various assessments our organization uses. But I also have several cautions.

First, just because a task isn't my best contribution, doesn't mean I can't contribute. For instance, at our church plant, we highly value our children's programs. I haven't worked with kids for years and I don't think I'm best suited for it. But it is a purposeful contribution. I have discovered that I enjoy teaching the kids (even when I'm a bit startled when they ask about the Apostle Paul pooping!). By the end of the lesson, I feel tired. But what a delight to invest in these young lives for the kingdom. I pray for them faithfully. Praise God that I can contribute.

Second, we should try new things so that we don't become overly confident in ourselves. What adventures await when we must depend on someone else. I am terrible at crafts.

My younger teammate helped me make a necklace. Another gal helped me construct a Christmas ornament. Situations outside of my comfort zone force me to learn from others, strengthening our relationship while benefiting from their skill sets.

I (Eva) have seen that we naturally narrow our focus as we get older. When young, we attempt many things to find out what we like to do and where we excel. The confirmation of others and our own personal joy and success help weed out areas of less effectiveness. In our middle years, we try to work in those areas of strength we have discovered. But as we get older, our time and energy become more precious. We need to give ourselves permission to say no to things we used to do or no longer want to do. The older we get, the more we often concentrate on fewer activities.

If we don't know ourselves well, we won't feel energized in our ministries, especially if we church plant in resistant areas where spiritual fruit ripens slowly. We may feel we are wasting time, but we aren't. We are investing time as God develops strengths in us by his power and grace.

As you consider going or staying, evaluate how new information about yourself affects this decision.

REFLECTION

What might be holding you back from pursuing knowing yourself?

What are your strengths? What are your weaknesses?

How would you describe your best contribution? How else can you contribute?

What can you learn this year that isn't a part of your gifting or strengths?

What things do you want to focus on as you get older? What things do you want to let go of?

RESPONSE

Take five minutes at the end of the day to reflect upon the situations and circumstances of the day. Reflect upon one or two of the following (no particular order) from Tim Bias:

The meetings you attended.

The people with whom you had interaction.

What emotions did you experience?

Was anything said or done that triggered a negative response from you?

When did you have to stand on your values or beliefs? Did you give in?

When were you aware of your strengths or weaknesses? How did you respond?

When did you experience joy?

How did you cultivate relationships today?

Who do you need to contact to express appreciation for helping you become more who you are created to be?

Who do you need to contact to ask forgiveness for your lack of self-awareness?[1] Share what you discover with a mentor or friend.

PRAYER

God, I offer my life to you again, today. I have some preconceived ideas of what I should be able to do and some of those ideas aren't where I am gifted. Thank you for the gifts you've given to me. Thank you for the way you've gifted others. May we all work in unity as we offer ourselves to you to do your will joyfully and devotedly. Amen.

FOR FURTHER REFLECTION

Romans 12:1–8:
Therefore, I urge you, brothers and sisters, in view of God's mercy, to offer your bodies as a living sacrifice, holy and pleasing to God—this is your true and proper worship. Do not conform to the pattern of this world, but be transformed by the renewing of your mind. Then you will be able to test and approve what God's will is—his good, pleasing and perfect will.

For by the grace given me I say to every one of you: Do not think of yourself more highly than you ought, but rather think of yourself with sober judgment, in accordance with the faith God has distributed to each of you. For just as each of us has one body with many members, and these members do not all have the same function, so in Christ we, though many, form one body, and each member belongs to all the others. We have different gifts, according to the grace given to each of us. If your gift is prophesying, then prophesy in accordance with your faith; if it is serving, then serve; if it is teaching, then teach; if it is to encourage, then give encouragement; if it is giving, then give generously; if it is to lead, do it diligently; if it is to show mercy, do it cheerfully.

Reflect on Romans 12:1–8. How do the first two verses change your perspective about ministry? What is the foundation that verses 1 and 2 lay as you look to serve? What are the guidelines for self-assessment? How are we to use our gifts?

---

1 Bias, "Six Ways to Know You Are Growing in Self-Awareness."

RESOURCES

https://clarionmodel.com/ _____

https://www.gripbirkman.com/ _____

https://www.godswordforyou.com/living-for-jesus/knowing-yourself/908-
understanding-your-strengths-and-weaknesses.html _____

https://www.desiringgod.org/articles/weakness-may-be-your-greatest-strength

Bob Goff, *Dream Big: Know What You Want, Why You Want It, and What You're Going to Do About It* (Nashville: Nelson Books, 2020).

Chapter 30

What Changes Need to Occur for Me to Stay?
Making Adjustments

Our energy is drained by Activity Without Direction (doing things that don't seem to matter), Burden Without Action (not being able to do things that matter), and Conflict Without Resolution (not being able to deal with what's the matter).

—ABCs Energy Drain, adapted from John C. Maxwell

After all the work you've put in to get to your current state or position, leaving too soon would be a loss. Perhaps you feel stuck as though nothing will make a difference and leaving is your only way out. Maybe you have tried to maintain an unsustainable load, working long hours with high demand and low support. Maybe you feel life is unfair because you put in the same effort as your teammate yet see less results.

The messenger life also earns few tangible rewards. We don't receive regular pay raises or much recognition for our efforts. And working with unhealthy leaders who show little empathy or concern about our well-being can drain our grit to stay.

We propose that some adjustment to life and work may make it possible for you to stay:

First, you may need to change your ministry focus. Suppose after you've arrived, learned the language and culture, and stepped into ministry, the team then changes focus. What if you discover that your gifts could be used more effectively on a different team? Rather than leaving too soon, we suggest you thoroughly explore other options with your team, regional, and international leaders. My (Eva's) husband changed roles frequently in order to keep things fresh and challenging, which enabled us to remain on our team longer than we might have.

Many times, working together and loving one another through differences makes teams more fruitful. But sometimes, the team you joined no longer fits you well. You may need to change teams or start a new one. If an issue exists with another team member, enlisting mediation might prevent a premature departure.

Second, your angst may also come from your home or location. When my (Sue's) daughter and her family lived in an apartment in their host country, my granddaughter suffered recurring asthma attacks. Someone suggested mold might be an issue. They moved to a different flat, and she hasn't had an asthma attack for quite a while. Another family struggled because of their child's consistent nightmares. Their team prayed through their house, asking for God's cleansing and protection. The nightmares ceased. Maybe you prefer the town, and you live in a village. Or you grew up in a small borough and the megalopolis you now inhabit overwhelms you. Maybe you love flowers but live in a cement city with little charm. One woman lovingly filled her apartment with silk flower arrangements that brought her joy.

Third, perhaps you need to make changes to your daily life. Purchasing a vehicle and hiring a chauffeur might relieve the stress of navigating the city. Decide which parts of daily life you need to keep doing because you love doing them and give the parts that you don't enjoy to hired staff. Make small or large adjustments that enable you to control some parts of your already unpredictable life.

Fourth, for those feeling like they can't keep going, try adjusting your boundaries. Say "no" more often. Choose wisely in investing your time. Sometimes we can do more; other times we must do less. We have varying energy levels and personalities, and we keep experimenting until we find a healthy balance. Make changes to ensure good emotional and physical health.

Whatever you face, we encourage you to explore other possibilities before returning home. Some of these may feel beyond your reach. We encourage you to not let lack of finances or hesitation to spend money keep you from making the changes necessary to stay. Rather, as you evaluate your ministry focus, location, team fit, daily life, and boundaries, ask God to provide what you need if he desires you to remain. Use the worksheet in Appendix Seven to help you reflect on how making changes to your work might enable you to stay.

REFLECTION

What changes do you need to make in order to stay?

How can you implement those changes?

If you could make those changes, how would that affect your desire to leave or stay?

What adjustment to your boundaries might enable you to stay?

RESPONSE

Decide if there are any changes you need to make and implement one this week. Share your intentions with a trusted friend or mentor.

PRAYER

Lord, I'm tired. We have so many needs and too little resources. Everyone works diligently and when I say no to an opportunity, I feel so guilty I end up saying yes to almost everything. I can't keep going like this and I need to know what to change. Help me make necessary adjustments so I can remain invested in your calling on my life. Amen.

FOR FURTHER REFLECTION

Exodus 18:13–26

The next day Moses took his seat to serve as judge for the people, and they stood around him from morning till evening. When his father-in-law saw all that Moses was doing for the people, he said, "What is this you are doing for the people? Why do you alone sit as judge, while all these people stand around you from morning till evening?"

Moses answered him, "Because the people come to me to seek God's will. Whenever they have a dispute, it is brought to me, and I decide between the parties and inform them of God's decrees and instructions."

Moses' father-in-law replied, "What you are doing is not good. You and these people who come to you will only wear yourselves out. The work is too heavy for you; you cannot handle it alone. Listen now to me and I will give you some advice, and may God be with you. You must be the people's representative before God and bring their disputes to him. Teach them his decrees and instructions, and show them the way they are to live and how they are to behave. But select capable men from all the people—men who fear God, trustworthy men who hate dishonest gain—and appoint them as officials over thousands, hundreds, fifties and tens. Have them serve as judges for the people at all times, but have them bring every difficult case to you; the simple cases they can decide themselves. That will make your load lighter, because they will share it with you. If you do this and God so commands, you will be able to stand the strain, and all these people will go home satisfied."

Moses listened to his father-in-law and did everything he said. He chose capable men from all Israel and made them leaders of the people, officials over thousands, hundreds, fifties and tens. They served as judges for the people at all times. The difficult cases they brought to Moses, but the simple ones they decided themselves.

Read Exodus 18:13–26. What do you see Moses doing? How did his father-in-law step in and help? What makes you hesitant to delegate? What changes do you want to make in light of this passage? Who will you talk with about needed boundaries?

RESOURCES

https://team.org/blog/thrive-on-the-mission-field _____

https://www.alifeoverseas.com/5-mistakes-i-made-my-first-year-
on-the-mission-field/ _____

https://www.dahlfred.com/index.php/blogs/gleanings-from-the-field/
691-friends-a-key-to-survival-on-the-mission-field _____

https://themissionexperience.weebly.com/blog/archives/07-2020 _____

Wayne Cordeiro, *Leading On Empty: Refilling Your Tank and Renewing Your Passion.*
(Bloomington, MN: Bethany House Publishers, 2009).

Chapter 31

What Key Scriptures Can Encourage and Guide Me?
Biblical Guidance

Let us not become weary in doing good, for at the proper time we will reap a harvest if we do not give up.

—Saint Paul

We believe engaging with God's Word encourages our souls and strengthens us in our journey of faith. When I (Sue) wanted to give up, God's Word gave me the power and hope to stay. No surprise, as Paul reminds us that God gives encouragement and Scripture teaches us endurance:

> For everything that was written in the past was written to teach us, so that through the endurance taught in the Scriptures and the encouragement they provide we might have hope. May the God who gives endurance and encouragement give you the same attitude of mind toward each other that Christ Jesus had, so that with one mind and one voice you may glorify the God and Father of our Lord Jesus Christ. (Rom 15:4–6)

We must consult Scripture too when making hard decisions regarding transition. God has pointed me (Eva) to specific verses at the very times I've needed direction. I have taken comfort in the promise that "Whether you turn to the right or to the left, your ears will hear a voice behind you, saying, 'This is the way; walk in it'" (Isa 30:21).

As you seek to do his will regarding your future, may his Word be central in your thinking. Perhaps by searching Scripture, he will lead some of you to stay. You will need grit. Many of you who stay will say goodbye to teammates who choose to leave. Saying multiple goodbyes brings yet more opportunities to persevere. The Lord will guide others of you to leave. You, too, will need endurance. As believers in Jesus and as commissioned ministers for the gospel, we all need to persevere whether God leads us to stay, go, or say goodbye to those who leave.

Many Scripture verses and stories guide us when facing difficult decisions. If you feel overwhelmed by the number of verses below, pick only one or two. As you read them, check out their contexts, underline what is meaningful to you, and circle the promises.

As you explore these passages on endurance, faith, and guidance, don't rush. Be patient. Pray as you begin. Ask the Holy Spirit to teach you, work in you, guide you, encourage you, and make his nearness known to you. Sit at his feet, linger, and listen to what God is communicating to you through his written Word.

Perseverance

Romans 5:1–5: Therefore, since we have been justified through faith, we have peace with God through our Lord Jesus Christ, through whom we have gained access by faith into this grace in which we now stand. And we boast in the hope of the glory of God. Not only so, but we also glory in our sufferings, because we know that suffering produces perseverance; perseverance, character; and character, hope. And hope does not put us to shame, because God's love has been poured out into our hearts through the Holy Spirit, who has been given to us.

2 Corinthians 6:3–10: We put no stumbling block in anyone's path, so that our ministry will not be discredited. Rather, as servants of God we commend ourselves in every way: in great endurance; in troubles, hardships and distresses; in beatings, imprisonments and riots; in hard work, sleepless nights and hunger; in purity, understanding, patience and kindness; in the Holy Spirit and in sincere love; in truthful speech and in the power of God; with weapons of righteousness in the right hand and in the left; through glory and dishonor, bad report and good report; genuine, yet regarded as impostors; known, yet regarded as unknown; dying, and yet we live on; beaten, and yet not killed; sorrowful, yet always rejoicing; poor, yet making many rich; having nothing, and yet possessing everything.

Colossians 1:9–12: For this reason, since the day we heard about you, we have not stopped praying for you. We continually ask God to fill you with the knowledge of his will through all the wisdom and understanding that the Spirit gives, so that you may live a life worthy of the Lord and please him in every way: bearing fruit in every good work, growing in the knowledge of God, being strengthened with all power according to his glorious might so that you may have great endurance and patience, and giving joyful thanks to the Father, who has qualified you to share in the inheritance of his holy people in the kingdom of light.

2 Thessalonians 3:3–5: But the Lord is faithful, and he will strengthen you and protect you from the evil one. We have confidence in the Lord that you are doing and will continue to do the things we command. May the Lord direct your hearts into God's love and Christ's perseverance.

Hebrews 10:32–39: Remember those earlier days after you had received the light, when you endured in a great conflict full of suffering. Sometimes you were publicly exposed to insult and persecution; at other times you stood side by side with those who were so treated. You suffered along with those in prison and joyfully accepted the confiscation of your property, because you knew that you yourselves had better and lasting possessions. So do not throw away your confidence; it will be richly rewarded.

You need to persevere so that when you have done the will of God, you will receive what he has promised. For,

"In just a little while,
he who is coming will come
and will not delay."
And,

"But my righteous one will live by faith.
And I take no pleasure
in the one who shrinks back."

But we do not belong to those who shrink back and are destroyed, but to those who have faith and are saved.

Hebrews 12:1–3: Therefore, since we are surrounded by such a great cloud of witnesses, let us throw off everything that hinders and the sin that so easily entangles. And let us run with perseverance the race marked out for us, fixing our eyes on Jesus, the pioneer and perfecter of faith. For the joy set before him he endured the cross, scorning its shame, and sat down at the right hand of the throne of God. Consider him who endured such opposition from sinners, so that you will not grow weary and lose heart.

James 1:2–4: Consider it pure joy, my brothers and sisters, whenever you face trials of many kinds, because you know that the testing of your faith produces perseverance. Let perseverance finish its work so that you may be mature and complete, not lacking anything.

Faith

2 Thessalonians 1:3–4: We ought always to thank God for you, brothers and sisters, and rightly so, because your faith is growing more and more, and the love all of you have for one another is increasing. Therefore, among God's churches we boast about your perseverance and faith in all the persecutions and trials you are enduring.

1 Timothy 6:11–12: But you, man of God, flee from all this, and pursue righteousness, godliness, faith, love, endurance and gentleness. Fight the good fight of the faith. Take hold of the eternal life to which you were called when you made your good confession in the presence of many witnesses.

Hebrews 11:24–27: By faith Moses, when he had grown up, refused to be known as the son of Pharaoh's daughter. He chose to be mistreated along with the people of God rather than to enjoy the fleeting pleasures of sin. He regarded disgrace for the sake of Christ as of greater value than the treasures of Egypt, because he was looking ahead to his reward. By faith he left Egypt, not fearing the king's anger; he persevered because he saw him who is invisible.

2 Peter 1:3–9: His divine power has given us everything we need for a godly life through our knowledge of him who called us by his own glory and goodness. Through these he has given us his very great and precious promises, so that through them you may participate in the divine nature, having escaped the corruption in the world caused by evil desires.

For this very reason, make every effort to add to your faith goodness; and to goodness, knowledge; and to knowledge, self-control; and to self-control, perseverance; and to perseverance, godliness; and to godliness, mutual affection; and to mutual affection, love. For if you possess these qualities in increasing measure, they will keep you from being ineffective and unproductive in your knowledge of our Lord Jesus Christ. But whoever does not have them is nearsighted and blind, forgetting that they have been cleansed from their past sins.

Guidance

John 16:13: But when he, the Spirit of truth, comes, he will guide you into all the truth. He will not speak on his own; he will speak only what he hears, and he will tell you what is yet to come.

Psalm 32:8: I will instruct you and teach you in the way you should go; I will counsel you with my loving eye on you.

Isaiah 58:11: The LORD will guide you always; he will satisfy your needs in a sun-scorched land and will strengthen your frame. You will be like a well-watered garden, like a spring whose waters never fail.

Psalm 25:9: He guides the humble in what is right and teaches them his way.

Romans 8:26–27: In the same way, the Spirit helps us in our weakness. We do not know what we ought to pray for, but the Spirit himself intercedes for us through wordless groans. And he who searches our hearts knows the mind of the Spirit, because the Spirit intercedes for God's people in accordance with the will of God.

REFLECTION

Whose story in Scripture inspires you to persevere? To have faith?

What promises have been most meaningful to you in your life and ministry?

What warnings touched your heart?

Are you in need of encouragement to persevere? Courage to go?

Spend some time with God as you talk with him about your needs.

RESPONSE

Choose one of the passages you've read through and write it out. Post it where you can see it. Read over it daily. Share it and share why it is so meaningful to you with a friend.

PRAYER

Lord, your Word is rich with promise and meaning. My choices, direction, lifestyle all find their basis in your Word. I know your promises are sure. Your way is best. I take hold of your strength as I walk by faith. Help me keep my eyes on Jesus. May I fight the good fight, finish my race, and keep the faith. May I persevere to do your will and bring you glory. Amen.

FOR FURTHER REFLECTION

Read 1 Thessalonians 1:2–3; 1 Timothy 4:14–16; James 1:12; and Revelation 2:2–4. How do these verses encourage you? What would be a warning to take to heart?

RESOURCES

https://www.abwe.org/blog/10-reasons-god-entrusts-us-trials   _____

https://www.youtube.com/watch?v=u-LvOF4BNGA&list=RDLVyIOg
YPkNA7g&index=13 (How Do I Find God's Will for My Life)   _____

https://davidjeremiah.blog/5-principles-for-biblical-decision-making/   _____

https://www.watermark.org/blog/decision-making-principles   _____

Beth Moore, *Praying God's Word: Breaking Free From Spiritual Strongholds* (Nashville: B & H Publishing Group, 2009).

Jan Johnson, *Savoring God's Word: Cultivating The Soul-Transforming Practice of Scripture Meditation* (Colorado Springs: NavPress, 2004).

D. A. Carson, *Praying with Paul: A Call to Spiritual Reformation* (Grand Rapids: Baker Academic, 2015).

Chapter 32

How Do I Sense God Leading Me?
Seeking His Will

A saint realizes that it is God who engineers his circumstances; consequently there are no complaints, only unrestrained surrender to Jesus.

—Oswald Chambers

I (Sue) made a bust of Jesus out of clay in sixth grade vacation Bible school. While not artistic, my teacher was, so my attempt at sculpture turned out quite nicely. As I grew older, I kept that head of Jesus on my dresser in my bedroom. When I began dating a young man, I was unsure if he was "the one." I wrote a letter to God. If you could pick up that clay head today, you would see a hole underneath where I put the letter for safe keeping.

The letter is long gone, as is the clay head, but the memory lingers. In the letter, I told God that I thought this young man and I should be together. But I wasn't sure. So, I asked the Lord to guide me. If not this man, then would he please lead me to the one I would marry.

It wasn't him! However, I learned a lifelong lesson from that experience. I asked for guidance and trusted God to lead me, and he did. I struggled while navigating those waters. At times I was surprised, confused, and anxious—all the things we experience on the journey of life. But God proved faithful, and I remained open to his direction. I'm grateful today for the husband God gave me.

When my (Eva's) husband and I prayed about leaving our church staff and joining our current agency, I participated in a course which discussed the spiritual discipline of discernment. My facilitator asked me thought provoking questions. What do you want to do? Does your desire line up with God's design for your life? Do you believe God is wholly good? Will this decision produce the fruit of the Spirit in you? Will it enhance your love for God and for others?

She also introduced me to the spiritual formation prayer of indifference. This simple prayer, "Lord, I am indifferent to anything but your will," reminds me that if I expect God to be my guide, I must truly want to do his will, not mine. I must want his guidance in order to obey, not just to get his stamp of approval on my plans.

As I considered this input, I reaffirmed my belief in God's goodness. I could then completely trust that he would guide me into his best for me. I released my fear that I would miss his perfect will. For the first time, I considered my own heart when making a decision. Since then, I have listened to God in new ways. I ask for wisdom (Jas 1:5). I pray for God's love to abound in knowledge and depth of insight in me so I can discern his best for me (Phil 1:9–10).

Through the years, I've (Sue) had ideas about God's will, but also tried to keep my heart open in case God had a different idea. Missionary friends of ours closed their prayer letters beautifully. Above their names they wrote, "Holding tightly to his hands and loosely to our plans." What a beautiful way to put it: making plans, thinking we know what to do, and trusting God as we navigate the future.

Consider how God has led you in the past. As you've prayed, sought counsel, examined your circumstances, how has God pointed you in the way you should go?

When we seek to do God's will, look to him for guidance, and let his Word speak to us, we can be sure he will direct our steps. God doesn't purposefully hide his will from us, but he does ask that we seek his kingdom. He asks that we deny ourselves, take up our cross, and follow him.

As we do, we grow more assured of our firm foundation. And we get to know Jesus better as we spend more time with him, asking him what we should do.

REFLECTION

What do you want to do? What don't you want to do?

How can you "hold tightly to his hands and loosely to your plans"?

How can you remind yourself of God's goodness and deep love for you?

What choice will lead you into a deeper relationship and dependence on God?

How do you sense the Spirit drawing you in a particular direction?

RESPONSE

Make a timeline of your life. Draw a line on a piece of paper. On one side of the line mark your highlights. On the other side show the challenges.

How did God lead you through these times? How did he use them in your life?

Spend some time with a mentor or friend, thanking God for his faithfulness and his purposes for your life.

PRAYER

You have been faithful, Lord. Throughout my life, you have been at work. I look back and when I felt alone, I see now that I wasn't. You were there. When I look ahead and feel anxious, I know you go before me and that your faithfulness will continue. I praise you for your goodness and kindness to me. I entrust the future to you and know that you will guide me. Amen.

FOR FURTHER REFLECTION

Acts 9:10–19:

In Damascus there was a disciple named Ananias. The Lord called to him in a vision, "Ananias!"

"Yes, Lord," he answered.

The Lord told him, "Go to the house of Judas on Straight Street and ask for a man from Tarsus named Saul, for he is praying. In a vision he has seen a man named Ananias come and place his hands on him to restore his sight."

"Lord," Ananias answered, "I have heard many reports about this man and all the harm he has done to your holy people in Jerusalem. And he has come here with authority from the chief priests to arrest all who call on your name."

But the Lord said to Ananias, "Go! This man is my chosen instrument to proclaim my name to the Gentiles and their kings and to the people of Israel. I will show him how much he must suffer for my name."

Then Ananias went to the house and entered it. Placing his hands on Saul, he said, "Brother Saul, the Lord—Jesus, who appeared to you on the road as you were coming here—has sent me so that you may see again and be filled with the Holy Spirit." Immediately, something like scales fell from Saul's eyes, and he could see again. He got up and was baptized, and after taking some food, he regained his strength.

Reflect on Acts 9:10–19. How did God lead Ananias? What were his concerns? What were the outcomes of his obedience? What can we learn from this example of God's leading?

RESOURCES

https://ourdailybread.org/article/god-leads-us-along/   _____

https://www.youtube.com/watch?v=CJ3ZPukSriA   _____
(What does it look like to let God lead us?)

https://www.youtube.com/watch?v=wFxywgihThQ   _____
(How to Discern God's Leading)

https://transformingcenter.org/2011/12/advent-4-mary-and-the-prayer-of-indifference/   _____

https://www.infocusnet.org/how-to-make-a-prayerful-decision/   _____

Dr. Henry Cloud, *Necessary Endings* (New York: Harper Collins Books, 2011).

Chapter 33

Have I Already Moved On?
Staying Present

> *As we trust God to give us wisdom for today's decisions, He will lead us a step at a time into what He wants us to be doing in the future.*
>
> —THEODORE EPP

Living in the present while thinking of next steps complicates the decision-making process.

My husband and I (Sue) have made plans to repatriate to our home country in the near future. We look forward to living near two of our children and seven of our grandchildren. We anticipate future ministry opportunities. But we aren't living there yet. I've already caught myself planning what possessions to take and what to leave behind. We've had things in storage in the US for about twelve years, and I'm not sure I remember what we have and what we dispersed. I wonder where we will live and what life will look like after more than a decade away.

But I am still here. Not there. I resolve to live here, serve here, and stay focused here for as long as necessary. Of course, thoughts and concerns about our future flit through my mind. Sometimes I think about them and maybe jot down a note to myself. Other times I shelve them for another day. I need to fulfill my duties here until it's time to actually leave, not checking out too soon. If, however, those thoughts become uppermost in my mind, perhaps my soul has already moved on.

John Koessler, reminds us to stay in the present and not think too much about the past or future:

> Vocational mindfulness does not ignore the future or the past. But it does view them with a measure of sanctified skepticism. Both can be an unhealthy refuge for those who are disappointed with their present. Dwelling inordinately on the future or the past produces a state of denial. We avoid the present because we are disappointed with things as they are. We would rather run ahead to the future, which is the realm of our dreams and our ideal church. Or we prefer to take refuge in the past, so our work in the present becomes a monument to an earlier time.[1]

After thinking a lot about moving on, cross-cultural workers can begin moving unconsciously in that direction. At first, they don't admit it to themselves. They certainly don't say anything out loud because that feels too final. Thus, they end up living in a kind of limbo state where they've made their decision but haven't said anything or acted on it yet. If no one else knows, it doesn't seem definitive. But it is.

Be honest with yourself first. Where do you long to be? What place or ministry do you spend the most time thinking about?

---

1 Koessler, "Ministry in the Present Tense."

Then be honest with someone else. Choose this person wisely. Someone who focuses only on the ministry where you serve may seek to persuade you to stay and not really hear you. On the other hand, someone only concerned about you with no understanding of the ministry God called you to may too easily dismiss the idea of you staying. Find the right person with concern for you *and* the ministry.

As you honestly process where you long to be, things usually become clearer and enable you to decide proactively and intentionally.

REFLECTION

How often do you think about leaving? Have you told anyone? Why or why not?

If you have already made your decision to go, how can you prevent checking out too soon?

Who cares about you and your ministry and is someone you could talk to?

RESPONSE

Where does your soul live (here, there, past, future)? Write out your thoughts.

Invite a friend to go out for coffee and talk about what you've discovered about your soul's location.

PRAYER

Jesus, today I have everything that I need. I have life today. I am where I am today. I'm not sure I want to stay here, but I'm not sure I want to leave, either. Instability almost feels too normal. As I look to you, may I live today for you. Help me plan wisely for the future but live in the present. Amen.

FOR FURTHER REFLECTION

Matthew 25:14–30:

Again, it will be like a man going on a journey, who called his servants and entrusted his wealth to them. To one he gave five bags of gold, to another two bags, and to another one bag, each according to his ability. Then he went on his journey. The man who had received five bags of gold went at once and put his money to work and gained five bags more. So also, the one with two bags of gold gained two more. But the man who had received one bag went off, dug a hole in the ground and hid his master's money.

After a long time the master of those servants returned and settled accounts with them. The man who had received five bags of gold brought the other five. "Master," he said, "you entrusted me with five bags of gold. See, I have gained five more."

His master replied, "Well done, good and faithful servant! You have been faithful with a few things; I will put you in charge of many things. Come and share your master's happiness!"

The man with two bags of gold also came. "Master," he said, "you entrusted me with two bags of gold; see, I have gained two more."

His master replied, "Well done, good and faithful servant! You have been faithful with a few things; I will put you in charge of many things. Come and share your master's happiness!"

Then the man who had received one bag of gold came. "Master," he said, "I knew that you are a hard man, harvesting where you have not sown and gathering where you have not scattered seed . So I was afraid and went out and hid your gold in the ground. See, here is what belongs to you."

His master replied, "You wicked, lazy servant! So you knew that I harvest where I have not sown and gather where I have not scattered seed? Well then, you should have put my money on deposit with the bankers, so that when I returned I would have received it back with interest.

"So take the bag of gold from him and give it to the one who has ten bags. For whoever has will be given more, and they will have an abundance. Whoever does not have, even what they have will be taken from them. And throw that worthless servant outside, into the darkness, where there will be weeping and gnashing of teeth."

Reflect on Matthew 25:14–30. What do you learn about serving in the present? Which servant do you identify with the most? What does faithful service look like to you?

RESOURCES

https://lifehopeandtruth.com/life/christian-living/decision-making/   _____

https://www.alifeoverseas.com/the-idolatry-of-missions/   _____

https://www.alifeoverseas.com/resources/   _____

https://www.alifeoverseas.com/10-reasons-not-to-become-a-missionary/   _____

https://www.christianitytoday.com/pastors/2017/august-web-exclusives/
ministry-in-present-tense.html   _____

Chapter 34

What Would I Be Going To?
Next Steps

> *God wants you to get where God wants you to go*
> *more than you want to get where God wants you to go.*
>
> —MARK BATTERSON

As servants of the Lord, we often feel stuck when our future remains uncertain. What if we miss God's will? How will we know? What if the next steps aren't clear, but we feel led to leave? What if the next steps aren't clear, but we feel led to stay?

If we only come up with, "Whatever it is has to be easier than this!" we might be in trouble. Next steps may not be easier, or better. Any major adjustment will prove challenging.

After a year of home assignment, praying, and seeking counsel, we made our decision to leave the foreign field. My (Eva's) husband knew he wanted to pursue a counseling degree, but all other details remained vague.

An illustration my mother gave me years ago helped guide me. She said, "A car that sits parked beside a curb cannot be steered. In order to turn it left or right, it must be in gear and moving. Likewise, take the first step, start moving, and let the Holy Spirit steer you." We did that. We said goodbye, packed up, and moved to my husband's hometown. God revealed each step as we needed it.

On the other hand, my former teammates knew exactly what they were going to do before they even desired to go.

When we were first asked to consider leaving our fruitful and exciting ministry among a people that we loved for a role in mobilizing and training others, we entered into a deep struggle. Why would God take us from an isolated work among the unreached where he was doing something amazing? We felt compelled to pray.

In order to leave, God would need to resolve what felt like a list of impossibilities. God slowly and clearly began to answer. I will never forget the night I sat with my closest friend who had become family to us and shared that we were being asked to leave. I told him I would not leave unless God was already at work in his life. He looked at me and said, "God has been showing me that he was going to take you away so you can send others to the unreached to do what you have done here." There were many tears, but we all knew that God had spoken. Though with deep sadness of heart, we knew our only option was obedience.

Sometimes we know exactly what we're going toward. Other times we don't.

Sometimes what's ahead draws us. Other times we're asked to leave.

Sometimes, we're ready for God's leading and other times, we aren't.

Sometimes we want to go and other times we don't.

Sometimes the role drives the decision. Other times not.

Sometimes we want to stay, but shouldn't.

Sometimes we just know we need to go.

God uses all these scenarios.

Remember, God calls us first to himself. He goes ahead of us. Run toward him. Follow Peter's example when he said to Jesus, "If it's you, tell me to come to you on the water" (Matt 14:28). Only after hearing "Come" did he step out of the boat (v. 29).

Charles Haddon Spurgeon reminds us, "Jesus is the good Shepherd going before His sheep, bidding them follow Him, and ever leading them onwards with the sweet word, 'Come.'"[1]

God calls us to advance his kingdom. And he equips us for that ministry. While the specifics of how we do that change throughout our lives, we can be assured that he calls us to what is for our good and his glory. This includes challenges we face that shape us more into his image. This involves opportunities to serve him that are beyond our imagination. It may be different. It may be hard. And it may take some adjusting.

As you follow God's leading to remain or leave, go toward what is good.

REFLECTION

What do you think God may be guiding you to?

How can you obey God when the future is still unclear?

What supernatural things must God resolve before you can move ahead?

---

1 Spurgeon, "Morning and Evening Devotional."

RESPONSE

Set aside one day to go back over your reflections on the questions posed in this section. Consider your observations and ask yourself, "What is my decision?"

Share what God may be saying to you with a trusted friend, mentor, or teammate. Then do it!

PRAYER

Lord, I am so encouraged that the people listed in Hebrews 11 weren't commended for their perfect lives or flourishing ministries, but for their faith. I feel so uncertain about my future. Yet I have faith in you. May I continue to trust you. One day I will see you and I won't need to walk by faith anymore. Until then, I will believe and follow your voice, my shepherd and my God. Amen.

FOR FURTHER REFLECTION

Read and reflect on Hebrews 11:4–39. Make a list of the people mentioned and what you know about their lives. What do you observe about what they "went to"? What strikes you about their faith? What can you apply to your own decision-making process?

RESOURCES

https://christianhomeandfamily.com/tag/christian-life-planning/ _____

Ruth Haley Barton, *Invitation to Retreat: The Gift of Necessity of Time Away with God* (Downers Grove: IVP Books, 2018).

Chapter 35

Whether I Stay or Go, How Do I Say Goodbye Well?
Healthy Goodbyes

> *The global transnational family has developed an amazing capacity to adapt, to move forward, but sometimes we need to just stop where we are and honor that moment, honor the goodbye.*
>
> —MARILYN GARDNER

Goodbyes are hard enough; poor goodbyes are even worse. Lack of closure or bad goodbyes increase the difficulties for those who stay as well as those who leave. Short term, it may seem easier to avoid the goodbye, but long term, hurt ensues.

Since goodbyes are uttered frequently in our world, we may become blasé and not take them as seriously or as intentionally as we should. Even in healthy relationships, saying goodbye is heart-wrenching. I (Sue) hate crying in front of people. I try so hard to hold it all in until I am alone or with Don. Accordingly, no one knows how hard goodbyes are for me. I appear to handle the loss well. Even for my family, had I not written about how much I cried, they might never have known.

I (Eva) have discovered that I pre-grieve. As soon as I sense a goodbye on the horizon, I begin to mourn. I journal, feel sad, think of all the things I'm going to miss, and cry a lot before I give that last hug or step on the tarmac. But as soon as I've waved the last time, I'm ready to look ahead with minimal grief.

Some folks are post-grievers. They go about the process of packing up, attending final events, and saying goodbye with little emotion. But as soon as the airplane door closes, the emotion dam bursts, and the mourning begins.

Knowing your grieving style will help you and those around you. You can then give grace to those who seem either indifferent or overly emotional.[1]

When relationships have been challenging, we may want people to leave already. No need for goodbyes, we just want it over with. Saying goodbye can feel also like a relief. But if the goodbye is poorly done, that relief can be short-lived. The baggage left behind may affect future relationships and our own emotional well-being. R. J. March reminds us, "A good goodbye helps you to transition into the next situation. Transition is real. And it can hurt. Goodbyes help you—and the people in your life—make that transition well."[2]

---

1 Young, *Looming Transitions*, 78.

2 March, "Ten Tips for Good Goodbyes."

Sorting, packing, and preparing to move can be physically and emotionally exhausting. We may not feel up to adding the stress of goodbyes to the mix. Closure can feel like just one more thing to do and not a pleasant thing.

However, we encourage you to not neglect your goodbye. We want to leave or stay with relationships intact. We want to be grateful to God for how he leads and works in our lives, in the lives of teammates, and in the ministry. Keep in mind that we model spiritual family for national believers we work with. R. J. March also says, "Remember, goodbyes are generally harder for those left behind."[3]

Mission leaders have long advised that a healthy goodbye can be achieved by following the R.A.F.T. method. Be sure to try to *reconcile* any relationship issues, *affirm* those that matter to you, say *farewell* to people, places, pets, and possessions in culturally appropriate ways. And even while saying goodbye, *think ahead* to your new destination, making plans and discovering what life will be like.[4]

Whether leaving or staying, we all need good closure.

REFLECTION

What do you need in order to say goodbye well?

Consider some of your previous goodbyes. How might you have done it better?

If a teammate is leaving, what do you need from them in order to say goodbye well?

If you have decided to leave, how might you implement the R.A.F.T. principles?

Discern your grieving style.

---

3 March, "Ten Tips for Good Goodbyes."

4 Pollock, van Reken, and Pollock, *Third Culture Kids*, 240–46.

RESPONSE

Get together with your teammate who is leaving (or staying) and discuss what you have learned about saying goodbye and what you need from each other.

PRAYER

Father, thinking about staying and leaving causes me grief. Neither seems good to me and yet I want to do both. How to choose? I don't know, and I feel stress. May I follow your leading and would you give me and others grace as we struggle to decide what to do. Sometimes I wish you gave flashing lights and clear directions for the future. Yet, this is a walk of faith and I desire to follow you—however you lead—with courage that you supply. And when I do decide, help me say goodbye well. Amen.

FOR FURTHER REFLECTION

Acts 20:22–38:
And now, compelled by the Spirit, I am going to Jerusalem, not knowing what will happen to me there. I only know that in every city the Holy Spirit warns me that prison and hardships are facing me. However, I consider my life worth nothing to me; my only aim is to finish the race and complete the task the Lord Jesus has given me—the task of testifying to the good news of God's grace.

Now I know that none of you among whom I have gone about preaching the kingdom will ever see me again. Therefore, I declare to you today that I am innocent of the blood of any of you. For I have not hesitated to proclaim to you the whole will of God. Keep watch over yourselves and all the flock of which the Holy Spirit has made you overseers. Be shepherds of the church of God, which he bought with his own blood. I know that after I leave, savage wolves will come in among you and will not spare the flock. Even from your own number men will arise and distort the truth in order to draw away disciples after them. So be on your guard! Remember that for three years I never stopped warning each of you night and day with tears.

Now I commit you to God and to the word of his grace, which can build you up and give you an inheritance among all those who are sanctified. I have not coveted anyone's silver or gold or clothing. You yourselves know that these hands of mine have supplied my own needs and the needs of my companions. In everything I did, I showed you that by this kind of hard work we must help the weak, remembering the words the Lord Jesus himself said: "It is more blessed to give than to receive."

When Paul had finished speaking, he knelt down with all of them and prayed. They all wept as they embraced him and kissed him. What grieved them most was his statement that they would never see his face again. Then they accompanied him to the ship.

Reflect on Acts 20:22–38. Describe the emotions exhibited in this passage. How did Paul know when it was time to leave? How did Paul say goodbye well? What did Paul include in his goodbye? How did others say goodbye?

RESOURCES

https://www.missionarycare.com/saying-goodbye.html _____

https://velvetashes.com/goodbye-for-now-and-for-good/ _____

https://www.alifeoverseas.com/goodbye-making-a-hard-word-easier/ _____

https://www.alifeoverseas.com/honor-the-grief-honor-the-goodbye/ _____

https://www.alifeoverseas.com/to-the-one-who-is-left-behind/ _____

https://www.thecultureblend.com/the-transition-that-never-ends-the-ongoing-cycle-of-expat-stayers-goers-and-newbies/ _____

https://www.christianitytoday.com/women-leaders/2019/august/should-i-stay-or-should-i-go.html _____

https://thirdculturethriving.libsyn.com/69-leaving-and-loving-well _____

Chapter 36

A Closing Challenge

As we come to the end of our book, we want to leave with you with some closing thoughts.

Don't Leave Too Soon

Stay awhile. Don't run from. Accept the challenges. Try new things. Change what isn't working. Experiment and be willing to succeed or fail. Grieve when you need to, but don't rush through the grief.

In an online seminar on disappointment, Amy Galloway said, "You can't grieve what you haven't acknowledged."[1] Take the time to acknowledge and grieve. Rejoice when you can. Rely on the Spirit of God. If fruitfulness flourishes at about the eight-year mark, don't leave in seven and a half. Keep growing in your walk with God. Find your niche as you discover your strengths and embrace your giftings. Love others well. Forgive often. Learn the language to the best of your ability. Serve even when no one notices.

Keep going even when you don't have a clue how God is using you. Sometimes God gives us a glimpse into how he uses us, and that is delightful. Other times, we won't know until we reach heaven and see how God worked through us. Remember, God uses our little offerings for his big name.

Don't Stay Too Long

Don't stay just to stay. If you need a sabbatical, a change of pace, or a new direction, be open to leaving. Get the resources you need to be healthy. Talk with your team, your leaders, trusted friends, or professional member care staff as you consider a change. When a family or health crisis strikes, trust God as the orchestrator of circumstances and follow him as he leads you.

When leaving feels unbearable, but you know you must, move forward by faith. If you get deported and sent off in disgrace for the name of Christ, you are honored and blessed in the kingdom. If you or others see a different area or different ministry where you might fit and be able to serve in your strengths, be open to go. If everything has fallen apart or remaining risks your health, be willing to go. Grieve as needed but don't rush through the sadness. Rejoice in God's faithfulness.

Prayerfully and Intentionally Decide

As you or teammates decide to stay or to go, pray. Consider. Seek counsel. Know the Lord will direct your steps. Grieve what you must say no to even as you say yes to something new.

Love well, no matter what. Celebrate one another and God's leading. Trust God together. Walk by faith. Serve faithfully wherever you live and with whatever gifts God has given you.

Say Goodbye Well

If you stay, stay well with healthy goodbyes to those who leave. If a teammate leaves, honor them. Acknowledge their efforts. Celebrate life and ministry. If you are leaving, don't rush off. Spend time with people. Revisit memorable places. Review your time with thanksgiving. Remember your hard times and grieve while remembering God's sustaining presence. Promote good closure for all. Honor one another in love.

---

1 Galloway, "Keeping an Open Heart."

May God guide your steps as you look to him. We can think of no better way to close out this book than to pray for each of us the benediction from Hebrews 13:20–21:

> Now may the God of peace, who through the blood of the eternal covenant brought back from the dead our Lord Jesus, that great Shepherd of the sheep, equip you with everything good for doing his will, and may he work in us what is pleasing to him, through Jesus Christ, to whom be glory for ever and ever. Amen.

Appendix 1

Soul Care Rhythms Worksheet

Use the following questions to assess your current soul care rhythms. The activities listed are merely ideas to get your thoughts flowing.

Master Care

List the activities you do daily. (*i.e., read the Bible, pray, and journal*)
Weekly. (*i.e., worship, take a sabbath or quiet day*)
Monthly. (*i.e., read a spiritual book, memorize verses, take a half-day retreat*)
Annually. (*i.e., take a spiritual retreat, try a new discipline or devotional*)

Self-Care

List the activities you do daily. (*i.e., eat healthy meals, get eight hours of sleep*)
Weekly. (*i.e., play games, do a life-giving activity, go to a gym*)
Monthly. (*i.e., do a hobby, get a haircut, do something fun*)
Annually. (*i.e., take a vacation, get a dental, eye, or physical exam*)

Mutual Care

List the activities you do daily. (*i.e., eat family meals together, call a friend, hug someone*)
Weekly. (*i.e., meet with prayer or accountability partner, have coffee with a friend*)
Monthly. (*i.e., meet with a coach or small group, go on a date or outing*)
Annually. (*i.e., take an anniversary getaway, attend a conference or family reunion*)

Evaluate your current rhythms

- What changes to your self-care do you need to make?

- Are you connecting with God and others regularly?

- How are your rhythms causing you to love God and others more?

- Do you have enough rest for the work you are doing?

Appendix 2

Sample Team Covenant of Relationship

By Daniel Bethel, Christar Church Planting Director[1]

Our desire as a team is to effectively model the body of Christ to others through our interaction. Therefore, as we extend grace and show love to one another, we commit to do the following:

- We will keep each other accountable in our personal lives and ministry.
- We will pray for each member of the team and their families.
- We will have fun together and enjoy the uniqueness of each member of the team.
- We will be honest about our own lives and flaws and open concerning the lives and flaws of individual team members.
- We will not slander one another or gossip about each other, even to a spouse or close friend outside of the team.
- We will respect and listen to the views and opinions of each team member.
- We will keep all team and interpersonal issues confidential from those outside the team, except in extraordinary circumstances.
- We will value each other as individuals that are created in the image of God.
- We will be kind to one another and patient with one another.
- We will resolve conflicts quickly and not let strife or bitterness linger among the team.
- We will seek to clearly understand the feelings and opinions of each team member.
- We will show concern and empathy for each other's needs.
- We will challenge each other in our thinking and methodology.
- We will appropriately prioritize relationships before task.
- We will affirm and celebrate individual and team success.
- We will spur each other on toward the vision and encourage individual initiative.
- We will generously serve each other with our time and resources.
- We will honor and support each family's parenting philosophy.
- We will seek to honor our commitments to one another.

---

1 Used with permission.

Appendix 3

Six Lessons for Good Listening

Adapted from David Mathis[2]

David Mathis, in his book *Habits of Grace*, gives six lessons for good listening.

- Good listening requires patience. It avoids "a kind of listening with half an ear that presumes already to know what the other person has to say."

- Good listening is an act of love. Poor listening rejects, good listening embraces.

- Good listening asks perceptive questions. Good listening asks open-ended questions.

- Good listening is ministry. There will be days when the most important ministry we do is listen.

- Good listening prepares us to speak well. Sometimes good listening only listens, but typically good listening readies us to minister words of grace.

- Good listening reflects our relationship with God. Our inability to listen well to others may be symptomatic of a chatty spirit that is drowning out the voice of God.

---

2 Mathis, *Habits of Grace*, 150–55. A free download is available here: https://www.desiringgod.org/books/habits-of-grace.

Appendix 4

Loss and Grief Worksheet

Acknowledge Loss—Pray about and list your losses, large and small.

- Who or what have I lost? (*person, place, thing, event, job, pet, dream, health, opportunity, identity, life-stage*)
- Secondary losses? (*what I loved about them, memories, potential experiences, hopes, dreams, details*)

Process Loss—Feel the loss and release the emotions appropriately.

- How will I mourn? (*cry, release anger, lament*)
- Who might I need to forgive? (*those who hurt me, or are responsible for my loss*)
- Have I confessed and accepted forgiveness for my part? (*blaming myself, not doing enough, believing lies*)
- What have I gained? (*what was not lost, will be kept alive, memories, lessons learned*)
- How will I remember what I lost? (*write a story, continue traditions, create a collage, hang photos*)
- What will I do with this list? (*cross off each item as it loses power over me; then, in time, burn, flush, toss, or tear up and create something new*)

Use your Resources—You are not made to grieve alone.

- What Scripture will I turn to? (*passages that give comfort and renew hope*)
- Who in the body of Christ will I tell? (*friend, pastor, counselor*)

Nurture Yourself—Do more activities that bring life to your soul.

- What life-giving activities will I engage in? (*crafting, hiking, spa day, sitting by the beach, playing music, sports, reading, gardening*)
- When will I do them? (*make a plan and do it*)

Appendix 5

Exit Interview

Not every question needs to be asked. Instead, use them as a guide to allow the transitioning missionary to talk, process, and be heard.[1]

Ministry

- List all your assignments with dates and reasons for reassignment, including your current one. What are the main reasons for leaving this assignment, location, or organization?

- As you look back, what was the single most significant and/or fulfilling accomplishment of your whole missionary experience? What were some other highlights and victories? What brought you joy?

- What, by God's grace, is different about your life today than when you first became a missionary? (We often view accomplishments as the work we got done, souls saved, churches planted, etc. We forget the victories that God has done in our lives, the years of perseverance, plugging away at a language, etc.)

- What were the greatest hardships, challenges, or defeats that you faced? What objectives were you unable to accomplish? What do you feel you have left undone? What were the reasons for not accomplishing those objectives?

- On a scale of 1 to 10 (10 being the highest), rate your satisfaction with your role or ministry on the field. What would you change if you could do it over again?

Relationships

- Describe your relationship with your team, field leadership, mobilization center, and home church. In what ways were you supported by them? In what ways did you lack support?

- For married couples, describe your spouse's and/or your family's cross-cultural experience.

Organization

- What advice would you give a person just arriving on your field or your team?

- What have you learned from your experience that you would like to share with others?

- What advice do you have for your organization based on your experience?

- Under what circumstances might you want to go back?

- What unfinished business might need to be addressed before leaving (hurts to be healed, relationships to be mended, etc.)?

---

1 I would like to acknowledge Ron McLain of LinkCare Center, Lois Dodds of Heartstream Resources, and Ken Williams of SIL for providing the first materials on debriefing which I, and many others, have taken and adapted over the years. For more debriefing resources, see https://www.mmct.org/debriefing/ and www.heartstreamresources.org/shop.

Future

- What's most challenging or fearful for you (and your family if you have one) as you look ahead? What lessons from your field experience might help you face those challenges?

- What are you most passionate about now? What do you hope to spend more time doing? How has this changed from when you first went to the field?

- What do you sense is God's future plan for you? What are your short-range goals? What are you most excited about?

- As you look ahead, do you need further education? Financial resources? Counseling? Medical care? Rest? What next steps will you take to find these resources?

- Who might mentor you as you move forward? How might your organization assist with your transition? What prayer requests do you have?

Appendix 6

Losing a Team Member Team Debriefing

Adapted from Losing a Team Member Team Debriefing, by Elizabeth Corbin, PsyD[1]

Preparation

Inform team members that this debriefing will be a time to process their experience of X leaving so that the group can move forward free of unresolved issues, and to learn from the experience.

Before the open debriefing discussion begins, the leader should briefly (5 minutes) explain the process leading to the decision of X's departure (such as X was given warnings, a decision made by the whole leadership team, X was given an opportunity to tell their side of the situation, what help has been provided for them after they leave, etc.). This will reassure the remaining members they are not in danger of being suddenly asked to leave without warning.

The Debriefing (Approximately 60 Min)

Ideally, the facilitator leading the debriefing has training in helping people process emotions. Members will likely speak more openly if the debriefing facilitator is not their immediate supervisor, due to members' experiences with authority and differences in power. The facilitator should encourage both members and leaders to answer the questions and then summarize. To enable open discussion, the leaders of the team should refrain from explaining their actions and decisions.

Possible Questions

- How did the decision of X being asked to leave impact you?
- How does it affect the team?
- What will you miss about X?
- What can a team do differently in the future to improve? What did we learn from this?
- Are there things that we collectively as a team did that we need to ask X forgiveness for?

Closing

When the discussion is finished or on a different occasion, the leaders can provide further explanations if they think it would be helpful. Encourage individual follow-up meetings with the facilitator, a mentor, or a counselor, if further processing is needed.

Individual Mentor Meetings

Discuss any unresolved issues with X that the team member needs to either confront or ask forgiveness for. Feelings of anger, grief, resentment, guilt, and relief can be processed.

---

1 Corbin, "Losing a Team Member Team Debriefing." Used with permission.

Appendix 7

Work Matters Reflection

Evaluate Your Current Workload

- Identify three work related things that you could put on hold or let go of.

- How might your margin and rest be adequate or inadequate for the work you are doing?

- If you need help, who can you ask? When can you do this?

- Identify any values you hold that differ from your organization, your team, or your role.

- Identify any unfairness in your work environment that bothers you.

- Describe any unhealthy leadership that has hampered your work.

- What would it look like to have adequate reward and affirmation for your work?

Read the Following Testimony

I'm a volunteer firefighter as well as being a pastor. Obviously you have to push yourself physically when fighting fire. It's a stretching experience that is uncomfortable and physically difficult. You have to know your limitations while making the sacrifices needed to get the tasks done that must be done.

It's foolishness to ignore your limitations, try to be the hero, and cramp up, pass out, or have a heart attack while in a burning structure because you're beyond the limits of what God has supplied you with the capability of doing. It's a form of heroic suicide that is counterproductive because you're now no longer effective in fighting fire and the resources that were dedicated to fighting the fire are now dedicated to saving you.[1]

Reflect and Respond

- What metaphorical fire(s) are you fighting?

- What sacrifices are necessary, and which are simply being "heroic?"

- How might you be choosing "heroic suicide?" How is this affecting your work?

- What resources are being directed to "saving" you instead of toward the ministry?

- What are your physical, emotional, and spiritual capabilities? How are you utilizing them?

- What are your physical, emotional, and spiritual limitations? How are you dealing with them?

- Considering your answers to the above questions, what changes do you need to make regarding your work to make it more sustainable?

- How will you make these changes?

---

1 Ash, *Zeal Without Burnout*, 25.

Acknowledgments

Sue Eenigenburg

I am grateful for God's grace and patience throughout my life. He gives strength and wisdom when needed. At times, I thought I needed them sooner. God knew best and strategically used that waiting time to teach me more about patience, faith, myself, and him.

Eva's insights have proved invaluable. I am thankful for her gift of writing and her experience caring for beloved colleagues in ministry.

I'm thankful for my husband Don. His partnership in life and ministry remains one of my greatest blessings. Our four kids, their spouses, and our dozen grandkids give me joy. Living far from them has been a pull-on-my-heart sacrifice, but a worthy one.

I'm grateful to peer readers who helped improve our book. Thank you to Dorcas, Hadassah, Karla, Kristi, and Don.

God has always provided what we needed. He has used faithful, generous friends and churches to partner with us in ministry—some for more than thirty-seven years. I am blessed.

Eva Burkholder

Thank you, to Sue who asked me to collaborate with her. I have loved this process and echo her assessment at the start, "We do better when we work together."

To fellow global workers who answered our survey, commented in chat boxes during webinars, and willingly shared your stories in interviews and emails. Your testimonies enhance our words.

To our readers, for taking time to give us helpful feedback and encouragement: Suzi, Mark, Esther, Joan, Jayme, Eunice, Beth, and Lula.

To the missions experts and authors who read our rough draft and endorsed our words with enthusiasm.

To my ministry partners, colleagues, friends, Tuesday morning Bible study—all who prayed, asked me how the book was coming along, and told me they couldn't wait to read it. You have kept me going.

To my sons, who I tore away from their comfortable island home when we followed God's leading back to the US. Thank you for loving our Lombok life and enjoying the ride.

To my husband, Mark, the other half of my beautiful, blessed alliance, without whom I would not have experienced the cross-cultural life. Thank you for taking me along on the journey.

And mostly, to my Lord for giving me grace for my own process of growth and grit to serve cross-cultural workers.

Bibliography

"4 Truths to Help Overcome Loneliness on the Mission Field." May 12, 2021. https://withinreachglobal.org/4-truths-to-help-overcome-loneliness-on-the-mission-field/.

Ash, Christopher. *Zeal Without Burnout: Seven Keys to a Lifelong Ministry of Sustainable Sacrifice.* UK: The Good Book Company, 2016.

Austen, Jane. *Pride and Prejudice.* England: Penguin Popular Classics, 1994.

Befus, Connie. *Sojourner's Workbook: A Guide to Thriving Cross-Culturally.* Orlando: BottomLine Media, 2018.

Bias, Tim. "Six Ways to Know You Are Growing in Self-Awareness." *Transforming Mission* (blog). Accessed March 29, 2023. https://www.transformingmission.org/six-ways-to-know-you-are-growing-in-self-awareness/.

Challies, Tim. "Gift Envy and Gift Projection." *Challies* (blog), October 7, 2017. https://www.challies.com/christian-living/gift-envy-gift-projection/.

Chambers, Oswald. "Those Borders of Distrust." My Utmost For His Highest, April 4, 2023. https://utmost.org/classic/those-borders-of-distrust-classic/comment-page-1/.

Collins, Jim. "The Stockdale Paradox." Accessed March 29, 2023. https://www.jimcollins.com/concepts/Stockdale-Concept.html.

Dahlfred, Karl. "Should Missionaries Use Facebook and Twitter." *Gleanings from the Field* (blog), June 3, 2010. https://www.dahlfred.com/en/blogs/gleanings-from-the-field/351-should-missionaries-use-facebook-and-twitter.

Dowsett, Carol. "Forbearance: A Greater Grace." *Engage* (blog), November 24, 2018. https://blogs.bible.org/forbearance-a-greater-grace/.

Duckworth, Angela. *Grit: The Power of Passion and Perseverance.* New York: Scribner, 2010.

Eenigenburg, Sue, and Robynn Bliss. *Expectations and Burnout: Women Surviving the Great Commission.* Littleton: William Carey Publishing, 2010.

Ellis, Linda. "The Dash Poem." Accessed March 29, 2023. https://lindaellis.life/.

Freeman, Emily P. *The Next Right Thing: A Simple, Soulful Practice for Making Life Decisions.* Grand Rapids: Revell, 2019.

Freeman, Emily P. "03: Make the Most Important List." Produced by Emily P. Freeman. The Next Right Thing. August 22, 2017, Podcast, MP3 Audio, 18:00. https://emilypfreeman.com/podcast/03-make-important-list/.

Galloway, Amy. "Keeping an Open Heart when Faced with Chronic Disappointment." Webinar at Gather, 2022, March 30, 2022. https://hub.thriveministry.org/gathering-sessions/a1G8h000009ygpyEAA.

Hay, Rob, Valerie Lim, Sarah Hay, and Jaap Ketelaar. *Worth Keeping: Global Perspectives on Good Practices in Missionary Retention* (Pasadena: William Carey Library, 2006).

James, Carolyn Custis. *Half the Church: Recapturing God's Global Vision for Women.* Grand Rapids: Zondervan, 2011.

Jones, Jerry. "Going Nowhere: Ten Tips for Expat Stayers Who Want to Stay Well." *The Culture Blend* (blog), January 13, 2016. https://www.thecultureblend.com/going-nowhere-ten-tips-for-expat-stayers-who-want-to-stay-well/.

Koessler, John. "Ministry in the Present Tense." August, 2017. https://www.christianitytoday.com/pastors/2017/august-web-exclusives/ministry-in-present-tense.html.

Kotesky, Ronald. "Missionary Single Issues: Loneliness." Missionary Care. Accessed March 29, 2023. https://www.missionarycare.com/missionary-single-issues-loneliness.html.

Kotesky, Ronald. "What Missionaries Ought to know about Relationships." Missionary Care. Accessed March 29, 2023. https://www.missionarycare.com/relationships.html.

Kraft, Marguerite. *Front Line Women: Negotiating Cross-Cultural Issues in Ministry.* Littleton: William Carey Publishing, 2012.

Lamp, Herbert F. *Journey With Me: Spiritual Formation for Global Workers.* Littleton: William Carey Publishing, 2021.

Lamp, Herbert F. *Journey with Me: Spiritual Formation for Global Workers* (Littleton: William Carey Publishing), 2021, quoted in Richard J. Foster, *Celebration of Discipline: The Path to Spiritual Growth* (San Francisco: Harper, 2000).

March, R. J. "Ten Tips for Good Goodbyes." *Serge Global* (blog). Accessed March 29, 2023. https://serge.org/blog/10-tips-for-good-goodbyes/.

Mathis, David. *Habits of Grace: Enjoying Jesus Through the Spiritual Disciplines.* Wheaton: Crossway, 2016.

McDaniel, Patrick. "Fear in Decision Making: How This F Word Messes You Up." Wise Insights. Accessed March 29, 2023. https://www.wiseinsights.net/fear-affects-decision-making/.

Miller, Dan. "Forbear with One Another." *9Marks* (blog), March 30, 2021. https://www.9marks.org/article/forbear-with-one-another/.

Nieuwhof, Carey. "Is It Time to Quit Ministry? How to Tell If Your Time As a Pastor is Over." *Carey Nieuwhof* (blog). Accessed March 28, 2023. https://careynieuwhof.com/is-it-time-to-quit-ministry-how-to-tell-if-your-time-as-a-pastor-is-over/.

Ortberg, John. *The Life You've Always Wanted: Spiritual Disciplines for Ordinary People.* Grand Rapids: Zondervan, 2022.

Ortberg, John. *The Me I Want to Be: Becoming God's Best Version of You.* Grand Rapids: Zondervan, 2009.

Ortlund, Dane. *Gentle and Lowly: The Heart of Christ for Sinners and Sufferers.* Wheaton: Crossway, 2020.

Piper, John. "Should I Ever Take an Action I Don't Have 'Peace' About?" Desiring God. September 17, 2018. Interview, MP3 Audio, 08:46. https://www.desiringgod.org/interviews/should-i-ever-take-an-action-i-dont-have-peace-about.

Pollock, David C., Ruth E. van Reken, and Michael V. Pollock. *Third Culture Kids 3rd Edition: Growing up Among Worlds.* Boston: Nicholas Brealey Publishers, 2017.

Scazzero, Peter. *The Emotionally Healthy Leader: How Transforming Your Inner Life Will Deeply Transform Your Church, Team and the World.* Grand Rapids: Zondervan, 2015.

Schutte, Shauna. "The Gift of Loneliness." Focus on the Family. February 1, 2007. Focusonthefamily.com.

Sears, Andrea. "Overview of Survey and Methodology." *The Missions Experience* (blog), August 28, 2018. https://themissionsexperience.weebly.com/blog/archives/08-2018.

Shaughnessy, Andrew. "Pandemic, Missions, and Loneliness: Q&A with MTW's Member Care Network." March 9, 2021. https://mtw.org/stories/details/pandemic-missions-and-loneliness-a-qanda-with-mtws-member-care-network.

Sheppard, Linda. "Juggling Multiple Roles as a Missionary." *Missionaries in Haiti* (blog), October 7, 2017. https://missionariesinhaiti.blogspot.com/2017/10/juggling-multiple-roles-as-missionary.html.

Sittser, Jerry. *A Grace Disguised Revised and Expanded: How the Soul Grows Through Loss*. Grand Rapids: Zondervan Books, 2021.

Spurgeon, Charles H. "Morning and Evening Devotional: December 16 Morning." https://www.crosswalk.com/devotionals/morningandevening/morning-and-evening-12-or-16-am-550644.html.

Stallings, Patty. "Build Your CABIN." *Velvetashes* (blog), May 28, 2015. https://velvetashes.com/build-your-cabin/.

Stephens, Dr. Elliott. "Webinar: Field Onboarding and Retention." MissioNexus, February 21, 2022. https://missionexus.org/webinar-field-onboarding-and-retention/.

Thompson, Craig. "Is Conflict with Teammates Really the Top Reason for Missionaries Leaving the Field?" *A Life Overseas* (blog), July 28, 2017. https://www.alifeoverseas.com/is-conflict-with-teammates-really-the-top-reason-for-missionaries-leaving-the-field/.

Tripp, Paul David. *Instruments in the Redeemer's Hands*. Phillipsburg: P&R Publishing Company, 2002.

Tripp, Paul David. *New Morning Mercies: A Daily Gospel Devotional*. Wheaton: Crossway, 2014.

"Tuckman's Stages of Group Development." West Chester University. Accessed March 29, 2023. https://www.wcupa.edu/coral/tuckmanStagesGroupDelvelopment.aspx.

Williamson, Mabel. *Have We No Rights?* Chicago: Moody Press, 1957.

Willis, Eric. *Sacred Conflict: Resolution Skills for the Follower of Christ*. Bloomington, MN: Westbow Press, 2018.

Young, Amy. *Looming Transitions: Starting and Finishing Well in Cross-Cultural Service*. Independently published, 2015.

About the Authors

SUE EENIGENBURG has been in cross-cultural ministry for over thirty-six years. She graduated from Moody Bible Institute and Lancaster Bible College. She has been married to Don since 1978. Their clan includes four children, their spouses, and twelve grandchildren. Sue has served on four different continents and is grateful for God's grace in every place. She enjoys reading mysteries, playing word games, and eating chocolate.

She delights in mentoring and teaching others who serve across cultures. Using life experience, humor, and the Word of God, she seeks to encourage and equip others in life and ministry. She wrote *Screams in the Desert* and *More Screams, Different Deserts*. Sue also co-authored *Expectations and Burnout: Women Surviving the Great Commission* and *Sacred Siblings: Valuing One Another for the Great Commission*.

EVA BURKHOLDER has been teaching and mentoring women for over thirty-five years. Her experience as a missionary kid in Papua New Guinea, cross-cultural worker in Indonesia, women's ministry director, and Bible College adjunct professor adds a global dimension to her study of Scripture and the stories she tells. Through her blog, *Pondered Treasures* (https://evaburkholder.com/), and her book, *Favored Blessed Pierced: A Fresh Look at Mary of Nazareth*, Eva invites readers to slow down, reflect, and practically apply God's Word to life.

Currently, she and her husband live in Richardson, Texas and promote the well-being of global workers in a church planting mission agency. A graduate of Baylor University, she also has a Master of Christian Education from Columbia International University in Columbia, SC. Crafting (specifically macramé) and spending time with her two married sons and their wives rejuvenates her soul.

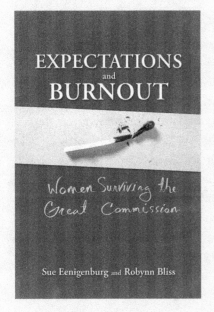

Expectations and Burnout:
Women Surviving the Great Commission

Sue Eenigenburg and Robynn Bliss, Authors

Missionary women have high expectations when they respond to God's call. These expectations are often times impossible to fulfill and can lead to mental and physical exhaustion. Eighty percent of missionary women feel they have come close to burnout. In *Expectations and Burnout*, Sue provides research and surveys from the field while Robynn lends her own personal experiences to demonstrate how burnout can happen and how God can bring life from ashes. Join them as they explore how to develop realistic expectations and yet maintain faith in our sovereign God who continues to accomplish the impossible.

Paperback & ePub

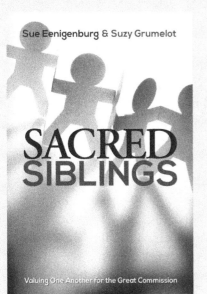

Sacred Siblings:
Valuing One Another for the Great Commission

Sue Eenigenburg and Suzy Grumelot, Authors

In *Sacred Siblings* we learn about how teams come together with varying expectations of what team life should be. The authors offer ideas and positive practices of valuing one another based on a survey from 289 missionaries, representing 12 mission agencies. These practices not only build unity and understanding of each other but enable greater effectiveness in ministry.

Paperback & ePub

WILLIAM CAREY PUBLISHING

visit us at missionbooks.org

Screams in the Desert: Hope and Humor for Women in Cross-Cultural Ministry

Sue Eenigenburg

Screams in the Desert is an invitation to participate in one woman's cross-cultural journey and the lessons she learns along the way. Sue Eenigenburg's poignant and humorous accounts of life overseas provide insight into issues that many women encounter in the mission field. Join Sue for trips to the zoo, bouts of illness, landmine fields, miscommunications, and other everyday experiences of life in a foreign country. Providing women with examples to learn by, Scripture to meditate on, and space to write about personal experiences, *Screams in the Desert* offers hope and humor to women working cross-culturally.

Paperback & ePub

More Screams, Different Deserts: Joy and Perseverance for Women in Cross-Cultural Ministry

Sue Eenigenburg

More Screams, Different Deserts is another invitation to join Sue on her adventures in cross-cultural living and biblical studies that have helped her along the way. Her stories and insights encourage women to look to Jesus, our only hope wherever we live. Stories, ranging from one corner of the world to another, include discovering a forgotten museum, protecting her children from chocolate, visiting a camel market, and meeting wild pigs on a nighttime walk. God has been her refuge, and his Word held her steady when all she really wanted to do was run away and hide. Questions and resources at the end of each chapter will help readers think through personal application and find additional help.

Paperback & ePub

Printed in the USA
CPSIA information can be obtained
at www.ICGtesting.com
LVHW051156110224
771538LV00009B/871